ASTROLOGY FOR LIFE

BY NINA KAHN

CASTLE POINT BOOKS
NEW YORK

ASTROLOGY FOR LIFE.

Copyright © 2020 by St. Martin's Press.

All rights reserved. Printed in the United States of America. For information,
address St. Martin's Press, 120 Broadway, New York, NY 10271.

www.castlepointbooks.com

The Castle Point Books trademark is owned by Castle Point Publishing, LLC.
Castle Point books are published and distributed by St. Martin's Publishing Group.

Cover design by Katie Jennings
Interior design by Melissa Gerber

ISBN 978-1-250-27106-8 (paper over board)
ISBN 978-1-250-27070-2 (ebook)

Our books may be purchased in bulk for promotional, educational, or business use.
Please contact your local bookseller or the Macmillan Corporate and Premium Sales
Department at 1-800-221-7945, extension 5442, or by email
at MacmillanSpecialMarkets@macmillan.com.

First Edition: 2020

10 9 8 7 6 5 4 3 2 1

YOUR PATH IS
ILLUMINATED BY
A ROAD MAP
OF STARS.

—Ambika Devi

CONTENTS

INTRODUCTION

Welcome to the magical, mystical, and endlessly fascinating world of astrology. Astrology is fun. It's magical. It's insightful. And I believe it gives us a little sense of home and interconnectedness within an otherwise very large (and often confusing) universe, especially when we learn how to apply it to our everyday lives.

Most of us are already quite familiar with astrology in the form of our Sun signs and horoscopes. Learning my Sun sign and reading about its stereotypical qualities was certainly enough to get me hooked on simple astrology in my preteen years, and had me flipping to the back of every new issue of my teen magazines to see what was in store for Libra in the coming month. But Sun signs and horoscopes are actually just the tip of an extremely vast, glittery sparkle of a cosmic iceberg, and astrology can be used for so much more than just a fun tip-off about what your day, week, or month may bring. It can also be used as a tool to make your day-to-day life more magical, spiritual, and in sync with the stars.

Astrology spans far beyond the overgeneralized horoscope page at the back of a print magazine. The rest of that cosmic iceberg is a vast and complex world of astrology that begins to feel really daunting really quickly. It can make the concepts of astrology feel just as distant as the stars in the sky. But once you take the time to get to know the basics of astrology, you'll get more familiar and comfortable with its archetypes and symbols—and suddenly, they won't feel so distant. In fact, you'll probably be able to feel their presence and effects quite strongly.

We're all on a quest to find ourselves and make sense of this thing called "life." Whether it's navigating our relationships, building a career and finding a life purpose, or simply getting to know ourselves on a new level, we can actively use astrology and the ever-changing placement of the planets to guide us.

> Astrology is a language. If you understand this language, the sky speaks to you.
>
> —Dane Rudhyar

Getting Cozy in Our Corner of the Universe

Astrology can help us feel connected to the mysteries of the cosmos in a way that wouldn't otherwise be possible. I mean, it's hard to feel at home in a solar system that's larger than our lil' human brains can even really comprehend. We're just a bunch of tiny beings that are inherently and intrinsically part of a much larger cosmic system—one that we, admittedly, can only begin to understand. Sometimes, when we're so hyperfocused on our phones and our in-boxes and our jobs and our schedules, it's easy to think that our daily dramas

> With astrology, the planets and other celestial objects in our solar system begin to feel less like foreign, alien concepts and more like our friendly celestial neighbors—neighbors who have the power to affect our planet in a gravitational sense, but perhaps in a symbolic sense, too.

are *everything*. It's easy to forget that we've all just sort of magically grown into existence out of thin air—or rather, exploded out of a star—along with everything else in our universe. It's both mind-blowingly spectacular *and* terrifying, when you think about it. I'm always struck by how incredible it feels to remember that I am really just a speck of stardust.

When we begin to think of the whole, wide universe (a concept so great it's difficult to even wrap your head around, really)—the fact that it's infinite, that its bounds are perhaps beyond what our minds can logically conceptualize—our lil' solar system begins to feel a *lot* cozier, doesn't it? In a universe that's boundless and full of an infinite number of solar systems, the planets, stars, and asteroids floating about in ours feel like home. There are *billions* of stars in our galaxy, but we (us and other planets) all revolve around just one. Of everywhere we could be in the whole wide universe, we're here. Together.

In teaching us ways that we can align ourselves with the energy of the planets in our solar system, astrology helps us feel so much more in touch with our celestial neighbors. For example, instead of thinking of Saturn as a distant, random concept of a planet, I now think of it as an amazing force in my life *personally*—an energy that interacts with my astrology to teach me lessons about responsibility, boundaries, and how to be an adult. We all orbit the Sun together, and when you take the infinite nature of the universe into account, this means we all live pretty close to each other, too, right? We're like a big, cosmic family. And through astrology, you'll learn how these celestial objects can affect your life, as well as how we can connect with these elements and call upon their energy to help in all different situations. It can help us feel more in sync with the boundless, cosmic universe of which we're *already* so much a part—whether or not we even realize it.

Astro Therapy

Astrology can serve as the springboard for deep soul-searching, self-reflection, and personal growth, which is why I often think of it as a sort of cosmic therapy. It is a tool, among many other tools in our spiritual toolboxes, that can be used to guide you in your life. For the record, I have a real, live, human therapist, too, but there's something different about exploring your innermost qualities by using the cosmos as your backdrop. There's something much more primal and ancient and exhilarating (and obviously, it's a lot more fun and magical, too).

But just like any other type of therapy, it requires work on our end. You're in charge of your own destiny, and you have free will—so you can certainly take in the wisdom offered by astrology and use it to prompt reflection and changes in your life, but you can't expect the planets to do the work for you. The planets may have influence,

Astrology is not a magic pill, and it can't change your life for you. Only *you* can do that!

Since we're all just little specks of stardust, why *shouldn't* we try to make our daily lives feel as magical as we possibly can?

but they don't have magical powers. Astrology is merely a tool that can help you align yourself with the cosmos and gain a deeper understanding of yourself and the circumstances that you (and we collectively) are working with. That's helpful, but the rest is truly up to you. Reading about astrology is one thing, but actually applying it to your life requires work, responsibility, and accountability on your end, too. Figuring out how to make it happen is the adventure.

Astrologers Just Wanna Have Fun

In addition to being helpful in your quest to become a more evolved version of *you*, astrology is also just *really* fun (not to mention endlessly fascinating). To me, there's nothing more exhilarating than the existential giddiness that comes with feeling ~one~ with the universe. Looking up at the stars and feeling like you are truly a *part* of that insane cosmic matrix—that those distant sparkles in the sky might actually connect directly to you—it makes life feel a thousand times more mystical and magical. If gaining a deeper understanding of astrology and developing relationships with the planets can help facilitate that feeling, then why not use it?

I can't even count how many nights I've spent drinking wine on the couch with my best friends, wavering between jaw-dropping awe and teary-eyed giggles until three in the morning talking about astrology—doing everything from analyzing the birth charts of our crushes to texting homemade astrology memes to our friends to tease them about their stereotypical Sun sign traits. With so much to explore, I find astrology to be a virtually endless source of entertainment and fun—but with the incredibly cool added bonus of helping you explore yourself more deeply.

How to Not Use Astrology

Astrology is an incredible tool to use for growth, spiritual connection, creative inspiration, self-improvement, and so much more. But even good things can go awry, and that's why I'm also going to suggest how *not* to use astrology. There are endless archetypes and stories, myths, narratives, and stereotypes in astrology, but

We're *so much more than a* sun sign, and astrology is about so much more than horoscopes.

Astrology should never make you feel boxed in and suffocated; it should feel empowering.

defining yourself by any single one of them probably isn't going to enhance your life—nor is thinking of astrology as a fated crystal ball that leaves you doomed to live out your horoscopes after they've been written, powerless to your own fate. That's not the case!

I can recollect a period in my life, back when I was just a teenage astrology novice, in which reading my daily horoscope each morning was a ritual—but not a particularly healthy one. At this point, I only really knew my Sun sign, so I didn't think much about what astrology offered beyond that. If I started my morning by reading a positive horoscope, I'd elatedly set off on my routine, feeling like a group of fairies had descended upon me from the heavens to ensure a magical day ahead. If it was negative, though, anxiety would kick in like a dark cloud. I'd feel doomed to endure a day full of bad news and mishaps, blaming anything negative that happened on my horoscope, and hoping that the bad things that happened would at least not be *that* bad. In retrospect, this was totally ridiculous: I was reading someone's interpretation of the planets' placements that day and how it might apply to my Sun sign alone (which really isn't enough to go on) and taking it as gospel.

Perhaps you've never been stuck in an anxious horoscope cycle, and that's a good thing (not everyone is as neurotic as I am, and I'm grateful for it), but either way, this must be said: *Astrology does not define you: You are a person with free will who creates your own reality. Astrology does not define your future: It is merely a tool you can use to help craft your future.*

Your future is yours. If you believe that the planets and the beautifully intricate system of astrology have an impact on your life, that's great—I believe it, too! But you are not a powerless person at the mercy of the stars. Using astrology in your favor to guide you and help you feel connected to the world (and universe) around you is where the practice and teachings of astrology can really sparkle and come alive, enhancing your life in myriad ways. Everyone's life, including yours, should benefit from it.

Astrology is like a *magical* cord that symbolically connects what's happening with the planets with what's happening to us here on Earth.

So . . . What Even *Is* Astrology?

Astrology is the study of the position of and relationship between the celestial bodies in our solar system and the interpretation of how they affect our lives. It means looking at the planets, noting where they are and how they're interacting with each other (all while applying the symbolism of astrology's aspects), and interpreting how that affects all of us Earth babies. It's similar to astronomy in that it's based on the study of the planets, but astrology is served up with a big ol' side of divination, mysticism, and mythology.

Astrology also connects our modern-day world with a *very* ancient practice. The history of astrology dates back thousands of years, and was practiced in various forms by people all around the globe. And back in the day, astrology and astronomy were actually considered one in the same. It was widely believed that the planets in our solar system directly affected worldly happenings and were intrinsically intertwined. Astrology was pretty much the be-all and end-all of cosmic study for centuries.

Today, of course, astronomy and astrology have gone off in wildly different directions. Astronomy is considered a hard science—no mysticism there to speak of. Astrology, however (while still incorporating many of the scientific elements of astronomy), still uses the symbols, mythology, and mysticism of the ancient craft to create the rich system of interpretation known as modern-day astrology. And the practice of astrology has continued to evolve and adapt to make sense in the modern world. As we learn more about the solar system around us, our use of astrology grows and changes.

Astrology as Science

Anyone who dives into astrology beyond a surface level will see that there is still a lot of science to it. You've got astronomy, along with a heavy serving of straight-up geometry (aspects, or the relationships between planets, are measured in degrees on a 360-degree wheel—a little throwback to high school geometry class). And have you ever glanced at an ephemeris? It's pretty astounding if you've never seen one before—and it makes it very clear why many people spend *years* studying this practice before they truly understand its vastness. There are *so* many moving parts that come together in order to create the rich and colorful world of astrology, and many of these parts can get quite technical. Astrology may be considered a pseudoscience, but it's surely got its roots in the real, tangible world of math and astronomy.

Astrology as a practice will never be outdated. It adapts amazingly well to our changing world.

What Is an Ephemeris?

An *ephemeris* is a giant guidebook full of numbers and glyphs that shows exactly where each celestial body will be at any given time.

Astrology Is Art

Of course, what makes astrology a unique and mystical *art* is the way it takes the tangible aspects of astronomy and combines it beautifully with the metaphorical and symbolic interpretations of how these planets affect our lives, relationships, and futures on a more divine and mystical level. Astrology attempts to explain how all the nearby celestial bodies influence *us*, which is beyond cool (because who *doesn't* want to feel more interconnected with the cosmos?). In this sense, astrology is an art form, too—it's about interpretation, creativity, and storytelling. You could go online right now and easily find a hundred different horoscopes for today's date, all written by different astrologers, and each will be different from the last. They're all based on the same planetary aspects, but how we interpret these and apply them to our lives can differ vastly. Just as a poem could be read in a hundred different ways by a hundred different people, so can astrology be interpreted into different stories, with different slants and different focuses.

Just as times have changed over the years, astrology has had to evolve to fit our modern-day world. It's an ancient practice, but astrology's tenets are based on archetypes—meaning it was designed with the bare bones and solid foundation needed to allow astrologers to constantly reinvent it. So for example, today we might note that Tauruses love a good food delivery app, or that Libras are particularly skilled at curating an aesthetic social media presence. But centuries back, food delivery apps and social media pages obviously weren't a thing. So in order to apply the timeless practice of astrology to daily life *now*, we must constantly interpret and reinterpret these symbols with a fresh, creative, and intuitive lens. We can easily look to the root of a planet or a sign's essence in order to see where something new and modern might fit into astrology, and that's open for interpretation, too. That's one of the many things that makes this practice so cool, and why even now, millennia after its invention, people are still excited about the art of reading the stars.

The cycles of our solar system are taking place whether we acknowledge them or not—they're beyond our control—but by actively acknowledging them, we're able to swim *with* the energetic tides instead of against them.

How Astrology Guides Us

Astrology resonates with me because it's based on the rhythmic, reliable, natural cycles of our planet and the solar system of which we're inherently a part. Immersing yourself in this world is also immersing yourself in the comfort of reliable cycles: the change of the seasons, the phases of the Moon, the Mercury retrograde cycles that inevitably roll around way sooner than we'd like. We're consciously aligning ourselves with the powerful cosmic entities that we share a solar system with, and with the cycles that govern life on this planet. By doing so, we can open ourselves up to synchronicity, feel more in tune with the planet (and surrounding planets!), and make life feel a little extra magical.

Why Believe in Astrology?

A lot of people ask me why I think astrology is real, and the answer is simple: because it rings true and makes sense to me. Because the more I learn about it, the more it proves itself to me, the more interconnected with the universe I feel, and the more I see what a useful tool it is in my life. And because symbolism and metaphor can be important tools when it comes to relating to the world, and astrology is chock-full of them.

One example that I've heard many people come back to, though, is the very measurable and tangible power of the Moon. The Moon's gravitational pull is what causes our oceans to have waves and tides—it's the Moon that causes the ebb and flow of the ocean, and causes the waves to crash upon the shore minute after minute, day after day, year after year. It's like a heartbeat. It's clockwork. And considering there are *hundreds of millions* of cubic miles of water within Earth's oceans and seas, being the catalyst for such reliable, measurable movement is obviously no small feat!

Consider also, then, that the human body is made up of approximately 60 percent water. If the Moon can cause an ocean that's made up of quintillions (*quintillions!!!*) of gallons of water to have steady, ongoing, powerful tides, then is it really so crazy to assume that this celestial body, which is approximately 238,000 miles away from the Earth, might have an effect on us, too?

It certainly seems to. While not many studies support it, many doctors, nurses, and hospitals still insist that they brace themselves for much busier shifts when there's a full Moon, and report noticing a major surge in emergency room visits, baby deliveries, and patients admitted for psychiatric care. And changes in the Moon cycle have long been believed to have an effect on people's moods, energy levels, and mental states. Take the word *lunatic*, for example, which is named after the word *luna*, and references the temporary mental instability that people were believed to have as a result of the lunar cycle.

Obviously, this isn't hard-core proof of anything—but then again, I'm not here to prove to you that you should believe in astrology. You should believe in anything that feels right! But if you're reading this book, chances are that astrology has caught your eye and sparked something within you, even if it's simply that you identify with the plentiful flow of astrology memes made for your Sun sign. And you're definitely not alone in that.

Astrology and Your Life

The goal of this book is to provide you with a fun and easy-to-understand introduction to the astrological scene, specifically the major planets and their distinct personalities, the twelve signs of the zodiac and their individual manners of expression, and the foundational elements of your birth chart (aka the astrological pie that is completely and totally unique to *you*). But beyond getting you more acquainted with the moving parts, this book aims to help you actually *connect* with astrology and use it to enhance your life.

Throughout this book, you'll learn to use the Sun's seasons to set personal goals and focus your energy. You'll learn how Venus's movement through the signs can help you plan dates and up the romance factor in your love life. You'll learn to work *with* the energy of a retrograde period, and to use it to your advantage rather than dreading it and trying to work *against* it. You'll learn how tracking the Moon's cycles can help you get better at self-care.

Astrology can be so much more than simply reading a horoscope. You can learn how to work with the energy of different planetary transits in a way that will allow you to foster an interconnection with the universe, and in a way that is also unique to *you*.

People have observed
the Moon's ability
to affect us on a
personal level for
thousands of years. If
the Moon affects us,
then it seems logical
that other celestial
bodies could, too.

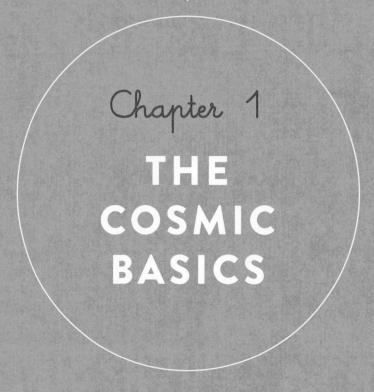

Chapter 1

THE COSMIC BASICS

THE PLANETS ARE GOD'S PUNCTUATION MARKS
POINTING THE SENTENCES OF HUMAN FATE,
WRITTEN IN THE CONSTELLATIONS.

—James Lendall Basford

For most of us, astrology exists in magazines, on social media, and in books (like this one!). But the *real* foundation of astrology exists up in the sky, in the space surrounding our planet—it's all based on real constellations and maps of the sky that we can observe from our little planet.

Of course, not all of us are astronomers and mathematicians with quality telescope access, so most astrologers use interpretations *based* on what's going on in the cosmos to guide us in our astrological studies. When it comes to our effective use of astrology on the daily, we'll use an astrology wheel or chart. It looks like a circular pie chart, each of which contains twelve **houses** (which represent different areas of our lives) that overlap with twelve **signs** (which represent the *vibes* we feel in those areas and *energy* we express ourselves through). Of course, each chart also contains the full rainbow of the **planets** (which represents different aspects of ourselves and our personalities), as well as points, asteroids, and other non-planetary celestial objects that represent the same. These elements come together to form the birth chart unique to you, and this cosmic pie chart is the key to your personal astrology. If you're new to this, it may sound complicated, but we're going to break down the basics.

Together, the planets collide and interact to create the whole of a person. We are *all* affected by the placement of each of these planets on a daily basis, and understanding their influence can help us feel more connected to the cosmos and ourselves.

Planetary Fundamentals

We begin with the planets, as they are some of the major players when it comes to the world of astrology. You can think of them as the zodiac's actors, each with its own unique and notable personalities, motivations, jobs, strengths, interests, and character flaws. The zodiac wheel (full of signs and houses) is the stage on which they perform and interact with each other. Some people like to think of this like a big ol' cosmic soap opera, which makes sense, given all the *insane* intensity and chaos that the planets sometimes decide to drum up on this little stage of theirs. It's as if they sometimes forget that this stage is actually our *lives*. But hey, *c'est la vie*. Life is dramatic, silly, exciting, mundane, terrifying, and beautiful all at once, and in astrology, the planets are some of the driving forces behind this range of experiences.

Planets represent different aspects of our *selves*—parts that we all share. Some planets focus on our physicality, others our ego, and others still our emotional states. They relate to how we connect with other people, how we work, and even our relationship to spirituality. You can think of each planet as parts of a whole. All are important when it comes to your personal natal chart, as well as the day-to-day astrological transits that affect us as a collective.

We all have the same set of planets in our charts and each represents the same things—but don't worry, you are *still* a unique snowflake. Each planet has a unique effect on *you* depending on where it falls in your birth chart and which zodiac sign it was in at the time you were born. The zodiac sign that a planet is in colors the way the planet's energy is expressed. The planet still has the same focus and job to do, but the way it goes about doing it will be different, depending on the sign it's expressing through. Planets' energies will also show up differently in your life depending on the house they reside within in your birth chart.

Every day, these planets are forming relationships to one another that can activate the energy in your personal zodiac chart and influence energies on the whole, so building relationships and associations with *all* the planets (and figuring out how their energy gets expressed in your chart) is a helpful way to start making astrology feel more personal to you.

Astrology works with a nice, solid handful of planets, but it also includes some stars, asteroids, and "points" (which I'll explain more about later). This is because the word *planet* is often used interchangeably in astrology with *celestial objects*. For example, in our everyday life, we know that the Sun is a star and not a planet. And in astronomy, we don't categorize moons as planets, either. As you may recall, astronomers booted out poor little Pluto from Club Planet back in 2006, deeming it a "dwarf planet" instead. But in astrology, the Sun, the Moon, and Pluto, too, are *all* categorized as planets. So as you read, try to kick back and avoid letting your inner NASA scientist get too bent out of shape over it. We're playing a new game here in la Casa de Astrology, so different rules apply.

Planets in Action: Orbits, Retrogrades, and Planetary Returns

As each planet moves along its orbit, it also moves through the areas of the sky that correlate with the twelve signs of the zodiac. This means that once a planet makes a full rotation around the Sun, it's generally completed a full journey through the zodiac, too. This takes a different (and quite varied) amount of time for every planet, given that planets' distance from the Sun and the pace at which it moves along its course.

But throughout most of the planets' journeys through the zodiac (all except the Sun's and the Moon's, to be exact), they'll encounter what are referred to as *retrogrades*, and these can have a major effect on our lives. Retrogrades are periods during which a planet temporarily appears to move backward instead of forward on its orbit. Obviously, the planet isn't *actually* pulling a fast one on us and defying the laws of physics—it just *appears* to be reversing course from our Earthly vantage point. Symbolically in astrology, retrogrades signify a time of reflection and slowing down in the areas governed by the retrograding planet.

If we work with the retrograde energy, we can make it a time of peaceful reflection. But if we work against it, retrogrades are known to cause mishaps, frustrations, and metaphorical traffic jams when it comes to the planet's reign. Retrogrades can be frustrating, but they're a regular part of almost every planet's orbit in astrology, so we may as well get used to them.

Once a planet *does* finally make its way through each of the twelve zodiac signs and completes a full cycle, it returns to the place where it started. When dealing with your personal astrology, this is notable—when a planet returns to the exact place in the zodiac that it was when you were born, this is known as a planetary return. The most celebrated of these planetary returns would be your solar return—aka your birthday! This is the day of the year on which the Sun returns to the exact degree of your Sun sign that it was in on the day you were born.

When a planet returns to our birth placement, it completes a cycle not only within the zodiac wheel, but also within ourselves. It's a time when the energy of the planet is reinvigorated and makes itself *very* known in your life. This could indicate the completion of one cycle and the beginning of a new one, and that can feel both exciting and also scary. The most infamous of the planetary returns is the Saturn return, which happens for the first time at around age twenty-nine. During this time, Saturn is believed to come down *hard* with a tough-love approach, causing people to face their responsibilities and the end of their youth, confront their life circumstances and decide whether they're honoring their truth, and deal with the restrictions and boundaries that reality is placing on them.

The Top 10: Luminaries, Inner Planets, and Outer Planets

LUMINARIES

In astrology, there are said to be two **luminaries**: the Sun and the Moon. These are both, quite obviously, the largest, brightest, and most notable celestial objects in the sky from our vantage point here on Earth, and perhaps the two most influential and symbolic. While the luminaries aren't known as planets in astronomy, they are two of the major planets in astrology. The luminaries are named such for their brightness, but they're also arguably the two most important celestial bodies in our skies—and this is true literally, but also symbolically in astrology. These two celestial bodies can also be differentiated from the other major planets in that they are the only two that don't orbit the Sun (the Sun *is* the Sun, obviously, and the Moon technically orbits around the Earth). And thus, the luminaries are also the only two planets that don't experience retrograde periods.

The luminaries may be differentiated in title and some qualities, but they are both part of a larger team of "inner planets" or "personal planets." The Sun is an inherently masculine planet, ruling over the ego, while the Moon is an inherently feminine planet, ruling over the emotions. Each of the luminaries rule a single zodiac sign. Naturally, the two luminaries happen to rule the signs affiliated with the most illuminated point of the summertime: Cancer and Leo, whose Sun seasons collectively span from late June through late August, when the days are longest. (In fact, Cancer season begins on the day of the summer solstice, also known as the longest day of the year!) Given that these two celestial bodies are named for their luminosity, it makes sense that they would rule over the two signs that express themselves during the brightest part of the year.

Retrogrades are that funky time of year (or years) when a planet (and its area of influence) appears to falter off course. If you know when a planet is in retrograde, you can hold off on any major moves in the planet's territory to avoid the mishaps retrogrades often cause.

22

INNER PLANETS

Moving beyond the luminaries, we enter the land of the rest of the **inner planets** to the five traditional planets in astrology. Beyond the Sun and Moon, these include Mercury, Venus, and Mars, and to a lesser degree, Jupiter and Saturn (although these last two are sometimes referred to as transpersonal planets). The inner planets are believed to affect us on a personal level, and are often called "personal planets" because of this. They move through the signs relatively quickly, although there's still quite a range. For example, the Moon switches signs every few days, whereas Saturn only switches signs every few *years*. Each of the inner planets is believed to have a great influence over us personally, meaning that we feel and experience their effects more intimately as they transit through the zodiac and form relationships with other planets.

> While the Sun represents the core of our identity, the other inner planets greatly influence the nuances of our personalities, and how we function and express in different ways.

The Moon reveals how we express emotions and seek comfort, Mercury indicates how we think and communicate, Venus shows how we experience pleasure, Mars shows how we take action and get sh*t done; Jupiter highlights how we seek growth and expansion; and Saturn teaches us how to set boundaries and take in life lessons.

This is a great testament to how we are *so* much more than our Sun sign alone (meaning that if you're a Taurus but you don't feel like one, that's *normal*—your Sun might very well be the only planet in that sign, meaning you have a ton of other influences to work with!).

In traditional astrology, before the "outer planets" were discovered, each of the five inner planets ruled over two zodiac signs—one traditionally feminine sign, and one masculine—while the luminaries each ruled one sign (masculine sign Leo for the Sun, and feminine sign Cancer for the Moon). The luminaries rule the two summertime signs of Cancer and Leo. Then, quick-footed and even quicker-thinking Mercury (the closest planet to the Sun) ruled the two signs *adjacent* on either side of the luminaries' signs: Gemini and Virgo. Next up in line from the Sun, flirty Venus fluttered in and took over the *next* set of adjacent signs: Taurus and Libra. And so on, applying to Mars, Jupiter, and then Saturn in the same fashion.

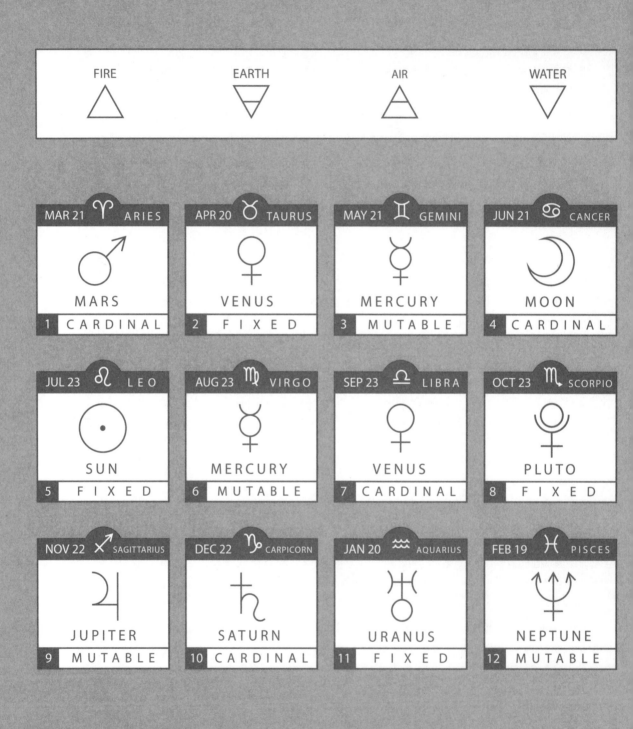

FIRE △   EARTH ▽   AIR △   WATER ▽

MAR 21 ♈ ARIES — MARS — 1 CARDINAL

APR 20 ♉ TAURUS — VENUS — 2 FIXED

MAY 21 ♊ GEMINI — MERCURY — 3 MUTABLE

JUN 21 ♋ CANCER — MOON — 4 CARDINAL

JUL 23 ♌ LEO — SUN — 5 FIXED

AUG 23 ♍ VIRGO — MERCURY — 6 MUTABLE

SEP 23 ♎ LIBRA — VENUS — 7 CARDINAL

OCT 23 ♏ SCORPIO — PLUTO — 8 FIXED

NOV 22 ♐ SAGITTARIUS — JUPITER — 9 MUTABLE

DEC 22 ♑ CARPICORN — SATURN — 10 CARDINAL

JAN 20 ♒ AQUARIUS — URANUS — 11 FIXED

FEB 19 ♓ PISCES — NEPTUNE — 12 MUTABLE

But today, the three outermost planets (all of which emerged *relatively* recently in the astrology scene) have usurped a sign each to exert their rulership over—meaning that in modern-day astrology, only Venus and Mercury still have full reign over a pair of signs. There's a *fascinating* theory held by some astrologers that we may still be awaiting the discovery of two more celestial bodies that will usurp yet another sign each (taking one from Venus and one from Mercury), which would mean all twelve signs would have a designated planetary ruler to themselves. Only time will tell whether this is true, but never say never in astrology! Part of the beauty of this mystical art is its ever-evolving nature. Just as we humans evolve and discover more and more about the not-so-distant universe around us, so does astrology grow, change, and adapt. And as astrologers (or just astrology lovers), we can choose which theories and schools of astrological thought resonate with us most. It's all up for interpretation, which keeps things exciting and fresh.

Once we pass the luminaries and leave Mercury, Venus, and Mars behind, too, we reach Jupiter and Saturn (known as the greater benefic and greater malefic, as you'll soon learn). Both of these planets are much further away from the Sun than the other inner planets, so they have a notably slower orbit. (We jump from Mars, which typically spends only up to a few months in each sign, straight to Jupiter, which spends more than a *year* in a single sign.) While I will be referring to both as inner and personal planets, some astrologers push these two giants further out toward the qualities of the outer planets and prefer to categorize them as "transpersonal planets," or beyond the realm of the personal. These two planets certainly do mark a thematic departure away from (and beyond) the more fundamental qualities of the other inner planets, dealing more in evolved and complex concepts of the human mind than the more simple, instinctual, personality-influencing energies of the others.

And because of this, Jupiter and Saturn are also sometimes called the "social planets." Some astrologers make this distinction in labeling because these planets are a little bit less personality related than the other personal planets, and a little more socially complex. Your Sun, Moon, Mercury, Venus, and Mars signs, for example, may be obvious in your personality from a young age, as they all represent somewhat basic and fundamental human qualities. But philosophical, growth-focused Jupiter and responsible, discipline-focused Saturn are a bit more socially developed in the themes that they deal with. This isn't to say they don't also have their hand in fundamentals—they surely do! But as you learn more about these planets, you'll see the way in which the themes and influences they work with might inspire some astrologers to put them in a category all to themselves.

BENEFICS AND MALEFICS

Within the inner planets, there's also a concept known as "benefic" and "malefic" planets, which, if we want to put it *really* crudely, labels certain planets as essentially good or bad. Jupiter and Venus are known as the benefics, or the planets that tend to bring a beneficial energy to whatever area they travel to in one's birth chart. Saturn and Mars, on the other hand, are known as the malefics, or planets that tend to bring a more malevolent energy. This makes sense, given that Jupiter is the planet of luck while Venus is the planet of love, versus Saturn as the planet of restriction and Mars as the planet of war. But in modern-day astrology, we know that *all* planets can be beneficial—even if their form of love is a tough one—and we know that all planets can end up in a more challenging area of your birth chart or can be negatively expressed at times, too. It's helpful to acknowledge both the benefic and malefic forces when trying to get better acquainted with the planets.

OUTER PLANETS

Expanding even farther outward, toward the edges of our solar system, we now enter the vast, foreign, and spacious land of the **outer planets** in astrology. These are Uranus, Neptune, and Pluto. The outer planets are sometimes referred to as "generational planets" given the slow pace at which they move through the signs, making it so that entire generations of people may be born before one of these planets switches signs (for example, it takes Pluto a whopping 248 years to cycle through all the signs of the zodiac, and it can spend up to thirty years in a single sign!). Thus, a whole generation of people will share a greater number of qualities regarding the way that planet's energy is expressed, which has a greater influence on society in general.

The outer planets are also sometimes referred to as "modern planets" in reference to it not being until relatively modern times that we even discovered these planets existed. For centuries, Uranus, Neptune, and Pluto were unknown to mankind. And how could we have known them? These planets are *way* on the outskirts of our solar system, and it even blows my mind today to think of the fact that we're aware of their existence. Unlike the inner planets, they're not visible to the naked eye and require higher-quality telescopes in order to come into view. But now

> Don't think of *malefic* planets like Saturn and Mars as all bad; sometimes their tough love is exactly what we need.

26

that we *are* aware of them, these planets have become an important part of modern-day astrology (specifically Western astrology).

We look at these planets' influence and their relationships to other planets just as we do with the inner planets now. In fact, despite only being discovered between the late eighteenth and early twentieth centuries, each of the outer planets have been given a sign to rule over in modern-day astrology, making them a massively important part of the zodiac. Each planet has also been assigned qualities and traits, just like the personal planets have. These qualities sometimes even coincide with the type of events taking place in the world at the time of the planet's discovery, as that timing is believed to be significant.

Each of the three outer planets are believed to operate at a so-called "higher octave" or "higher vibration" to one of the personal planets: Uranus is the higher vibration of Mercury; Neptune is the higher vibration of Venus; and Pluto is the higher vibration of Mars. Thus, each of the outer planet's qualities are considered to be a sort of evolution of its associated personal planet. While the qualities of the inner planets are personal, the outer planets take those same concepts and transform them into qualities that connect us to the collective consciousness, the group experience of humanity. The associated outer planet evolves the inner planet's qualities to apply on a more transcendental level.

Because of the slow movement of these planets through the zodiac as compared with the inner planets' cycles, these planets are believed to have a greater influence over the arc of time, causing more long-lasting changes within the themes that humanity faces on the whole rather than affecting us on an individual level. This isn't to say these planets *don't* affect us personally—they do, especially when they form strong aspects (relationships) to our personal planets! It's rather to note that these outer planets simply have a stronger influence over the collective rather than the individual, shaping global themes in a more powerful way than the quicker-moving personal planets are able to. Think about it: We weren't even aware of these planets' existence until relatively recent times in the history of astrology, so we shouldn't expect to feel these planets on a regular basis.

This makes sense, too, when we think about the outer planets' proximity from the Sun—they're incredibly and vastly far away from it, so far away that we weren't even aware of their existence during the majority of astrology's history! The Sun represents our ego and sense of individuality; it's the ultimate personal planet. The fact that Uranus, Neptune, and Pluto are such a significant distance from this energy—and really take their time traveling through the zodiac—speaks to their nature of having a more pointed focus on the collective, a slow-moving effort. They're far from the ego and the center of the *self*.

The outer
planets affect
bigger-picture issues
and tend to work
in the background,
but don't overlook their
influence in our personal
lives or chalk up their effects
to some other planetary
happening. Their effects are real.

Planetary Dignities

Just as we feel more comfortable at home than we might feel elsewhere, planets feel more or less comfortable, free, and dignified, depending on which sign they're in. These categories are called dignities, and they denote the signs that a planet is most comfortable or most spectacular in, as well as the signs in which a planet is *least* comfortable and least dignified.

That said, some astrologers feel that planetary dignities only apply to the inner planets, and aren't applicable to the transpersonal outer planets. It's believed by some that these planets deal in issues too intangible and nebulous, which makes categories such as dignities (and even rulerships) irrelevant. In fact, some astrologers follow traditional astrology so devotedly that they don't acknowledge the modern-day rulership of planets over certain signs (Uranus to Aquarius, Neptune to Pisces, and Pluto to Scorpio) and prefer to stick to the traditional rule that involved the inner planets only, which obviously eliminates the outer planets having a domicile or detriment. And similarly, some astrologers also reject the idea that the outer planets have a sign of exaltation or fall (and even among those who do, there is some debate and confusion around *which* signs represent their exaltation and fall).

While I like to acknowledge this deviation, I also believe that as modern-day students of astrology, it's nice to embrace the new systems. So in this book, we're going to include the domiciles and exaltations for *all* the planets, but we'll note any time there's a case of traditional rulerships versus modern-day interpretations so you're aware and can come to your own conclusions.

Here are the key words to keep in mind when it comes to dignities for each planet:

Domicile: This is a planet's home base. When we say that a planet "rules" a zodiac sign, that generally denotes that it's the planet's domicile. When a planet is in its domicile, it's *home*—and it feels good. A planet in its domicile is a planet at its most *effective*. All of its qualities, goals, and overall energy will be highly functional in its domicile. It's able to be completely itself, and nothing about the sign's energy will oppose, counteract, or throw wrenches in the way of a planet's wants, needs, and tasks. This is a planet's home sweet home, and the place where it's most comfortable.

Detriment: A planet's detriment is the opposite of a planet's domicile. When a planet is here, it feels restricted and inhibited. The energy of the sign of a planet's detriment opposes many of the qualities of the planet, making it much more difficult to express itself the way it would like to. It's a frustrating place to be—kind of like hanging out with someone whom you just don't jive with. We've all been around energies (in the form of people, places, or situations) that make us feel unable to express ourselves. That's exactly how a planet feels in its detriment. It's likely to hit roadblocks and yellow lights at every intersection while trying to go about its business, which is frustrating.

Exaltation: Every planet has a sign in which it's known to be *exalted*. This is different than its domicile, but is just as positive, if not even more so! When a planet is in its exaltation, it's like being a guest at its very best, most lovely friend's home—a friend that's *more* than happy to accommodate for its visit, and a home that it feels incredibly comfortable in; in fact, a planet feels pampered in its exaltation. Exaltations are each planet's chance to feel just as expressive as they do at home, but with a little extra sparkle and gleam. In exaltation, a planet gets to be the best, most dignified version of itself. It's a grand, freeing, and fun placement that makes a planet and its energy extra regal.

Fall: This is the opposite of an exaltation. It feels like being in the home of a person you don't know very well, maybe don't trust, and *definitely* don't want to stay with. When a planet is in its fall, it doesn't feel appreciated. The energy of the sign of its fall makes the planet question itself and feel self-conscious. It's as if suddenly, its qualities aren't seen as important or valid—even though, of course, they still are! It's an awkward placement that can even make the planet feel a little embarrassed. And *no one* is living their best life or shining the way they should be when they feel embarrassed and self-conscious. It's a frustrating and uncomfortable placement for a planet, as it's being poked in its weak spots and is questioning who it is.

Let's dive a little deeper into the ins and outs of each of the big ten, shall we?

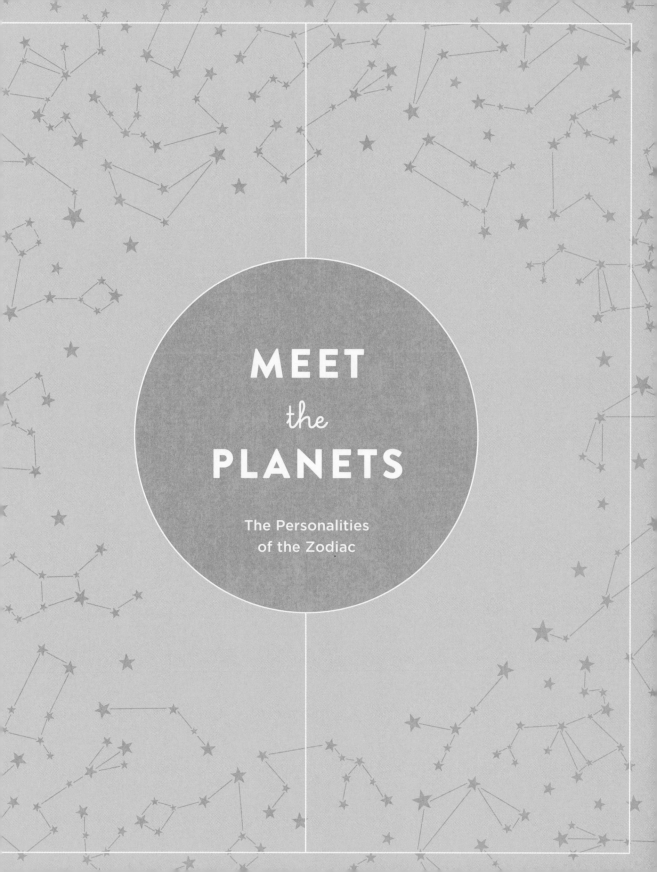

MEET
the
PLANETS

The Personalities
of the Zodiac

SUN

King of the Self; Center of the Solar System

HOME TURF	Leo
EXALTED IN	Aries
DAY OF THE WEEK	Sunday is, quite obviously, the Sun's day! This makes Sunday a great day to focus on yourself and your higher goals. Be creative!
KEY CONCEPTS	Vitality, ego, will, identity, the conscious mind

Meet the glittering, sparkling, blazing-hot ball of fire in the sky known as the Sun.

Really, this glowing luminary doesn't need much of an introduction, as you're likely *quite* familiar with it if you're a member of its solar system.

This baby has a lot of things going for it (well, it's not a baby, but rather a giant orb that could fit more than a million Earths inside of it—but I digress): It's the largest celestial object in our solar system (like I said, a million Earths!), the only star in our solar system (and thus, our sole provider of light, heat, and life itself), and the celestial body around which all the other planets orbit. Whew, that's quite a resume.

The life-giving Sun is always the brightest point in the sky (and from our vantage point here on Earth, it looks to be the brightest star in the whole *universe*).

It's no wonder the Sun is perhaps the most well-known of all the planetary figures in astrology, too. After all, almost everyone knows their Sun sign, whether they're interested in astrology or not. It's the sign most horoscopes are written for, and the sign that you'd answer with when someone asks you, "What's your sign?" While all the planets are important, we mustn't forget that the blazing Sun is the center of this show. And how could we? We see it every day, and we couldn't live without it. There are billions of stars in our galaxy, but the beautiful Sun is *ours*.

In astrology, the Sun represents our identity. It's the core of ourselves, the center around which all of our other quirks and qualities orbit, and the foundation on which we build the rest of our complex and wonderful personalities. As the planet that represents the power of the self, the Sun is dripping in purpose and self-awareness. It's bestowed with an unshakable sense of power, free will, and the creative energy of the spirit. The Sun is our *soul* (and I should note that the Sun is affiliated with the Roman god *Sol*). It's the fire inside us that wills us to keep going.

Without the Sun, we simply wouldn't exist. In other words: He's *kind of* a big deal.

> The *Sun* is the burning core of our being that tells us who we are, after everything else is stripped away.

It's our drive, motivation, and will to *live*. The Sun represents vitality, health, and vibrancy, and is our source of life force energy in astrology.

Humans revere the Sun in the sky as the force of life on Earth, and there's endless religious and spiritual symbolism surrounding this luminary that spans far beyond the ancient realm of astrology. As the ruler of the daytime (as well as the singular force of warmth, safety, and visibility that we long for during the night), the Sun is the part of our zodiac makeup that wants to be *seen*. It *is* the OG source of all light on our lil' blue planet, after all, so naturally it feels good in the spotlight. It is shining in all its glory when it's able to express itself freely and openly, without restriction. In that sense, the Sun is both what we truly are and what we should *strive* to be. Being ourselves isn't always easy, but we'll always be happiest when we're able to be authentic. This is why it's believed that most people are happiest and most content when they're able to fully express their Sun sign's qualities. The Sun wants to *shine*, baby, and we'll be happier if we allow it to.

Just as the Sun in the sky is what lights up the daytime, giving us the power to see with our eyes what is right in front of us, the Sun in astrology is what lights up our conscious mind—our *awareness* of the physical world around us, as well as our sense of who we are. In the mental daylight of our conscious mind, matters are less esoteric and more straightforward. Our sense of self, as well as our thoughts, are rooted in reality, and we relate to these matters with our ego. This is the Sun's *thing*, what with it being at the core of our solar system and all. It's no wonder that we human beings often feel so ruled by our egos! The Sun knows exactly who it is, at its core, and is driven by a will to be itself.

One of the main qualities of the Sun's shiny personality? Its sheer will. The Sun rules our ego, and our ego gives us *will*. We must not confuse the Sun's strong will with Mars's action-oriented and bulldozer-like power to take charge. Rather, the Sun's extraordinary will blossoms from its deep-rooted sense of self. If we think of the zodiac as a business, then we could think of the Sun as its founder or CEO. The Sun wants to express its vision, share its viewpoint, and shine as an individual. So while any business obviously requires many moving parts in order to be successful, *this* guy's in charge. It is the Sun's vision and purpose that drives the rest of the zodiac—it's a power source *and* a powerful force.

Speaking of power sources, the Sun is also *the* great source of masculine energy among the planets (while the Moon, conversely, is the great feminine symbol). While there are other planets that are authoritative, paternal, and embody stereotypically masculine qualities, the Sun is the true father figure and divine masculine force of the zodiac. It represents leadership, the ability to trust ourselves and tap into our soul power. In our birth charts, it can also reveal information about our relationship to masculine authority figures or other prominent male figures in our lives.

While the other planets speak to how you do or feel or conceptualize or relate to things, the Sun speaks to what you *are*. This planet is the essence of you since you became you.

This luminary is the core, the foundation, and the centerpiece around which everything else *you* is built. So you can build yourself a fancy mansion, a bohemian love shack, or even a tent in the woods—but at the end of the day, it's still *your* home, filled with *your* things, and inherently imbued with the essence of *who you are*.

None of this is to say that the other planets are not important—because they are, vastly so, and without them the zodiac (and we) would be incomplete! You can think of the other planets in our charts as representative of moving parts. They govern the various ways in which our personalities and preferences are expressed. But at the center of it all, at the very core of it, is still the Sun. It is the singular, shining ball of fire around which everything else orbits—it's the source of life as we know it.

We also know that the Sun, in all its fiery power and glory, could burn us alive. If we merely stared at it for too long, we'd go completely blind. The astrological Sun is just as powerful, as it represents our ego, our sense of self, and our individuality. But if we become *too* swept up in the realm of our conscious mind and ego, neglecting the shadow parts of ourselves and putting forth an imbalanced amount of energy toward this part of the whole being, we may get burned and find ourselves unable to see things clearly—as if we stared into the Sun. An ego that's grown too large can make a person self-obsessed and disconnected from the forces that bind them to their surroundings. On a bad day, the Sun can be judgmental, overly individualistic, and egotistical.

But honestly, if the Sun has a larger-than-average ego, I don't blame him. That *is* kind of its thing. As the only star in our solar system, the Sun *literally* has star power! This makes it a bit of a showy character—or at the very least, a self-assured one. It loves to be seen, loves to express itself, and above all, loves to *shine*. And why wouldn't it? Shining is perhaps the Sun's most noteworthy day-to-day accomplishment, right? That said, you can think of the Sun as being quite dignified and perhaps even a little bit *royal* in nature. It knows damn well its importance in our corner of the universe, and thus it feels it's owed respect, dignity, and attention because of it.

So on the one hand, being the all-important center of the solar system makes the Sun's sense of self-importance quite grandiose. But on the other hand, being the all-important center of the solar system is a seriously *major* responsibility that not all planets have the will and confidence to take on. Without the generosity and life-giving power of the Sun, we wouldn't have warmth or light or the incredibly breathtaking beauty of the sunrise and sunset. Again, without the Sun, we wouldn't exist at all. The Sun works in an equally integral symbiosis with the other planets in astrology as it does in astronomy. Its light energizes and gives life to the qualities of each of the other planets as it interacts with them, and provides a spotlight that illuminates them from their best sides.

The Sun moves through the zodiac signs in astrology like any other planet, despite it *actually* being a fixed star that doesn't orbit anything in astronomy. Its astrological "orbit" is instead based on Earth's orbit around the Sun. This means it completes its full cycle through the zodiac once per calendar year, and spends approximately thirty days in each of the twelve signs. This clearly mirrors the Gregorian calendar, which has approximately thirty days in a month, and twelve months in a year (although the Sun's new year begins at the spring equinox rather than on January 1). When we refer to things like "Aries season" or "Leo season," we're referring to the monthlong period that the Sun spends in that zodiac sign each year. With this in mind, you can now justify celebrating your solar return for the *entirety* of your Sun sign's season. So yes, demanding extra attention for your whole birthday month has an astrological basis, too—the Sun is in your sign, and as we know, the Sun *demands* attention. So sweet sixteen it up during your entire Sun season, no matter *how* old you're turning.

It is understandable that the Sun requires a little more attention and space in astrology than the other planets do. This giant luminary is a glowing core at the center of our *own* personal astrological solar systems—aka our birth charts—and we must honor this regal planet for giving us a sense of self and the will to be authentic and express the highest versions of our true selves out in the world. The Sun is the planet that helps you maintain a sense of personal identity, your purpose as an individual, the core of what makes you *you*. Obviously, you are the sum of many different parts (or for today's purposes, many different *planets*), but el Sol is *the* soul. Many things about us change throughout our lives as we mature, learn, grow, and evolve, but beneath it all, the movement and orbiting and shifting of the tides, we still have our all-powerful Sun, showing us who we are at the very bottom of everything.

MOON

Queen of Our Feelings; Ruler of the Night

HOME TURF	Cancer
EXALTED IN	Taurus
DAY OF THE WEEK	The Moon rules Mondays (aka Moon-days), which *fully* justifies your desire to take things slow and be gentle on yourself post-weekend.
KEY CONCEPTS	Emotions, feelings, intuition, nurturing, comfort

Prepare to meet the second of the two bright 'n' shiny luminaries in astrology—although, like the first, I can guarantee you've met before.

I'm talking about the Moon, astrology's gentle, emotional, nurturing mother figure. This planet is affiliated with Luna in Roman mythology, the goddess who divinely personified the Moon in the sky.

The Moon is the ruler of the night, and generally makes its ethereal presence scarce during the consciousness of daylight, only coming into full view once the skies are dark and the Sun (or the conscious mind) has set itself to rest. Only then does this lovely luminary emerge to cast its dreamy (and occasionally eerie) glow over the tides of the sea. In astrology, the Moon rules over similarly enshadowed realms: our deepest emotions, our vulnerabilities, our intuition, and the most private sides of ourselves. As one of the luminaries, it has a significant effect on our personalities—the Moon governs over the sensitive heart and the soul of our inner self.

The Moon *feels* its way through the universe, down to the very center of each of its molecules. It's all about feelings—our emotions, our sensitivities, and what makes us feel nurtured. It's all emotion, all intuition. Unlike the powerful, self-assured Sun, the Moon doesn't feel any desire to run from or try to suppress its sensitivities, emotions, and vulnerable points. Instead, it wants to *nurture* them and create a cozy space where they can air out, heal, and feel acknowledged. This is why the Moon only comes out at night: In the darkness, this planet has created that cozy, safe atmosphere where these private and delicate parts can emerge and be themselves, and where they don't have to hide, don't have to feel shame, and don't have to worry about the rational, ego-driven critiques of the powerful Sun.

It's all about feelings—
our emotions, our
sensitivities, and what
makes us feel nurtured.

Our emotional side truly does need some mothering, because it *is* delicate—and our patriarchal society is pretty rough on it, not leaving it much space to explore, process, and grow. This makes the Moon's role even more significant: It's the divine feminine in all of us. Both the divine feminine *and* the emotional side within each of us need coddling, cuddling, and a gentle loving touch in order to feel comfortable revealing themselves to others. The Moon rules a world within ourselves that favors feelings over facts, intuition over logic, and comfort over function. In this world, these more hidden parts of us can dance, sing, or cry (of course) in the safety of the dark skies, without fear of prying eyes or ego-based judgments. The Moon, and its blanket of shadowy night, provides this safe haven for these extraordinarily intimate and tender pieces of our psyche. It is the guardian and ruler of our feelings and our vulnerable side. In the quiet of the night, this luminary can be itself—it can feel its feelings and freely embrace emotional, sentimental, and maternal qualities—and it can help us do the same.

The Roman Moon goddess Luna is affiliated with femininity and fertility, and the Moon in astrology deals in similar themes. This planet is considered the zodiac's mother and is inherently maternal. And what do mothers do? Well, a hell of a lot of things, but one notably maternal force is the way mothers nurture and care for others. And this is a big one for the Moon. This planet is primarily focused on how we *nurture*, how we bring a sense of comfort to ourselves and others. When you (or someone you love) need an emotional pacifier, here comes the Moon. This planet is the cup of hot soup delivered to your bedside when you have the flu, or the security blanket you sleep with on nights when your heart aches. Emotions and intuition go hand in hand with the Moon's protective desire to nurture: These are parts of ourselves that require protection and nurturing to feel safe. We struggle to process our feelings if

The Moon's nature is to nurture.

39

we're unable to nurture them. And we struggle to remain in touch with our intuition if we don't feel like we're in an accepting and comfortable place to do so. The shadows of the night offer us this safety, and we have the gentle light of the Moon to guide us.

Of course, we also have a tendency to *fear* what lurks in the shadows, don't we? The Moon's night can be a warm, validating blanket of security over our most vulnerable feelings, or it can be thought of as a dark and dangerous place, where monsters or other imaginary evils may hide out, waiting to launch a surprise attack. This luminary rules over the dark side of our emotions and vulnerabilities, too—sadness, heartache, insecurity, jealousy, and any heavy emotions or memories that we carry with us but feel unable to express due to shame or fear. The Moon can guide our shadow work, that is, the time we spend exploring dark and "undesirable" or shameful parts of our personalities. Your Moon sign can point to the way in which you hide or act out. On a good day, the Moon brings out the nurturing mother in us. On a bad day, the Moon makes us act like a total baby in dire *need* of a mother to stick a bottle in its mouth.

The fact that the Moon is the planet closest to the Earth (and revolves around it) illustrates its rule over the most intimate, domestic, and closely guarded parts of ourselves. It rules our private inner worlds as well as our private lives in general (which makes sense when you think about the emotions, feelings, and memories that go hand in hand with lunar energy). This rule over private and intimate realms also extends to the concept of home and family. Our home is our safe haven, and our families are the people we can be our truest selves around, showing both the good and the less-good. Like the relationship between a mother and child, the Moon is our motherly protector, keeping our emotional sides safe from harm and exploitation.

Other realms that the dreamy Moon rules over are things like our past—this includes our most precious memories, deep-rooted feelings, and the emotional growth we experience throughout our lives. The Moon is often willing to indulge in the pleasure and pain of a little nostalgia. Getting lost in old sepia memories, feeling your heart flutter or tears well up in your eyes when hearing an old favorite song—these are the beautiful moments that can take

Your *Moon* sign can point to the way in which you hide or act out.

place under the light and care of the Moon's rulership. When thinking in terms of the purposeful Sun, it may not seem like the most productive use of our time, but humans are the sum of many parts. And without these emotional, complex, private moments that take place between us and our feelings, or us and our memories, we wouldn't have the rich and complex foundation on which to launch ourselves into the future. Thus, a balance must be struck. Existing only in the ego-driven spotlight of the Sun's daylight *or* only in the emotional and sensitive cocoon of the Moon's night would make *anyone* feel imbalanced. We need time to be *on*, and then we need time to recharge. The Moon offers us that recharge refuge, but we must beware of getting swept away in its waves of emotion and drowning in its feelings, too.

Because the Moon is the fastest-moving planet in astrology, speeding through the zodiac wheel and switching signs every two and a half days, it is incredibly adaptable. And to use a word that speaks to its watery nature, its ever-changing state makes it fluid. Think of the way in which it changes form on a nightly basis, switches zodiac signs every few days, and completes its entire run through the zodiac's spectrum every month. This, of course, also indicates that the Moon's qualities may not be the most reliable. Just as the Moon moves quickly through the sky and the tides that it rules over pull constantly back and forth, so do our emotions have the capacity to (and often do) change, fluctuate, and transform entirely. If we always favored feelings over facts, we may not have the most secure and trustworthy foundation on which to build something long term, would we?

The Moon's placement in our charts (and the relationships it has with the other planets there) can show us a lot about the way we nurture and *feel* nurtured, as well as the way in which we typically process and express our emotions. It can also illuminate the relationships we have with our family and the concept of "home"—or in other words, where we feel comfortable, safe, and nurtured—as well as the nature of some of our earliest memories and life-shaping experiences. Because it is associated in general with mothers (or maternal figures), the Moon in our chart can also point to how we relate personally to significant feminine influences in our lives, as well as how our own maternal instincts are expressed. The house in our chart in which the Moon resides may be an area of our life where we feel particularly emotionally sensitive or protective, and it may also be an area where we crave privacy and feel extra vulnerable.

The Moon is all heart. It's the core of our feelings-center and the amalgamation of every experience that has come together to form the emotional being that is *you*. The Moon is simultaneously us at our most loving and maternal, as well as us at our most childish and oversensitive. The Sun may be our spirit and our essential life force, but the Moon is our heart and soul.

MERCURY

Your Go-to Cosmic Calendar, Cell Phone, and Search Engine

HOME TURF	Gemini and Virgo
EXALTED IN	Virgo
DAY OF THE WEEK	Mercury rules Wednesday, the midpoint of the week. This is a good day to clean up your calendar and get organized (the week ain't over yet!) and perhaps start planning some social outings (as the weekend ain't far off, either!).
KEY CONCEPTS	Intellect, communication, transportation, technology, information sharing

Don't kill the messenger! Because, well, if you did, then we wouldn't very well have the planet Mercury. And we like him, so let's keep him around. Mercury is the innermost planet of our solar system, meaning it's both the closest to the Sun and the fastest moving in its orbit (next to the Moon, of course, since technically the Moon orbits the Earth). As the messenger planet, Mercury must be quick on his feet. It's named for the Roman god Mercury, the messenger of the gods. Depicted as a fleet-footed, winged-capped messenger in Roman mythology, Mercury is just as much the swift-moving, reliable, and always clever character in astrology, tasked with the delivery of information and much, much more. Mercury has a very large load to manage in its astrological duties. When you need to put together a schedule, plan out your day, or communicate with other people, here comes Mercury—your astrological planner/taxi driver/communications department and so much more.

The Sun obviously likes to keep his errand boy close, and there's no better planet suited for the task than the quick-moving and even quicker-thinking Mercury. It's important that Mercury not only be quick on its feet but also that it stay on its toes, as this is the planet of communication, so *anything* could come up and Mercury would have to find a way to respond and deal. And Mercury is a fabulous first responder. Always rational

Mercury is the internet of the zodiac's planets in the sense that it's *full* of information and serves as a direct line of connection with so many other things.

and objective in its method of thinking, this planet is constantly observing its surroundings and taking things in with computer-like precision. Mercury, in its highest evolution, is the ultimate objective observer—always factual, always correct, and always with a keen eye for details. Mercury is the information-gathering and processing center of the zodiac, and it's a fabulously run one at that.

But Mercury is much more than just an observer and a processor of incoming info. It is also tasked with managing all *outgoing* communications just as equally. So Mercury takes in information, processes it, and then puts out a response, and it governs how *we* do the same. Mercury is the essential planet of communication. It rules, on the most fundamental level, how we express our thoughts and ideas to other people. This starts at birth, when babies communicate by crying, laughing, and using facial expressions. Then we gain the ability to use language, and Mercury rules that, too. Mercury also rules your speech patterns, choice of slang, texting style, and even handwriting! If it's unique to the way you communicate and express *ideas* to the world, then you can bet Mercury has its hand in it.

Adding to the long list that comprises Mercury's astrological resume, this planet also governs the realm of short-distance travel, scheduling, and transportation. While world traveling and big, fancy trips are growth-focused Jupiter's jurisdiction, Mercury rules over how we get from place to place on a more regular, day-to-day basis—cars, buses, trains, rideshare apps, planes, and even our GPS and phone maps are major points in Mercury's rule. This planet governs the way we conceptualize our schedules and how we map out our days logistically. It helps us manage our responsibilities and expectations and organize them into a nice and well-timed schedule (timing is another major area that Mercury rules). So Mercury helps you create your schedule, and can then assist you in *sticking* to it by whisking you from place to place, keeping you on top of timing and plans, and helping you communicate more clearly so that misunderstandings don't get in the way of your smooth sailin'. As you can see, Mercury is a very busy bee—and when this planet lights up in your chart, you'll likely be a busy bee, too!

This planet represents a big part of the rational brain when it comes to the body of the zodiac. And besides our brain, what tools do we use to collect information, store information, process information, and share information? Why, technology, of course! That said, it's no surprise to learn that Mercury rules over tech gadgets on top of all the other things it manages (although, I must note that *future* technologies are ruled by innovative Uranus, which we'll get to later).

In fact, if you want to behold what is perhaps the most Mercury vibed-out object of modern times, simply grab that beloved (or perhaps deeply loathed but relied upon nonetheless) little techno-brick that we carry around with us everywhere we go. Yeah, I'm talking about your cell phone. We use it to check the date and time (timing), manage our calendars and set reminders for upcoming events (scheduling), call rides via apps and map out our drives (transportation), make calls and send texts and check e-mails (communication), and access the well of information that is the World Wide Web (information sharing). This is *all* classic Mercury stuff, and this is why Mercury is known to govern technological devices. Communication and information sharing aren't just done via the written or spoken word, like it was during centuries past. We now communicate regularly via our phones, e-mail, social media accounts, photo sharing—and memes. We cannot forget memes. A good meme is an intersection between technology, communication, and (in most cases) wit, all of which are areas of Mercury's expertise. So yes, Mercury rules memes, and you can expect that this planet would *definitely* be sliding into your DMs with the dankest memes around if it had its own social media account.

But Mercury is much more than a simple errand boy to the Sun's wishes, even with all its proficiency in the realms of communication and transportation. Mercury also rules over the esteemed and ever-important realms of intellect and thinking. So while the Moon, for example, *feels* its way through life, Mercury couldn't fathom doing anything but using objective thinking to identify with the world around it.

What's great, too, is that Mercury isn't one of those intellectual types who lacks social skills. Oh no—this planet excels when it comes to communicating, so the act of observation, then processing, then expression of thought is a seamless activity for this guy. And remember, we communicate not only with people, but also with our *surroundings* constantly, in all different ways—and Mercury governs all of them.

Just like the element mercury, which is an amazing liquid-like metal at room temperature, planet Mercury is a somewhat slippery, hard-to-pin-down type of fellow, as I'm sure you're realizing. This planet is speedy, sharp as a tack, and *ever* clever—as it has to be, with its rulership of so many different facets of our daily life. This busybody planet shoulders a *lot* of responsibility, so it's necessary that it's both quick moving and sharp of mind. Mercury is your PR person. Your messenger. Your driver. And the most rational *thinker* you know. Intellect, scheduling, transportation, technology, and communication comprise a rather varied bag o' tricks for a single planet to hide up its sleeve, but if any one of them could pull it off, it's Mercury, with its clever and intellectual edge.

The various things that Mercury is in charge of each has a pretty significant influence in our day-to-day lives, no matter our age or occupation. We all have a schedule to stick to, have to get from place to place, and have to communicate with others and the world around us. This is partly why Mercury's tri- to quad-annual retrograde periods are so damn dizzying for most of us. To be honest, I'd be remiss to discuss Mercury without also noting the planet's infamous retrograde periods. The concept of "Mercury retrograde" has entered the

Fickle Mercury

Mercury experiences the widest gap between high and low temperatures of all the planets in the solar system. The highs are due to its close proximity to the Sun, while the lows can be blamed on its lack of a proper atmosphere to keep in any warmth during the planet's nights. So yes, the planet is indeed rather mercurial by definition—and some astrologers note that Mercury rules over and makes us aware of opposing forces in our environment, such as light and dark, cool and warm, night and day. A mercurial fellow indeed.

mainstream canon over the past years, and it's essentially synonymous with life getting messy. I'm sure you've heard people ask if Mercury is retrograde when plans go awry, apps crash, or other various scheduling mishaps or misunderstandings occur. During a Mercury retrograde (which is when the planet appears to move backward in the sky for a few weeks), we experience a major slowdown in the Mercury-ruled sectors of our life. This can result in poor communication, crumbling plans, tech malfunctions, travel snafus, and myriad other Mercury-related dramas.

In your personal natal chart, your Mercury sign can tell you a lot about how you handle information processing and communication on a daily basis. It's revealing of our communication styles, as well as the way we think, process facts, make short-term plans, and operate socially. Mercury also rules over things like studying (although higher education falls under Jupiter's reign), as well as short trips, so we might see revelations about these areas by looking to a Mercury sign, too. The house in which Mercury resides in our chart points to an area of our life where we can easily utilize our rational thinking skills, and are likely to feel more analytical and objective in the way we consider things there. We may find it easier to communicate our thoughts in the area ruled by Mercury's house, and notice that we're more curious about matters in that area, too.

If Mercury is retrograde, it's time to back up your laptops and phones, think before you speak, read all the fine print on everything, and avoid making any major final decisions.

VENUS

Goddess of Love; Empress of Pleasure; Queen of All That We Value

HOME TURF	Taurus and Libra
EXALTED IN	Pisces
DAY OF THE WEEK	Venus rules Friday, the beautiful day of the week that's full of hope and excitement for the weekend. This makes Friday a lovely day to pamper yourself and up the luxurious self-care factor, Venus style—or to plan a fun and romantic evening with a date or friends.
KEY CONCEPTS	Love, beauty, pleasure, value, luxury

She is beauty, she is grace—and she's got impeccable taste. Welcome to the luxuriously sensual, incredibly beautiful, endlessly expensive, and mind-bogglingly romantic realm of planet Venus. Named aptly for the Roman goddess of love, beauty, and desire (also known as Aphrodite in Greek mythology), Venus is the gorgeous planet that rules over these lovely realms and more—romance and pleasure, beauty and aesthetics, and money and luxury all fall under Venus's jurisdiction. Welcome to the church of endless pleasure, aka Venus's domain. It's a beautiful place to be.

Ultimately, Venus is about what we *value*, how we *love*, and what brings us *pleasure*. These are the main things that this planet points to in our charts. Venus shows us the things we find valuable—in life, love, relationships, *everything*. It shows us how we love and how we want to be loved, and how we want to be swept off our feet. It shows us what we find beautiful, pleasing, tasteful, and *why*. The powerful Sun keeps two planets very close to it: sharp and objective Mercury, which carries out its important day-to-day tasks, and then beautiful Venus, the planet of value. But Venus leads not with her mind, but rather with her *senses*, and without her, life simply wouldn't taste or look or smell or sound or feel as sweet.

What Venus is perhaps *most* famous for is her rulership over our love lives. Venus rules over our desires as well as our values, and love hovers right over these two areas, incorporating them both into its warm and rich realm. Venus loves to be in love—and when it comes to being in love, there are several different aspects to consider, all of which are equally Venusian in nature. First, there's the part of love that's pure *romance*. The butterflies in your stomach, the lovey-dovey

Venus appears when we're falling in love, when we need to beautify something, and when we take in our surroundings in a sensual, pleasurable fashion.

48

gifts of chocolate and flowers, the sticky-sweet showers of compliments, the luxurious date nights (along with the hours of beautifying and primping that come before them), and the endless sensual pleasures that chime when so closely sharing yourself (and your body!) with another. This pleasure concept with Venus extends *way* beyond the sensual pleasure of lovemaking—Venus rules over how we give, receive, and experience pleasure in any and *all* ways, using all of our senses! But if we're talking about being in love, then yes, these romantic, pleasure-filled aspects are very much what Venus is all about.

Money is *luxury* and value, and therefore Venus rules it.

Second, there's the part of love that's less butterflies-in-your-stomach and more about *value*, which is another of Venus's big key words. When we're in a healthy and loving relationship, we often reach a point where we find a deep sense of value in our love with our chosen partner. It's deep, it's meaningful, and it gives us a profound kind of pleasure that is perhaps beyond the purely sensory pleasures that we're dealt in spades during the romantic courting process that Venus treasures so dearly. Venus deeply enjoys feeling *pampered* (physically, financially, and beyond), and a loving relationship can often provide such a feeling of luxurious comfort in myriad ways. The surface-level pleasure of a budding romance combined with the deep-rooted pleasure of a trusting, valued relationship makes Venus one happy love goddess.

Venus also rules over aesthetics and beauty, which makes her a lover and an aficionado of everything from fashion to fine art. Venus is your art dealer, your interior designer, your personal stylist, your hairdresser, your makeup artist, and your matchmaker, all bundled up in one beautiful package. This planet rules your fashion sense, your taste in art, your makeup bag, the way you decorate your home, your hairstyle, and everything else that has to do with adorning your appearance or the appearance of your space. Your highly curated Instagram grid? Also Venus. Venus is the great beautifier of the zodiac. She loves being beautiful, but as a planet of sensuality, she's just as equally interested in being *attracted* to beautiful things. That's what Venus's love of aesthetics and beauty comes down to: attraction. After all, we generally style our outfits and make ourselves up in order to look attractive in some way, right? Perhaps the goal is to attract the attention of another person, or perhaps it's simply to express what *we* find attractive. Venus rules over what we're attracted to and how we attract others, as well as all the showy, excessive performances that come along with it.

Venus's focus and emphasis on value also makes her the planet of *money*, honey. While the concept of money and finance may feel cold and calculating when compared with Venus's other flowery and beauty/pleasure-centered qualities, that's simply our conditioning, as most of us are forced to take a rather rational approach to money in our society. It just takes a quick adjustment of perspective to see why money is a Venusian concept. Money is inherently a form of *value* in our society, and what we value is what Venus is all about. Money is also what we often think of as our doorway to *luxury*, which is another one of Venus's big key words. So while it's true that having a disciplined budget and savings plan might be more Saturn's territory, and that being ambitious and cutthroat in the workplace might be more Mars's jurisdiction, money as a *concept*—a form of value, a currency of luxury, and a gateway to freedom and pleasure—is very much a Venusian cup of tea.

If Venus were a soap opera character, she'd be the female lead—painfully beautiful; probably wearing an expensive, imported silk robe; enjoying a cigarillo from a long, slender cigarette holder like Hollywood starlets of the past; drinking a martini made from only the finest ingredients. And if Venus had a home, I'd imagine it to be draped in a Valentine's Day palette of reds and pinks, with ornate Victorian-style decor. Walls lined with sensual, expensive artworks. Curtains on giant, scenic windows made of delicate lace, and blankets piled atop giant, cloudlike daybeds made of the softest velvet. Every surface would boast vases of fresh, fragrant, luscious roses, and a warm breeze through an open window would carry their pungently sweet scent through the rooms, along with the sounds of birds chirping like an eternal spring.

In our birth charts, Venus can tell us a lot about what kind of lover we are, based on the sign that it's in. It can also point us toward the things in life we value, how we give and receive pleasure, what our relationship with money is like, and how we prioritize beauty. People who identify as women may embrace their Venus sign's qualities more fluidly, seeing their femininity clearly expressed through the energy of the sign. If you're attracted to feminine people, you might also look to your Venus sign to tell you more about what you find sensual and attractive in a romantic partner, and *why* you feel this way. Our Venus sign rules our aesthetic sense and the things we find beautiful in the world. The house in which Venus falls tends to be an area where we easily find pleasurable experiences.

Because of its proximity to the Sun, Venus moves through the signs relatively quickly, switching zodiac placements every month or so, and only ever moving up to two signs away from the Sun. It's no surprise that this planet is known as one of only two "benefic" planets, denoting that it has a tendency to bring about positive, enjoyable, benevolent influences wherever it travels in the zodiac. As the "lesser benefic" (the greater being lucky Jupiter), Venus is celebrated for being her pleasurable, love-lovin' self almost anywhere she goes.

MARS

God of War and Passion (Rawr)

HOME TURF	Aries (also the traditional/co-ruler of Scorpio)
EXALTED IN	Capricorn
DAY OF THE WEEK	Mars rules Tuesday, which makes Tuesday a great day to get *really* motivated for the week, start chopping away at your to-do list, and pick up the slack after a sleepy Monday.
KEY CONCEPTS	Action, passion, defense, boldness, animalistic instinct

Be on your best behavior for this one, kids, because hotheaded Mars is not to be f*cked with.

Mars is known as the red planet because it's red in color. And what exactly do we think of when we think of the color red? Passion. Anger. Heat. Rage. Blood. Danger. Just to name a few. Each and every one of these words could be applied to the qualities that Mars rules in astrology.

Mars is a force to be reckoned with, a powerhouse of action, a whole army of one. The red planet indeed packs a punch—and it's willing to throw a punch, too. Often labeled the "warrior planet," Mars rules with physical strength and is high in physicality and energy. It's perhaps the most energized of all the planets, and because its nature is so deeply rooted in energy and physicality, its qualities are also rather primal in nature. Think of the animalistic instincts that all of us experience—everything from our sex drive to rage to the *fighting* of fight-or-flight. These are all super Mars-y realms.

Mars is also known as an inherently masculine planet, given the stereotypically masculine energy it encompasses. If the zodiac were a teen drama, Mars would be the school bully on a bad day. But on a good day, it would probably be the jock. Hot. Muscular. Maybe with a little bit of a rage problem. Definitely the star of the football team. And speaking of football, Mars is competitive as all hell, so it's not advisable to stand in his way once he's set his mind to something (this planet also rules over sports and other physical activities, so go figure). Mars plays to win—even if it means bull-dozing anything and everything in his path—and he isn't afraid to play dirty, either.

In addition to Mars's physicality and strength, he's got all the ideal personal qualities needed to bring home the prize. Mars is brave, fearless, bold, aggressive, and ambitious. This planet's courage is boundless. While his problem-solving abilities won't involve any intellectual or

Mars is most certainly in touch with its inner beast. It's full of adrenaline, physical power, intensity, and has an insanely high pain tolerance.

rational thinking, they will indeed involve an amount of ambition, strength, and zeal that can be delivered by no other planet, and that energy can help us achieve wondrous, superhuman things if applied when the time is right. Mars brings us the energy to compete and put forth even the most Herculean of efforts.

Mars could easily be the hero *or* villain in any story, depending on how he's aspected by other planets and whether he feels like saving the day with his zealous bravery or destroying everything in his path with his brute strength. This means Mars doesn't just lash out in a blind and unstoppable rage for no reason (I mean, he *does*, not gonna lie—just not *always*). When it comes to self-defense, Mars is our go-to guy. Mars is animalistic in his protective nature, too. Think back to the role of most men in primal times: Hunting and protecting the family from danger was kind of the *thing*. And honestly, Mars is *still* about that life, even to this day. (And yes, Mars rules hunting—as well as sharp objects in general, for that matter, interestingly enough.)

Sex is a big one for Mars, but its dominion over the act of sex shouldn't be confused with Venus's rulership over the sensual pleasures. While Venus rules love, romance, and sensuality—or the sweet, tender, romantic part of lovemaking—Mars is all about the primal, raw, animalistic side of sexuality.

Sex with Venus is lovemaking; sex with Mars is basic instinct. For Mars, sex is just sex. It's an act of passion that's hardwired into us mammals as a means of reproduction and carrying on our species—an act as natural as breathing, and something that's not unique to us but to all animalkind. We can look to Mars in our birth charts to point us toward what ignites our passion-fire when it comes to sex, what really gets us hot and bothered. This is a good gauge of what we like in sex, as well as the role we may tend to take on in sexual relationships.

The Red Planet

The planet Mars is red in color due to the high amount of iron in its surface layer—this is the same reason that our blood is red. It's no wonder, then, that this planet is named for the god of bloodshed, war, and destruction. The color red, in and of itself, is known to be able to raise a human's blood pressure and metabolism, and speed up our breathing—just by laying eyes on it!

Mars's exaggerated masculinity makes the planet's character in the theater of astrology feel like a bit of an action figure come to life. Imagine bulging muscles, a warrior's garb, and an unmistakably intimidating swagger. Oh, and a major taste for danger, of course. This dude would certainly make for an entertaining lead in an action-genre blockbuster, at the very least. Such exaggerated masculinity does indeed put us on a slippery slope toward *toxic* masculinity, though, which is likely part of why Mars is known as one of the two "malefic" planets in astrology—meaning it's often associated with bringing some element of difficulty, negativity, and even malevolence into a situation. As the "lesser malefic" (the greater being big-daddy authoritarian Saturn), Mars has the potential to be a destructive, overpowering force of toxic masculinity, sometimes bringing an undue level of intensity to a situation or causing a disruptive eruption of emotion. Accidents of all sorts also fall under Mars's jurisdiction, thanks to the reckless, impulsive, act-first-think-later nature of this hot-tempered and sometimes violent planet.

As far as the physical body goes, Mars is known to rule a few different areas. And it turns out Mars's territory is to be expected. This planet rules the sex organs—no surprise there, since Mars is a super horny planet. Sex, violence, sports: Mars rules all the most popular things on TV. It also rules the adrenal glands, which produce adrenaline, primal and energetic Mars's best friend. And of course, it rules our muscles. Major muscle-y, super fit, physically strong Mars vibes. *Do you even lift, bro?* That was yoked-out Mars asking, not me.

When you need to kick your ass into high gear, get stuff done, and crush a goal, here comes your Mars sign, diving in headfirst with a spear in hand, ready to charge forth.

In your natal chart, your Mars sign shows you the way that you take *action*. Mars is inherently active; it's our most impulsive nature come to life. It's the way we act on our passions, instincts, and ambitions—essentially how we *do* things.

Mars is extremely energizing to any part of the zodiac chart that it happens to hit and can bring in a lot of strength and motivation, but beware, because a poorly aspected Mars can also bring explosive feelings and overly impulsive (if not downright dangerous) actions.

Mars is all action; it doesn't have to rationalize and think like Mercury, nor does it get swept away in the wave of beauty like Venus. It simply *acts* and *does*. Mars is a doer, and this energy can help us take action and kick-start important projects in our personal lives, too.

JUPITER

The Great Planetary Thinker; Our Cosmic Good-Luck Charm

HOME TURF	Sagittarius (also the traditional/co-ruler of Pisces)
EXALTED IN	Cancer
DAY OF THE WEEK	Jupiter rules Thursdays, which makes it a great day to learn something new, think big, and let your imagination run wild with big plans. Break up your week on this day by consciously trying to look at life from a more philosophical and spiritual perspective.
KEY CONCEPTS	Expansion, luck, fortune, growth, knowledge

Jupiter is the behemoth planet of our solar system, by far the largest of the bunch (other than the grand Sun, of course). Jupiter checks in at several hundred times the size of our little blue planet, and is nearly twice the size of all the other non-Sun planets of the solar system *combined*. This big boy is *not* afraid to take up space and use its immense gravitational pull to its advantage! It's a gentle giant, though, as its gargantuan stature doesn't seek to intimidate, but rather simply to communicate a few things to the world: how much knowledge and experience it seeks (a lot), the size of its aspirations and faith (huge), and the amounts of fun it wants to have along the way (*massive*). Jupiter's here for a good time, but also an enlightening one.

Named for the all-powerful and esteemed Roman king of the gods (better known as Zeus in Greek mythology), the planet in astrology most certainly lives up to its royal title. Jupiter's areas of rulership—luck, fortune, growth, world travel, and higher education, to name a few—are fit for a king. But rather than ruling with fear, as his father Saturn did back when *he* was king of the gods (more on *that* juicy drama later), Jupiter proves that he rules with benevolence, fairness, and understanding. Jupiter's the *good* kind of royal. The planet is made up of mostly hydrogen and helium—it's a giant ball of gas rather than mass—and it's interesting to note that this is also *exactly* what the Sun and other stars are made of. This only speaks further to the symbolism of Jupiter's regal godliness: As far as actual planets go, this planet is the closest to becoming a *star*.

Jupiter is synonymous with expansion in astrology. It's so physically large that it only makes sense that this planet deals in the high quantities of things. Jupiter loves anything that has to do with growth: It rules over the growth of our minds, as well as the physical growth of our bodies (like, literally—don't be shocked if you end up gaining some weight when Jupiter transits through your appearance-focused rising sign or first house!). But more so than a growing body, Jupiter finds itself preoccupied with mental, spiritual, and philosophical growth in a much more profound way. Just as the planet's surface is covered in an ethereal,

When it comes to growth of any kind, Jupiter is king.

56

expansive layer of beautifully colored clouds, Jupiter astrologically represents a similar form of expansive, nebulous, enlightening, and boundless form of human thought—thoughts that are philosophical and spiritual in nature, thoughts that pose questions about the abstract, the metaphysical, the intangible. Jupiter helps us elevate beyond basic forms of thinking and begin to explore, form, and solidify our own personal moral codes and ethical views. Elevated forms of thinking are deeply important to this massive planet, and it rules over higher educa-tion and the acquisition of knowledge (Jupiter definitely has, like, a

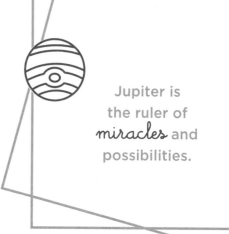

Jupiter is the ruler of *miracles* and possibilities.

minimum of *three* PhDs and probably a few honorary degrees thrown in, too). Jupiter also rules over concepts such as religion and the justice system, which makes sense, given its penchant for pondering the spiritual and philosophical sides of life.

Getting back to expansion, Jupiter is also concerned with the expansion of our bank accounts, as it rules over wealth, prosperity, and material abundance. Jupiter is known as the "luckiest" of the planets, and thus has very good fortune in all ways imaginable. And speaking of luck and material abundance, Jupiter loves to gamble (hey, if you had the kind of luck he does, wouldn't *you*?), and also rules over partying and celebrations. I *told* you Jupiter's here for a good time.

Combining Jupiter's passion for mind expansion and wealth, we've also got another concept that this planet rules: long-distance travel. Yes, the growth of our passport stamp collection is yet *another* type of growth that Jupiter is all about. Jupiter is worldly and idealistic, and its open-mindedness knows no borders, meaning this planet very much influences our desire to travel to experience new cultures, landscapes, languages, people, and ways of life. Jupiter's affinity for world travel and higher knowledge make him very wise indeed.

Another one of Jupiter's key qualities? It's sheer optimism and idealism. Clearly Jupiter's been dealt a rather lovely, prosperous, and fortunate hand in the game of astrological planet-dom, so its positive attitude and confidence in good outcomes isn't totally unfounded. But there's also this magical sort of *je ne sais quoi* element to Jupiter that's just plain *lucky*. Jupiter is charmed. Underneath the thick layer of clouds we see from Earth, this planet may as well be covered in endless fields of four-leaf clovers and countless rainbows with overflowing pots of gold at each end. Luck is always on Jupiter's side. It's as if no matter what it does or how it does it, things tend to work out okay—and perhaps even, somehow, work out perfectly.

As slightly bitter as we all may be when someone gets away with something out of sheer luck, we don't hate Jupiter for its perpetual fortune—we actually love him for it, because this planet's generosity knows no bounds! Jupiter's luck is meant to be shared with *all*. This planet genuinely wants to spread joy wherever it goes, and exhibits great amounts of gratitude (which according to the law of attraction, probably reels even *more* luck his way). The possibilities are endless when Jupiter comes 'round—so endless, in fact, that you needn't even rule out a full-blown miracle. A well-aspected Jupiter in someone's birth chart, for example, is believed to be able to counterbalance even a whole *slew* of negative aspects from other planets. That's how powerful (and generous!) this good-luck planet can truly be.

All things considered, it makes sense that in traditional astrology, Jupiter is one of two planets known as a "benefic"—and in Jupiter's case, it's the "greater benefic" (as opposed to the "lesser benefic," Venus). This means that it's influence among the planets is almost always viewed as being a positive and benevolent one, and honestly, Jupiter is pretty damn benevolent. This planet is kind, generous, understanding, and just—and it has a great sense of humor to boot. Jupiter is a blessing to all that it touches.

When Jupiter travels through your Sun or rising sign, expect for your whole life to shift into the fast lane, and watch opportunities bloom like wildflowers on your path. Jupiter jingles with good luck, or is that just all the money in his pocket? The symbol representing the god Jupiter is also fitting astrologically. It's a lightning bolt: powerful, electric, exciting, revitalizing—and like luck itself, impossible to contain, predict, or control. Jupiter has a comparable effect on whatever part of the zodiac chart it happens to be hitting. Like a lightning bolt of excitement and good fortune, it has the power to light things up in a most electrifying way.

Of course, this isn't to say that a poorly placed Jupiter can't result in any negative qualities. Can you have too much of a good thing? Of course you can have too much of *anything*, and when excessive Jupiter gets excessively excessive, things can get out of hand. What's left after a huge party? A floor full of confetti, deflated sad-looking balloons, red plastic cups sticky with punch, cake-covered paper plates, and *way* too many black trash bags full of cans and bottles and napkins that we're all too hung over to properly sort through and recycle. A scene like this one is what you might refer to as Jupiter's dark side, if he had one: Excessive. Wasteful. It's the potential aftermath of overindulgence. A hangover and a cleanup job could easily ensue. That said, Jupiter's negative sides almost *always* result from its being overly optimistic, and almost never because of having bad intentions. This is the greater benefic we're dealing with, after all, so even at his worst, we can say he gave it his best.

If we go back to the planetary teen movie scenario (wherein I likened Mars to the jocky star of the football team), I might just have to double-cast Jupiter as the cool, worldly professor who mentors the students all while maintaining a positive attitude and sense of humor, *and* the head cheerleader. Jupiter is a cheerleader in the sense that it *believes* in you. Jupiter wants you to win, and is jumping for joy by your side when you do, ready to throw you a party to celebrate afterward. Jupiter is the friend who is genuinely *happy* for you when good things happen, never jealous, never bitter. It wants you to succeed, think big, and seek improvement. Part of the joy of being such a big planet is that Jupiter knows that there's plenty of space for everyone at the top, and that one person's success doesn't have to mean another person's failure.

Jupiter also marks a noteworthy point in the order of the planets in which we begin to expand our consciousness and reach toward higher growth and maturity in general. It's really a turning point in the themes and qualities by which planets rule. Up until now, all the planets we've met have represented rather basic tenets of our being—parts of us that have either existed since birth or formed in childhood, parts that are somewhat necessary to our survival. The Sun is our ego, the Moon is our emotion, Mercury is our communication, Venus is our pleasure, and Mars is our action and defense. Jupiter, though, is *knowledge*. This planet encourages us to go above and beyond, to think about things on a higher, more philosophical level and seek a larger and deeper meaning in life.

There can sometimes also *appear* to be a wee bit of overlap between some of Jupiter and Mercury's jurisdictions, so let's clarify, as these planets are actually quite different in nature. Mercury rules information, but Jupiter rules *knowledge*. Mercury rules the observation and processing of facts, but Jupiter rules higher education and mind expansion. Mercury rules basic thinking and communication, but Jupiter rules our philosophical and spiritual thinking and expression. And Mercury also rules over modes of transportation and day-to-day traveling, but Jupiter rules long-distance travel.

Your Jupiter sign represents the way in which you grow and expand, how you take up space, and also tends to speak to your approach to philosophy, higher thinking, and even success. Whatever house Jupiter resides in within your birth chart is likely to show you a rather lush and blessed area of your life that sees a lot of success—a part of your life where perhaps you even have it easy. Jupiter's good-luck blessings always apply. This planet switches signs approximately every thirteen months, which means that only the closest peers within your generation, born within a year of you, will share your Jupiter sign. When you experience a "Jupiter return" every thirteen years, expect to feel earthshaking blessings and tons of good luck.

SATURN

The Master of Time; Cosmic Teacher of Patience

HOME TURF	Capricorn (also the traditional/co-ruler of Aquarius)
EXALTED IN	Libra
DAY OF THE WEEK	Saturn rules Saturday (aka Saturn-day), which makes it a great day of the week to prioritize structure, organization, and get yourself whipped into shape after a busy workweek, ensuring your affairs are in order before heading into another one.
KEY CONCEPTS	Discipline, patience, structure, boundaries, time

We now move on to the final and most remote of the "inner planets": Meet Saturn, the zodiac's elder and teacher and authoritarian, which rounds out the list of the traditional seven planets in astrology. Further away from the Sun than any of the aforementioned planets, Saturn can be cold and distant—this applies both literally and figuratively in astrology. Saturn is a rather rigid and paternal authority figure in astrology, dishing out life lessons via a tough-love approach at every turn. This planet represents structure, limitations, restrictions, discipline, hard work, commitment, and a desire to do things *right*. It also governs time, which means it forces us to slow down, helps us mature by teaching us lessons, and shows us the importance of patience.

As the furthest traditional planet from the Sun's generous warmth, Saturn can be an icy one, in every sense of the word. Like a drill sergeant, Saturn wouldn't be caught dead acting warm 'n' fuzzy. In fact, this chilly-to-the-bone planet has the power to freeze you dead in your tracks with a cold, hard, reality check. Whether you're falling down a tunnel of love à la Venus, impulsively charging forth with Mars's firepower, or leaping across oceans to follow a dream inspired by Jupiter, you can guarantee one of Saturn's infamous Life Lessons is lurking around the next corner, ready to hold up a metaphorical "STOP" sign, forcing you to hit the brakes. When we get carried away and start moving too quickly in life, especially if we're trying to take shortcuts or avoid putting in the hard work, Saturn swoops in and asks (or rather *forces*) us to stop, drop, and check ourselves. Is what you're

Saturn keeps it *super* real—it gives us boundaries, shows us life's restrictions, and makes us aware of our limits.

doing sensible and responsible? Are you being lazy, immature, or trying to skirt by on something other than raw effort? Is your plan well-thought-out? Are your goals even within a realistic realm of possibility, or are you being delusional? These are the types of questions Saturn and his obstacles will force you to face.

Saturn is also a *very* large planet, second in size only to the powerful expanse that is Jupiter. And mythologically, Jupiter and Saturn have some *history* with each other, too. According to Roman mythology, before lucky Jupiter became the king of the gods, it was actually his father Saturn who ruled. But when Saturn became privy to the prophecy that he'd eventually be overthrown by his own offspring, he decided to *eat his own children* after they were born to ensure he could properly rid himself of such competition. Gnarly story, right? Jupiter ended up surviving and taking over the throne in the myth, but let this tale be a testament to the fact that Saturn's energy does *not* f*ck around. Threaten his rules, authority, and power structures, and he'll *eat* you—even if he's your literal father.

Speaking of fathers, have you picked up on the major dad vibes that Saturn brings to the table yet? While the Sun is the true father of the zodiac, Saturn has many of the qualities you might expect from a stereotypically stern, strict, authoritarian father figure. And this makes sense, as Saturn is the great teacher of the zodiac—here to teach us valuable lessons through its own particular brand of harsh punishments and severe roadblocks. If this were a teen movie, Saturn would *definitely* be the female lead's tough and rigid father, the one who might ground her for bad behavior *right* before prom night to teach her about responsibility, and who is *definitely* harshly judging any not-good-enough high school boy she brings home who might distract her from getting into a good college. Because of its lesson-teaching style, Saturn has the unique ability to bring out the angsty teenager in *all* of us. This planet can make life *really*

Sometimes referred to by astrologers as the "lord of time" (a cute, casual, not at all daunting nickname for this totally chill planet, right?), Saturn forces us to slow our roll.

62

difficult and frustrating, slowing us down and making us feel punished. But misery is not the intention. Life lessons are! The tough-love approach is Saturn's way of showing you that he cares. Saturn is teaching you to be more disciplined in your behavior, exhibit patience, and get real about life so that you can *succeed*. Saturn is teaching you how to grow up.

Saturn is perhaps best known for its iconic and easily identifiable rings, icy structures that encircle this giant planet like a collar wrapped tightly around a dog's neck, like a symbolic shackle that's constantly ready to confine—a visible reminder of the fact that, yes, *boundaries exist*, and they are all at once cold and hard and very intense, and *you must work within their confines*. The rings symbolically remind us that we're not necessarily limitless, and that in order to succeed we must *acknowledge* our limits rather than attempting to ignore them. In the case of Saturn, these giant rings of ice and stone ensure that the binding nature of reality will never go ignored.

You might think of this sort of blatant reality check as a buzzkill, and honestly? You'd be right. Saturn is absolutely the buzzkill and killjoy and cold fish of the zodiac in every way. When Saturn shows up, expect a stern reality check to take place and burst any delusional little bubbles you've been blowing for yourself, but before you lose your cool over it, remember that reality checks aren't inherently a *bad* thing. Because without a reality check here and there, we'd likely not have many *actual* checks to cash, would we? Saturn may be a Debbie Downer sometimes, but it's also a disciplined and highly productive taskmaster, so it's doing *something* right. We have to trust that.

Saturn also rules over the passage of time in its many different facets—think time-related concepts such as tradition, maturity, and respecting your elders. On a more literal timing level, it often forces us to *slow down*, to check ourselves before we wreck ourselves. Shortcuts are *not* Saturn's style. At all. Saturn values long-term commitment, good old-fashioned hard work, and a level of discipline that borders on militaristic—it's a real blood/sweat/tears kind of planet.

If we're trying to *skate* through life without putting in the work, Saturn is likely to throw an obstacle in our path, but this is *always* done with the intention of forcing us to grow.

Saturn ensures we don't rush to the finish line at the expense of our own maturity and wisdom. It challenges us in order to teach us valuable lessons that we'll carry forth into our future, even if it means we have to work twice as hard and for twice as long to get to where we're going. Patience is a virtue that Saturn wants to drill into our psyches until it *sticks*. It doesn't always work, of course (most impatient Mars-ruled folk can attest to this!), but Saturn will give it his best shot.

Saturn can be harsh in the manner through which it imparts life lessons to us, but it's ultimately all about structure, and forcing us to focus on this type of structure within ourselves is what ensures we have a solid foundation on which to persevere, grow, and actually achieve what we want. Without Saturn, honestly, sh*t would fall apart. Not surprisingly, Saturn rules over the skeletal system (which is the bare-bones structure that holds our bodies upright!), and also rules hierarchies and careers, all structure-oriented systems.

With all the focus on boundaries, restriction, and discipline, Saturn has a heavy cross to bear. It is often referred to as the "greater malefic" planet in astrology (one of only two planets put into this category, Mars being the "lesser" malefic). This title refers to the planet's ability to bring challenge, struggle, hardship, and other somewhat malevolent energies to whatever area of a chart it hits. Of course, calling this planet "malevolent" is harsh and not totally accurate, but it can certainly feel this way when you're in the thick of it. A perfect example of this is the concept of a "Saturn return"—the astrological phenomenon that occurs every 29.5 years, when Saturn returns to the same place in your birth chart that it was when you were born. When you experience your first Saturn return around age twenty-nine, expect your life to turn upside down. You may find that circumstances beyond your control force major changes in your life, or that you're suddenly questioning everything about your choices, considering changing course completely. And maybe you will change the course of your life (or already have, if you're over thirty)! It's a bit like a quarter-life crisis. This can be a super painful, transitional time, full of rapid change and utter confusion (Saturn is also the ruler of pain, by the way). But no pain, no gain, honey. You can count on coming out the other side of your Saturn return much more confident, wise, and sure of your footing, thanks to Saturn's trial-by-fire approach to teaching.

In your birth chart, Saturn can bring a somewhat serious and stern tone to whatever house it lives in and bestow a feeling of restriction and sometimes difficulty in said area. There are likely to be a lot of lessons to learn about yourself in this part of your chart, many of which might prove challenging and require a lot of self-discipline and responsibility to overcome. Your Saturn sign shows you how you execute long-term plans, how you strategize, the ways in which you commit to things and express a sense of duty and responsibility, as well as the rules and confines within which you work and express yourself. You'll share a Saturn sign with people born within the same two-and-a-half-year period as you, meaning you'll share your expression of duty and responsibility with your very closest peers.

URANUS

The Great Awakener

HOME TURF	Aquarius
EXALTED IN	Scorpio
DAY OF THE WEEK	Uranus rules Wednesday, alongside its inner-planet brethren Mercury. Think "hump day," 'cause Uranus is a weirdo.
KEY CONCEPTS	Evolution, originality, inspiration, innovation, sudden change

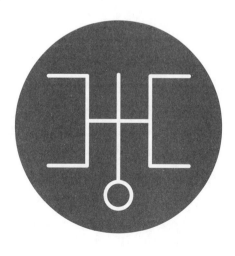

Surprise! We've left the homey realm of the personal planets and are now entering a whole new world of unexpected extra-Saturnian surprises, led by planet Uranus. Surprises and other unexpected flash happenings are what Uranus is *all* about—and *surprised* is exactly how astrologers felt when this planet was first discovered in the late 1700s. For hundreds of years, astrologers had carried on, dealing with what they believed to be the sole seven planets in our solar system. Until suddenly, Uranus made itself known and started shaking everything up (as it's wont to do), kicking off a century and a half of discovery, during which a whopping *three* additional planets would be identified by astronomers and taken in by the world of modern-day astrologers. And that's Uranus for you: Rebelliously leading the charge toward a revolution with no desire to ever look back. This erratic and eccentric planet is all about discovery, innovation, unexpected changes, radical new ideas, and embracing the future.

Uranus is the only planet in our solar system that spins on its side, which is really just a physical manifestation of its rebellious and maverick nature in astrology. This planet is a brilliant weirdo, not at all apprehensive about marching to the beat of its own drum. Perhaps Uranus is so confident in its personal compass because it knows that its march will lead it directly into the future—and this unknown futuristic realm, full of possibility and wonder and endless surprise, is where the unconventional Uranus is able to thrive. Because the future, my friends, is Uranus's happy place. This planet is preoccupied with looking forward, never backward, and is highly focused on innovation and evolution. Its rule-breaking, visionary power has the ability to usher in entirely

Uranus is believed by some to rule over the practice of astrology itself.

new eras—eras unimaginable to everyone else, except perhaps within an unpredictable flash of brilliance and creativity. Uranus is a revolutionary thinker, ruling over anything that's been recently invented, as well as all technology that's yet to come.

Uranus is often associated with being electric in nature, as it also rules electricity. Electricity, of course, has the power to shock us unexpectedly, frying us like a hot wire, and potentially leaving us burnt to a crisp. Electricity can be reactive, explosive, hard to control. In this sense, Uranus's high-voltage and disruptive nature can be a jarring, frightening, and even dangerous influence in our lives if we're not ready for it, or if it is badly aspected by other planets. It's no surprise that this planet also rules over destructive and sudden natural disasters, such as earthquakes. Electricity, like the planet Uranus, is a brilliant, shocking, sometimes even *blinding* force of nature. When it flashes, it strikes us with both fear and reverence.

But what else does electricity do, other than shock? It *illuminates*. It lights up a room, allowing us to see things in a revolutionary new light. We spent millennia without the power of electricity, but when it finally came into existence and became part of our lives, everything changed. It broke barriers and allowed us to evolve in ways we never imagined (just think of the way people used to be forced to live in darkness once the Sun set—now we can simply flip a switch in our homes, illuminate our surroundings as if it's the middle of the day, and carry on with our business!). It allowed us to overcome obstacles that we previously thought were impossible. Electricity also opened the door to new technologies, technologies that have carried us directly into the future. It's no surprise that Uranus is the planet that rules both new and future technologies. All the most innovative, cutting-edge, mind-blowing advances in technology can be attributed to Uranus in astrology.

Because Uranus rules electricity, the language used to describe Uranus often involves likening the planet to things like a spark,

Uranus Makes Its Debut

When Uranus was first discovered (with the help of a telescope) in the late eighteenth century, the timing aligned perfectly with the rise of romanticism in art, music, literature, and intellectualism. Romanticism's ideals included freedom and individuality, and was in a sense a reaction against the structure of the industrial revolution. It makes sense, then, that a creative, unconventional, individuality-focused planet like Uranus would make its grand entrance at such a period in history.

a flash, or a lightning bolt. This speaks to the quick-striking, sudden, unexpected energy of Uranus's influences. Unlike Saturn, which works slowly and calculatedly toward change, Uranus strikes fast and hot, like a thunderbolt of intensity and brilliance. Under a Uranus transit, this can come in the form of sudden and unexpected events that change the collective path we're on or the way we think. It can also, on a more personal level, come in the form of an unexpected burst of inspiration or creativity (as Uranus rules over our ingenuity and creativity, too). This is part of why Uranus is the planet of *genius*, whether it's creative genius or intellectual genius. A true genius is ahead of their time; they're thinking outside the box and shaping the future with their unique vision and innovative way of conceptualizing things. The symbolic imagery of a light bulb illuminating itself above someone's head to indicate a sudden and brilliant breakthrough idea is a 100 percent Uranus vibe. Genius, brilliance, and revolutionary thought are what this planet is all about.

This quirky planet is also the solar system's official nonconformist. Forever dedicated to its unique brand of independence and originality at all costs, Uranus will do whatever it takes to maintain this—even the most shocking and unexpected acts are on the table with this lightning bolt of a planet. Saturn may build structures, but Uranus will just as quickly break them down in order to usher in new eras and ensure its freedom.

If Uranus is badly aspected, it can certainly become a bit of a rebel without a cause, creating upset and disruption simply to shake up the conventional order of things. But usually, Uranus's causes are quite clear. Freedom is deeply important to this progressive planet, and given its revolutionary and radical nature, it is known to rule over humanitarian causes and social change, as well as groups and collectives in general, making it a very cause-oriented planet that's concerned with large-scale ideas and issues that affect society.

If we go back to the teen movie of the zodiac, one-of-a-kind Uranus could be a blend of many roles. Uranus might be cast as the nerdy but lovable but underappreciated teen genius who spends his days building strange little inventions in his bedroom and is destined to change the course of history with his brilliant, singular mind. Or perhaps the counterculture punk rock teen who plasters progressive and radical homemade political posters around campus and leads an anarchist revolution. Hell, I might even peg Uranus as the manic pixie dream girl of the bunch—but a super intellectual, trippy, and interesting one. It's the unconventional free thinker who steps in and rocks another character's world with their unique worldview and sense of individuality. Wherever Uranus is, you can bet that it's bringing a unique sense of brilliance and progressiveness along with it—and you can also bet that you won't be able to predict its next move.

★ The phrase "expect the unexpected" may have
very well been written with Uranus in mind.

Uranus is both highly intellectual and highly creative. It combines its endlessly sharp, analytical mind with an absolute trust in its higher intuition to create idea swirls that break all conventional barriers and offer the world a totally unique perspective. Uranus spends about seven years in each zodiac sign, which means we share our sign with many people who were born within a few years of us. It takes approximately eighty-four years to complete a full zodiac cycle through the twelve signs, meaning that some people will live to see Uranus transit through each of the signs and will subsequently experience their "Uranus return," which happens when the planet returns to the exact placement in the zodiac that it was when they were born.

In our birth charts, Uranus shows us how we shake things up and go against the grain, as well as the traditions we seek to break and how we seek to make changes in the world (and in ourselves!). It also shows how we ensure our freedom and independence, because with Uranus, independence is sought at all costs. The house that Uranus lives in your chart is likely to represent a part of your life in which sudden changes, shocking twists, and surprising turns almost come to be expected. While not always the most stable of influences, it certainly keeps things interesting. Pay closer attention to your Uranus sign if it's in a major aspect to one of your personal planets—in those cases, Uranus transits are likely to have a greater influence on your life specifically, rather than simply influencing generational themes on the whole.

All three of the "outer planets" are believed to resonate at a higher octave to one of the original seven inner planets, and in Uranus's case, it's Mercury. These planets are similar in that they're both intellectual thinkers, objective and unemotional in their thought processes, but while Mercury rules over basic thinking, Uranus rules over *revolutionary* thinking, flashes of brilliance, and inspiration. Similarly, Mercury is known to govern the land of technology, whereas Uranus rules *new* technologies specifically, as well as the future of technology, innovation, and all that's yet to be invented or imagined.

NEPTUNE

The Dreamer

HOME TURF   Pisces
EXALTED IN   Leo
DAY OF THE WEEK   Neptune rules Friday, a day it shares with its inner-
planet sister, Venus. No one *really* focuses on
work on Friday—Neptune thinks it's a good day to
daydream and fantasize about the weekend ahead.

KEY CONCEPTS   Dreams, illusions, the subconscious, magic

I hope you have both your scuba masks and sleep masks ready, because we're plunging into the deep, dreamy, and ethereal waters of planet Neptune. Named for the Roman god of the sea, who rules bodies of freshwater and oceans alike, Neptune is inherently otherworldly in nature. Just as the deep waters ruled by its namesake encompass a superfluity of mysteries beyond the realm of our wildest imagination, Neptune, too, in astrology, represents the mystical places and concepts that exist beyond the confines of our reality. Neptune rules the mental place we go when we dream, the state we enter when we meditate, and our evolution upon the dissolution of our ego. Neptune's realms aren't tangible or physical; these places are not accessed through the usual paths to experience that we typically travel.

Occasionally, because of distant Pluto's wonky orbit, Neptune ends up being the planet furthest out from the Sun, and symbolically, we could indeed say that this planet is very much *out there*. Neptune rules dreams, the subconscious, and even sleep (perhaps the most otherworldly state we enter on a regular basis!). The dreams that our subconscious creates for us as we sleep each night are ruled by Neptune, as are our daydreams and reveries—the little fantasies we imagine as we ponder to ourselves throughout the day. If you find yourself physically in one place but astrally projecting (or simply mentally wandering!) to another, you can likely cite Neptune's influence as the source. Neptune rules over our imagination and all things imaginary in nature, as well as our dreams, fantasies, and illusions of any sort.

To allow yourself to sink into Neptune's seas is to let go of the tangible, the ego-driven, and the rational world entirely.

71

All Dressed in Blue

If we're looking at the planet with our eyes (via a telescope's lens, of course!), Neptune is a brilliant shade of blue, the color of the deep ocean and the heavenly sky, and also the color most people associate with calmness and peacefulness. While astronomers project that this is hue is due to the presence of methane in its atmosphere, they cannot explain why Uranus (which has a similar amount of the gas above its surface) doesn't share the same vivid cerulean glow.

When we talk about Neptune ruling fantasies and illusions, this also includes how we alter our consciousness and blur the lines between our imagined worlds and reality. For example, Neptune rules over mind-altering substances—this rule includes using substances to go on spiritual "trips" or "journeys," but also applies to the lower vibration of abusing drugs and alcohol to escape the pain of reality. Escapist behaviors of any sort fall under Neptune's jurisdiction, so addictions are a big one (and this applies doubly for alcohol, given that Neptune is believed to rule liquids and beverages in general!). Drugs and alcohol can blur the lines of reality, or even cause us to totally dissociate and lose ourselves, Neptune style (this is also why Neptune rules over many mental illnesses and forms of depression). Neptune is all about blending energy, softening boundaries, and blurring the lines that separate me from you; us from them; ego from spirit. These experiences can be positive, inspirational, and spiritually awakening, but can also lead to confusion, fogginess, and delusion. Remember that Neptune doesn't necessarily deal in facts—so while its dreamworlds can leave us *endlessly* inspired, they shouldn't be confused with the *real* world.

It can be difficult to describe the realms that Neptune rules, quite frankly, because so much of what this planet governs is intangible, invisible, and spiritual in nature. Neptune rules over things like meditation, prayer, trances, shamanic and ritual work, divine inspiration, clairvoyance, and psychic connections of all sorts. All things magical in nature are under this planet's jurisdiction—think spirituality, mysticism, and the esoteric. This planet beautifully blends energy and fantasy with intention, which lends itself perfectly to the symbolic nature of manifestation spells and rituals, too. I know not all teen movies have a witchy, psychic character, but if they did, Neptune would be him or her. This planet is the zodiac's resident witch, energy worker, shaman, and clairvoyant.

Neptune may rule over "real" magic in the mystical and spiritual sense, but it also rules over sleight-of-hand and illusion-based magic "tricks" just as passionately! Anything that *appears* to be one thing but is *actually* another thing resides in Neptune's bag of tricks. Illusion and confusion are two of this planet's *favorite* things. For example, did you know that Neptune has rings? It's true—Neptune is encircled by halo-like rings, just as Saturn is! Except Neptune's rings are virtually invisible from Earth. They're there, but we can't see them; we just have to trust in the invisible force of knowledge. What's interesting still is that upon further study of Neptune's rings with powerful telescopes, they appear to be incomplete and impermanent compared to Saturn's, and have proven difficult for scientists to gain a clear understanding of in general. So it's hard to see the rings, but they exist, but then again, they're transient and ephemeral in nature. Following? These facts form a perfectly symbolic illustration of the planet's illusory nature and propensity to confuse and dilute us. This is Neptune's fantastical game.

In accordance with its mysterious coloring and elusive rings (and even the nature in which it was discovered), Neptune's physical qualities as a planet beautifully reflect its astrological qualities in many ways. The planet's astrological meaning is rich with symbolism, which is made all the more interesting when you consider that Neptune actually *governs* symbolism. A symbol appears to be one thing, but actually *means* another thing—this is Neptune's power of illusion in action. Neptune also rules all abstract forms of communication and expression, which includes all types of art, performance, and even entertainment. Think of the way notes in music can evoke a feeling; or the way poetry uses metaphors that *say* one thing but *mean* another thing; or the way a film or television show introduces us to characters who we relate to emotionally but are actually not even real—they're being played by actors. Neptune adores the power of nice, abstract, artistically charged illusion.

And Neptune is all about subtleties: Everything from subtle energy currents to subtle forms of communication fall under its rule. This planet is much more low-key in its approach to expression than many other planets; Neptune doesn't feel the need to be obvious or heavy-handed in its affairs. In fact, Neptune loves subtlety *so* much that it's almost never going to be clear, concise, or direct in its approach to *anything*! It would much rather leave things a little mysterious, nebulous, and up for interpretation. It favors intuition over rationality no matter the situation; the creative

> If it has the *power* to *enchant* and can connect us with other intangible realms of consciousness or experience, it is most likely something that's governed by dear Neptune.

right brain will *always* win Neptune's affection over the logical left brain. In Neptune's world, the left brain may as well not even exist.

It also rules anything that is intangible or hard to define. When did Neptune make itself known to the world? Well, it was back in 1864, when Europe was reaching the peak of the impressionist art movement, which was characterized by a painting style that favored fluid strokes depicting color and light rather than the rigid lines and forms that were considered traditional in art at the time. The impressionist art captured the *essence* of a subject, the color, and the light rather than literally interpreting the details of its physical form. This, of course, is all *very* Neptune, as this dreamy planet also works on a subconscious level to interpret energy, processing experiences through feeling and intuition rather than form and logic.

Neptune is named for the god of the sea, and the concepts affiliated with the planet are indeed watery and fluid in nature, too. You can't simply grab a fistful of water, for example—it'll just slip through your fingers, dripping away, seeping into things and eventually evaporating. Similarly, Neptune's concepts are elusive and impalpable. It seeks to rid us of the concept of otherness, instead focusing us on the concept of oneness.

It's nearly impossible to talk about Neptune's affiliation with the ocean and the sea without also considering the somewhat overlapping symbolism held by the Moon. In astrology and many other areas of thought, the ocean is symbolic of emotions and feelings. The compassionate Moon rules over our emotions and related areas, and some of Neptune's areas of rulership are fairly Moon-adjacent. But Neptune takes the Moon's emotion and transforms it into a sixth sense. It is through the Moon that we experience our own emotions, but Neptune helps us sense the emotions and experiences of *others*, both through emotional empathy and psychic sensitivity. Neptune, like the Moon, is also a deeply nostalgic planet. And while the Moon may rule over the private moments of our past, Neptune rules our proneness to getting *lost* in those reveries, sending us swimming through our thoughts and memories, perhaps so deeply at times that we risk getting swept away into a rose-colored fantasy version of the past.

> Neptune seeks to dissolve the boundaries of reality and the self, blending the tangible world around us with the intangible world of dreams, illusions, and imagination.

Because the outer planets were discovered so much later in the game than the personal planets, each of the three are considered to be the "higher octave" of one of the inner planets—in other words, each outer planet is believed to embody an extension and higher evolution of their assigned inner planet's qualities. In the case of Neptune, its higher vibration is that of the lovely planet Venus. As you know, Venus is all about beauty and pleasure. Venus loves to indulge in the worldly, earthly, and sensual pleasures—such as things that taste good, look good, sound good, and smell good—whereas Neptune indulges in the otherworldly and existential pleasures, preferring to get lost in a sea of fantasy: the ecstasy of spiritual enlightenment, the pleasure of a long daydream, the bliss of bathing in creative inspiration.

Neptune spends approximately fourteen years in each sign, which is about double the length of time that the next slowest-moving planet, Uranus, spends in each. This makes it one of only two planets (the other being outlier Pluto) that no single human is able to live to see transit through each sign—not even the luckiest or longest-living among us, as it takes more than 160 years for Neptune to cycle through the full spectrum of the zodiac. And because of this, we also never have the chance to have a personal "Neptune return," or to revisit any Neptune transit that we *do* experience in this life. On a personal level, this makes each Neptune transit feel rather eternal and perhaps even cherished, as we know that it's the only time we'll ever experience Neptune in that particular place in the zodiac in our lifetimes.

In your birth chart, Neptune represents how you dream and what inspires you. The house in your birth chart where Neptune resides is likely to be an area where you feel a great sense of idealism and inspiration, but your fantastical dreams could prove challenging to make real. This planet can bring beautiful fantasies, but also deep confusion. Learning to embrace the ideals that Neptune bestows upon us and tap into its well of inspiration *without* drowning in its dreamy illusions and losing sight of reality is key.

As the planet of *fantasy*, not everything Neptune shows us can be trusted or relied on.

PLUTO

The Alchemical Transformer; Ruler of the Underworld

HOME TURF   Scorpio

EXALTED IN   Aries

DAY OF THE WEEK   Pluto rules Tuesday, alongside his inner-planetary brother, Mars. Think #TransformationTuesday taken to a *frightening* new level.

KEY CONCEPTS   Power, transformation, crises, secrets, the unconscious mind

Okay, we're officially on the outskirts of the solar system now, out where it's infinitely dark, unfathomably cold, and incredibly solitary. Out here, in the vast expanse of darkness and nothingness and space, floats the strange and enigmatic Pluto, circling the Sun with its wide, unfamiliar elliptical orbit. Do not be fooled by this outer planet's stature: It is small, yes, but its energy is as mighty as they come. This planet rules some of the most intense, dark, and mysterious realms in all of astrology: power, transformation, death and rebirth, creation and destruction. For being such a small planet, it carries an *extraordinarily* heavy load, and it does so way out there in the darkness of our solar system's edges, all alone. Out here, it faces no distractions from the work that it knows must be done. And it's ruthless when it comes to making sure it gets its job done.

Don't be fooled, either, by the fact that this planet actually lost its official planet-dom in astronomy back in 2006 (this was when astronomers officially defined the terms of what makes a planet a planet, and deduced that according to these terms, Pluto actually could no longer make the cut, mainly due to its small size). While only discovered in the early twentieth century (making it the most recent planet to join the astrological ranks), Pluto has become an unshakable presence in the astrological scene since then, and its astronomical demotion didn't affect its astrological status. Here in the land of astrology, Pluto gets to keep its job—if not just because no one else would want to take it! Unmatched in its intensity (not even by rage-y Mars), Pluto works in the background in a way that no other planet—not even its fellow transcendental outer planets—even come *close* to.

> Pluto operates in the shadows and does the dirty work that no other planet seems willing to do.

Like it or not,
Pluto *forces* us to
grapple with the
darkest forces,
within and without.

Pluto is edgy in nature. It works on the edges of the solar system, but also symbolically lives its life on the edge—the edge of danger, chaos, power, and control. This planet is an outcast, but it couldn't care less. It's not a social planet in the least; it has transcended the realm of the social and is working instead within the realm of the unconscious mind. Pluto, given its proximity to the Sun, operates *so* far from the ego that we can barely see its workings with the naked eye of our conscious mind. Just like our unconscious mind has a massive influence over us (and the world around us), so does Pluto—on both us and our society. It's not always easy to see this influence by looking head-on because of the way it works in the shadows, lurking in the unconscious realm. Slow moving and generational, this planet controls the undercurrents of all things, not the overcurrents. But just because you can't see an undercurrent coming doesn't mean it isn't bound to knock you off your feet.

Named for the god of the underworld in Roman mythology, Pluto rules over the skeletons in our closets, the secrets we take to the grave, and the mystery monsters that make us afraid of the dark. (Note the paranormal, horror-movie-esque metaphors I used here. This is *not* a coincidence: We're in the underworld now!) But in layman's terms, things like shame, taboos, deep existential fears, and secrets are all tucked away in Pluto's mysterious chest of drawers. These are all things we inherently want to keep hidden—not only from the world, but often, even from ourselves (which is why the farthest planet from the conscious mind of the Sun reigns supreme in these parts). Pluto rules the underbelly of our minds, but also the underbelly of society. Crime falls under Pluto's rulership, too.

While Pluto rules sides of ourselves and our society that we'd all most likely feel more comfortable ignoring, that's not actually an option. It's impossible to fully suppress the power of Pluto's force. No matter how hard we try, the Plutonian-ruled "dark sides" in all of us (and in society on the whole) will come seeping out through the cracks, slowly poisoning us until we pay attention to its elephant in the room (fear, darkness, and shame) and address the issues. And that scenario is if we're *lucky*. If we're unlucky, they'll come *exploding* through the cracks, leaving behind nothing but a pile of ashes where something new can grow.

This sense of regeneration, the cycle of death and rebirth, is classic Plutonian subject matter. Transformation is one of the key words associated with this planet, and it's the ultimate representation of massive, critical, crisis-inducing, power-structure-crushing shifts in the zodiac. Often likened to the imagery and symbolism of the Phoenix (a bird that is believed to combust and burn to death in flames, only to be reborn again, regenerated from the ashes of its predecessor), Pluto is all about the transformational energy of big themes, like birth and death. We're talking about the *big* transformations: the alchemical ones. Creation and destruction. Life and death. This is part of why Pluto transits are known to cause change on such fundamental and omnipotent levels—this planet forces change through destruction and then regeneration. It's known to be ruthless in its power. There are certainly planets that are not to be messed with—like the malefics, war-starting Mars and rule-enforcing Saturn—but Pluto is perhaps the most feared of all planetary forces due to the mysterious and chaos-inducing nature of its power. Mess with Pluto, and you might be destroyed on a cellular, existential, or alchemical level.

Pluto is entropy in action. It is the measurable, almost orderly descent of things into disorder—and then, slowly but powerfully, back again. This is how Pluto operates: It destroys in order to renew. It brings death in order to bring life. Pluto is extreme in both its duties and its methods of execution, but that's the nature of this planet. It rules in extremes. Think about some of its notable qualities: It's the farthest planet from the Sun, the coldest planet, the planet with the most unusual orbit, and it's so small and far away from us that it was discovered, inaugurated as the ninth planet in the solar system, and then demoted to "dwarf planet" status all within a single century. The extreme ends of a spectrum make Pluto feel most at ease.

Pluto also rules all that is subterranean, both literally and figuratively. Obviously, Hell is within the planet's domain (aka the *other* great down under!), as it's named for the god of the underworld. And we know Pluto also rules things that are hidden below the surface of society—things like underground crime and conspiracies. On a super literal level, Pluto even rules things like plumbing (pipes hidden out of sight) and waste (which we flush away, again whisking it out of our awareness), as well as the roots of plants, trees, and vegetables that grow beneath the soil. It makes sense that it also rules things like viruses and bacteria, which are invisible to the naked eye but can obviously wreak havoc on our lives, both on a personal level (by making us ill, inducing transformations within our physical bodies) and on a societal level (by causing an outbreak of illness or even being used in chemical warfare).

It's interesting to note that things like precious stones and metals (such as diamonds and gold) are buried deep in the Earth's crust and nestled in caves. In mythology, Pluto was also viewed as the god of wealth, and now it makes sense why that is. The root of wealth, historically, was based on minerals that had to be uncovered (like the gold standard, which still applies to money today). So Pluto's reign over financial matters isn't to be confused with Venus's rule over money, which is tied to value. Nor is it related to Jupiter's reign over wealth, which is tied to abundance. Rather, Pluto rules money in the sense that it is an undercurrent of society. Money is currency, giving us access to abundance and luxury, but it's also an undeniably destructive force in the world. For example, what tends to drive people to commit crimes? Often, it's money. What's the basis for many wars? Also money. Money (and subsequently debt), for many people, can also be a source of shame and secrecy, something they feel they must hide and keep private.

Speaking of things that are often kept private, Pluto also rules certain aspects of sexuality, and on a more literal level, the reproductive system itself. Pluto is not affiliated with the emotional side of sexuality, nor the desire, but rather the transformational act of reproduction, creation, and generation. Because conception is really just the beginning of death, right? The alchemical magic that creates a human life from sperm plus egg is absolutely Pluto in action—an ultimate transformation. Pluto also rules any part of sexuality and sexual desire that's considered taboo, shameful, or deviant. Because sexuality as well as our sex organs themselves are considered private matters (and can sometimes even be a source of shame), you can be sure that they fall under Pluto's jurisdiction.

In the ongoing theme of all that is subterranean and hidden beneath the surface, Pluto also rules the unconscious mind. While fellow transcendental planet Neptune deals with the dreamy (or feverish) illusions of the *sub*conscious mind, Pluto deals with the animalistic, dark, and shrouded realms of the *un*conscious. Interestingly, the planet's discovery occurred right around the time prominent psychoanalysts were bringing notable ideas about the unconscious into the mainstream—think Freud's deconstruction of what he referred to as the unconscious mind, and Jung's theories about the collective unconscious.

While Pluto certainly rules over all that is hidden, it also rules over the *revelation* of what is hidden—the digging up of secrets and the unmasking of that which is obscuring the truth. And just as Pluto rules over crimes and unsolved mysteries, it also rules over detective work and sleuthing. Yet again, we see Pluto residing on the far ends of intense spectrums.

There's a massive permanence attached to Pluto's influences and transits. Because this planet moves so slowly, its meetings with other planets—and transitions into new zodiac signs—are always significant, and will rarely ever be repeated in an individual's lifetime. This brings a severe and drastic edge to any Plutonian influence in our society. This planet has the power to permanently alter the course of history in a large-scale way. Think of the invention of nuclear weapons (which are ruled directly by Pluto and came into the public sphere within fifteen years of the planet's discovery). This destructive force changed the way we fought (and threatened to fight) wars, and we're still living with the consequences of this invention to this day. Human beings invented a source of power so great that it could obliterate the existence of our entire species and end the world as we know it. Once again, we've arrived at Pluto's spectrum of creation and destruction.

As the outlier of the solar system, Pluto has the longest orbit around the Sun of any planet, and it takes a whopping 248 years to complete a full zodiac cycle. This means that like Neptune, no human has ever lived through a complete Plutonian orbit. In fact, we're lucky if we even experience Pluto in a handful of different signs throughout our lifetimes. It can spend up to three decades in a single sign, making this a true generational planet. Wherever Pluto resides in your birth chart tends to be an area where you seek deep, psyche-altering transformation and growth experiences. You might also experience power struggles and control issues in this area of your life. Your Pluto sign shows you how you (and your peers, or perhaps your whole *generation*) experience the transformational processes of pain, death, healing, and rebirth, metaphorically and otherwise.

Pluto is considered to be the higher octave of Mars (as each of the outer planets is considered to vibrate off of the energy of one of the inner planets). Pluto takes many of Mars's themes and applies them on a far deeper and grander scale. Both planets are associated with power as well as primal energies. For example, Mars is primal in a very animalistic sense—like the way it rules over the urge to have sex and the passion and desire to procreate. Pluto, on the other hand, is primal in a more ancient and mysterious way. It rules sexuality in the sense of it being an act of ultimate creation, as well as a source of ultimate shame in many modern-day societies (and old-fashioned societies, too). Mars may be the god of war, which is a dark, intense, and power-driven theme here on Earth, but Pluto is the god of the entire *underworld*, the themes of which are also dark, intense, and powerful, but in a much more mystical, symbolic, and transcendental form.

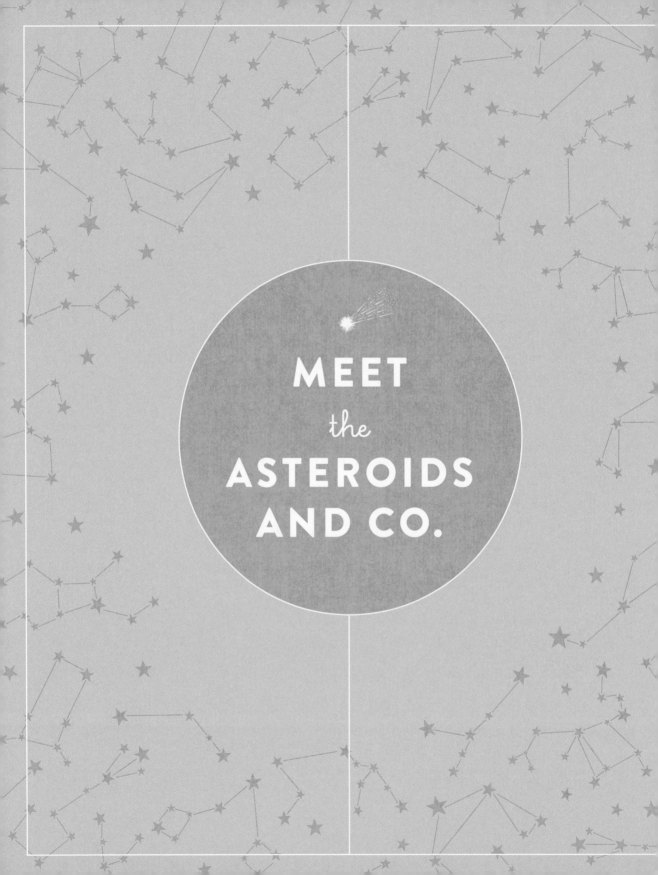

MEET
the
ASTEROIDS
AND CO.

Congratulations, you've officially been introduced (and hopefully made nice with) each of the ten major planets in astrology. While the ten major planets are the most notable and influential celestial objects in astrology, as they collectively rule over the twelve signs of the zodiac, there are other cosmic bodies that carry astrological significance as well. Although most astrologers focus their energies on the planets' more heavy-handed influence, there are a number of asteroids, fixed stars, and even dwarf planets that are also considered significant. Our solar system in general is chock-full of identified flying objects (there are *thousands* of asteroids in the asteroid belt, for example), so no need to overwhelm yourself. But there *are* a handful of them that are worth bringing into your cosmic awareness because of their astrological significance.

Firstly, there are the asteroids. The four that are most commonly studied in astrology—Ceres, Juno, Pallas, and Vesta—are all named for mythological female relatives of Jupiter, king of the gods (but Ceres is perhaps the most well-developed and studied in the astrological world). The asteroids are named for goddesses, and therefore represent more energetically "feminine" themes in astrology. But this doesn't mean their influence only applies to female-identifying people. When we talk about feminine and masculine aspects, we're talking about *energies*, and not actual gender- or sex-related subject matter.

That said, you may have noticed that most of the major planets in astrology are named for gods, not goddesses (the exception being Venus, and of course the feminine Moon, which is the mother figure of the zodiac). We live in a patriarchal world with a very long and patriarchal history, so it's no surprise that feminine energy is a bit underrepresented in the ancient practice of astrology.

There's also Chiron, which is not technically an asteroid but rather what is known as a centaur (or a small cosmic body that's not technically an asteroid but not quite a planet either). These objects are named for mythological centaurs rather than the goddess ladies of Jupiter's mythological family tree, and Chiron is the most influential among them in the astrology world. Fair warning: You may often hear astrology refer to Chiron as an asteroid despite it not technically being classified as such in astronomy. But no need for confusion, as this is a matter of semantics and simply refers to its status as a small celestial object that's not technically a planet—that's all.

While the asteroids don't officially rule over any zodiac signs, they do represent different concepts that affect us both personally and collectively, and can be *very* interesting to consider. Different astrologers put more of an emphasis on different selections of these smaller cosmic forces (or in some cases, none at all!), so we're going to explore just a few of the main ones.

We *all* have a yin and yang balance of masculine and feminine energies within us. Asteroids represent our feminine energies.

CHIRON

The Wounded Healer

Chiron is best known by its nickname, "the wounded healer." I'm sure we're all familiar with the archetype of the healer who could ironically help everyone except for himself. In mythology, Chiron was exactly that—a renaissance man (well, actually, he was a centaur, not a man, but I digress) and respected and skilled healer. He suffered many traumas in his life (he was abandoned by his parents, as he was conceived out of wedlock *and* his mother was disgusted by his form) but was eventually adopted and revered for his skills in the mystical, healing, and philosophical arts. Tragically, Chiron ended up being pierced by a poison arrow and suffered so greatly that he chose to trade in his immortality for death. He couldn't heal himself like he could everyone else, but perhaps ultimately *did* heal himself by transcending beyond the realm of the living.

Similarly, in astrology, Chiron represents deep sources of pain or hurt in our lives (emotional and spiritual pain, as well as physical), our ability to heal from wounds, *and* our ability to pass on the wisdom we gain *through* that healing to others. Because Chiron's symbolism ties in deeply with the concept of healing, it is also associated with wellness, sickness, and health in general, and our ability to grow from such experiences.

Chiron's placement is interesting to take note of, as its irregularly shaped orbit carries it on a path that falls between restrictive Saturn and revolutionary Uranus. Because of this, Chiron symbolically serves as a sort of intermediary between the personal and transpersonal inner and outer planets, bridging the gap between the literal, foundational, and conscious sides of ourselves (our pain and suffering) and the collective, transcendent, and spiritually evolved sides of ourselves (our healing and wisdom). Chiron's presence in astrology reminds us that even if we're hurting, struggling, and suffering, that we still have plenty to give, and that by giving to the world, we can perhaps eventually find healing for our ourselves, too.

According to myth, Chiron was more than just a healer (I didn't call him a renaissance man for nothing!); he was also a great and wise teacher, philosopher, soothsayer, and, believe it or not, astrologer. In astrology, this planet uses its colorful spectrum of gifts to fuse and heal the very different (and often opposing) influences that Chiron's planetary neighbors bring to our lives. Because of this, Chiron has been referred to by astrologers as a "bridge" between Saturn and Uranus, using its spiritual knowledge and healing powers to connect the strict, traditional, rule-making Saturnian energy with the rebellious, eccentric, rule-breaking energy of Uranus.

In our birth charts, Chiron can represent a deep wound and source of pain—likely one that could affect us throughout our lives or even be karmic or spiritual in nature. Unfortunately, sometimes instead of treating a wound when we're hurt, some may have a tendency to try to avoid it altogether, quietly hoping it goes away on its own. This is a common reaction to Chiron's influence in astrology; it can manifest as a quiet but lethal wound that we may choose to ignore out of fear. But nothing good can come from letting a wound fester; it all has to be dealt with eventually. Astrologically, you might be forced to address such issues if Chiron gets activated by other planets or points in your chart, or perhaps it will lurk until your Chiron return at around age fifty—the critical point when Chiron returns to the exact place in the sky that it was when you were born—forcing you to face your wounds. Alternatively, if you've been doing the work, step into the wisdom and healing powers that you've acquired throughout your journey thus far. Let's hope for the latter!

But don't get me wrong: Chiron is *so much more* than some wound in your zodiac chart. Ironically, Chiron's placement also

Chiron's Rise to Fame

This small *celestial* body, known as a centaur (given its mythological namesake), is not quite a planet astronomically, but orbits among the outer planets. And despite being a major newb in the official astrological scene (it was only discovered in 1977 and is definitely the most recent widely accepted addition to the astrology family), Chiron has become surprisingly significant among the asteroids and asteroid-like objects, and is considered within the practice of many modern-day astrologers.

> Sometimes the source of the deepest pain is also the site of the most transformational healing and growth, and this is the realm in which Chiron does its work.

represents an area where we have great ability to heal others and ourselves. Chiron is, at the end of the day, a healer.

If we dress the wounds that Chiron highlights for us, we have the opportunity to find immense power and great wisdom through our healing. Chiron's mythology brings a sense of humbleness to its efforts. The deeper and more intense the struggle, the more evolved you'll be once you come out the other side. Because of the maturity and wisdom that Chiron can bestow, you likely won't need accolades or pats on the back for the altruistic giving of your gifts, either.

As Chiron travels through the zodiac, it may put a spotlight on festering wounds, yes. But it does so with the pure and simple intention of *healing* those wounds, and it brings a magical power to soothe our suffering through growth and wisdom. Because even if we can't heal ourselves, as Chiron couldn't, perhaps by healing those around us we will find a sense of peace or be healed in return for the gifts we've been willing to give.

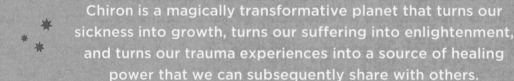

Chiron is a magically transformative planet that turns our sickness into growth, turns our suffering into enlightenment, and turns our trauma experiences into a source of healing power that we can subsequently share with others.

CERES

Hippie Earth Mama

Ceres is the largest of all the space rocks traveling through the solar system's asteroid belt, which is located between Mars and Jupiter's orbits. That said, it's technically not an asteroid, but rather the smallest of the "dwarf planets" (a classification that has also included Pluto ever since its 2006 astronomical demotion). Named after the goddess of the harvest and fertility, Ceres represents similar themes in astrology. This asteroid, like the other official asteroids in this section, is thought to be feminine in nature. Due to its affiliation with fertility, it's often associated with our ability to be maternal (in a practical sense), and is seen as influential on the major cycles and milestones of women's lives specifically. It was discovered on New Year's Day in 1801, and has since become a very important force in the practice of many astrologers.

This mini-planet is a total Earth goddess and hippie mama. Ceres rules crops, harvests, the land, and Earth's natural cycles, as well as related things, like growing our food and cooking. If this asteroid were a person, she'd likely live on a commune, practice a nature-based faith, care for animals and children wonderfully (as well as her crops!), and be that person you know who is most in tune with the land and nature's cycles. Oh, and she'd have a most impressive green thumb. Ceres is often associated with environmentalism and the need to preserve the Earth's resources, maintain a tangible connection with the planet, and care for the plants and animals with whom we share the world. Because Ceres is about physical nurturing in this way, it makes sense that it would emphasize a focus on environmentalism, because by nurturing the planet we live on, it will subsequently be able to continue nurturing us.

Because of Ceres's maternal nature and symbolic representation of fertility and motherhood, it's often thought to share some themes with the Moon, our solar system's most powerful motherly force. Like the

Moon, Ceres is all about nurturing ourselves and others. But while the Moon's focus on nurturing is often emotional in nature, Ceres's focus is on nurturing ourselves in a much more literal and earthy sense. The intuitive, feelings-centered Moon shows how you self-soothe, manage your feelings, and process your emotions. Grounded Ceres, on the other hand, is more focused on the tangible ways that we care for ourselves. This asteroid wants to ensure you're eating nutritiously, spending enough time in nature, connecting with the Earth, and staying grounded.

Ceres is also associated with hard work, and you can consider this in relation to the hard work it takes to truly *nurture* something, whether that's a person, a plant, or just an idea—it takes hard work to keep something alive. Being a mother (or parent in general), for example, requires constant attentiveness, devotion, and self-sacrifice. It also brings out the fierce warrior inside a person, whether that's via the immense endurance it requires to physically birth a child or the fierceness and adrenaline-fueled strength that takes the wheel if a mother feels her child faces danger. In many ways, you can tie this back in with farming and living in tune with the Earth's cycles, too: it takes year-round work, patience, and focus to successfully and sustainably farm and harvest crops. Ceres can point to an area in your chart where you're willing to bring on that fierce yet maternal and nurturing energy—to stay grounded enough to take the actions necessary to keep something *alive*.

If you had to assign Ceres to a zodiac sign, which would you choose? Some astrologers affiliate it with the sign of Virgo, the earth maiden, due to its practical-minded and earthy nature, its affinity for the pure and natural, and its symbolism of femininity and the harvest; others see it better suited to other feminine signs, like Taurus or Cancer.

Ceres knows all about the importance of the beautifully symbiotic relationship that we have to the planet on which we live, and thus, it motivates us to do our part and maintain a deep connection with the Earth.

JUNO

Queen of True Love

Juno represents commitment and marriage, but also the many complicated trials and tribulations that come along with being in a deep and vulnerable relationship with someone (romantic or otherwise). Although Juno in your chart can point to several things, this is one of the most interesting astrological players to look at when it comes to romantic relationships. Juno is not simply about the pleasurable bliss of romantic love (ahem, *Venus*) or an animalistic sexual attraction (lookin' at you, Mars). Juno's territory is a bit deeper and more complex, as it involves pain and struggle just as much as pleasure and attraction.

To truly understand Juno's place in astrology, it helps to look to her namesake in Roman mythology: the goddess of marriage. Goddess Juno was married to Jupiter, the king of the gods (better known as Zeus in Greek mythology), and was a deeply devoted, fiercely faithful, and completely committed wife (and I'd like to note that this type of loyalty speaks volumes when you're an immortal goddess—as a "forever" type of commitment takes on a whole new level of intensity if you never plan to die!). Thus, commitment, marriage, and all sorts of long-term partnerships are some of the most important aspects of Juno's role in astrology.

But love is pain, right? If you've ever been in a long-term relationship (or even a shorter but emotionally intense one), then you know this can be true, even in the most beautiful of unions. Thus, Juno's territory in astrology gets complicated. Let's go back to mythology: Juno was a fiercely loyal partner to her husband, as you know. Jupiter, however, was *not* faithful to his wife, and was notorious for taking many lovers and fathering many children out of wedlock. According to myth, Juno was ragingly jealous, vengeful, and vindictive, and was even known to take the lives of her husband's mistresses and the children they bore with him. Thus, in astrology, Juno also represents deep struggle, insecurity, conflict, and jealousy in relationships. Juno is believed to rule over divorce and separation just as she rules over marriage and commitment. She also rules over infidelity and abuse in relationships, just as she rules over faithfulness and devotion. It's a complex and complicated bag, but then that's how the most intimate and lengthy relationships tend to be.

In your birth chart, this asteroid can point you in the direction of the type of relationship that you can build a life around. Your Juno sign reveals the qualities you seek in a partner to fulfill your needs once the initial spark of attraction has waned, and the type of devotion and care that will make you feel truly satisfied in the long term.

Conversely, our Juno placement can also reveal some major trigger spots and areas of potential insecurity and self-consciousness, even beyond the realms of love and romance. Because the sign and house that Juno resides in your birth chart represents qualities that you value deeply in a long-term sense (and is likely an area that you seek fulfillment in, romantically and otherwise), then naturally if you feel exploited, betrayed, abused, or misunderstood in such areas of your life, you'll likely feel *extra* insecure about it. So yes, your Juno placement shows you the things you value in a long-term and commitment-focused way, but because of this, it is also a sensitive spot. That said, looking to the house that Juno resides in your birth chart can help you see the areas in your life in which you might be easily triggered, areas where any type of abuse, mistreatment, or toxicity is even *more* unacceptable and intolerable than it would be under normal circumstances. The sign that it's in can reveal the ways in which you want to be valued and, conversely, the ways in which being disrespected could feel like an even deeper betrayal.

Juno is the ruler of soul mates and true love.

Juno helps you identify the qualities you prefer in someone who will be there for you (and whom you will want to be with) in the long run, after the high of the honeymoon and the passion of a new love has long settled.

VESTA

Queen of Self-Care and Self-Sufficiency

Vesta is your new astrological self-care inspiration. Named after the Roman goddess of the hearth and home, Vesta represents our ability to take care of ourselves, clear our minds, and focus our personal energies. The goddess Vesta was an interesting case in mythology, as unlike many of her peers, she chose to remain a virgin throughout her life—despite being quite desired by many powerful gods—and instead focused her energy solely on her personal responsibilities, which included keeping the hearth fire alive and thriving. At this point, the hearth was considered the center of every home and was crucial to everyone's survival, as it brought warmth, safety, and nourishment. That said, the task of keeping this fire alive was not to be taken lightly—in fact, it was quite an ultimate responsibility. But Vesta devoted herself to her duties wholeheartedly and executed them with perfect focus and diligence.

This asteroid's symbolism marks a bit of a departure from the love, motherhood, and relationship-focused energies of Ceres and Juno (given Vesta's famed virginity and rejection of marriage). Instead, it is much more concerned with self-care, precision-like focus, and keeping on top of tasks. Vesta is known in astrology as the keeper of our own internal or spiritual flame. It rules the little spark of individuality, creativity, inspiration, and motivation that we all have inside of us that keeps us going in times of darkness. Because feminine energy is inherently creation-focused, you can think of Vesta as being representative of your ability to direct your creative energy toward the goals, aspirations, desires, and projects that light up your internal fire.

Vesta also represents absolute purity and clarity. Purity in the sense that yes, Vesta the goddess was a virgin, but also in the sense of being pure of intention and mind: clarity in the sense of being able to completely devote yourself to a cause and be of service. Vesta isn't distracted by the trials and tribulations of marriage or the tireless work of being a mother, which imbues the asteroid with a uniquely strong ability to focus on one's self and one's duties. So it's not that Vesta is asexual in nature, but rather it represents the channeling of sexual energy (aka creation energy) into something beyond the carnal—perhaps, even, in your own aspirations and goals. Vesta helps us see what we need to feel whole and balanced, and yes, how to check off tasks on our to-do lists.

> Vesta represents the *purest devotion* to service, a cause, and a clear-minded focus on whatever task is in front of you.

When Vesta travels through your chart, it brings along its broomstick and cleaning supplies (this asteroid rules the home, so that includes housework!) and reminds us that it's time to eliminate distractions, centralize our energy, and start cleaning house, and that could mean spiritually, emotionally, or literally. Vesta reminds us to clear our minds (and hearts and homes) of clutter so that we can *focus* and take care of business. This asteroid puts a great emphasis on self-care, too, as it encourages us to stoke our inner flame and keep our own *personal* hearth fire alive and hearty. It's about self-sufficiency and the ability to feel whole, useful, and accomplished. The Sun may represent our life force, but Vesta is the little spark of creativity that reminds us of who we are and what makes us unique. Vesta is known to be the brightest of all the asteroids, after all.

The house in which Vesta resides in your birth chart points to an area in your life that might require a more focused tending to. It asks how you might be more present and practice better self-care in that part of your life. Your Vesta sign also represents the nature of how you invest in yourself and your goals (it's no coincidence that "Vesta" sounds a lot like the world "investment," as Vesta encourages you to invest in yourself and devote focus toward the things that matter!). Conversely, Vesta may also point to an area where there's an overabundance of devotion that could cause an imbalance, in which case you'll want to check yourself (Vesta style!) and make sure you're upping the self-care and developing a healthier relationship to that part of your life. Vesta in your chart also points to an area of where you can provide service—the type of service that serves others or the greater good, but that is also fulfilling to *you*—that feeds your soul, that keeps the hearth of your heart burning brightly.

PALLAS

Wise Warrior (and All-Around Badass Babe)

Last but certainly not least, we arrive at the palace of Pallas—the asteroid named after Pallas Athena, goddess of warfare and wisdom in Greek mythology. In mythology, Pallas Athena was the daughter of powerful Zeus and was known for being a fierce warrior. Pallas Athena was also celebrated for sparkling intelligence, wit, creativity, a sense of justice, and wisdom. She had a brilliant, sharp mind just as she was a brilliant, strategic fighter. Pallas Athena is actually defined as the goddess of "prudent warfare" and "useful arts"—note the elevation there. She only rules warfare of the necessary sort. And the arts and ways of thinking she employs? They're useful. She used her wisdom when it came to fighting and her fierceness when it came to thinking. In astrology, Pallas the asteroid embodies the same. Pallas represents sage wisdom, sharp and creative intellect, independence (specifically of a female nature), and the same warrior-like strength that its namesake is known for.

Pallas is a warrior (according to myth, she was born fully armed), but what sets this asteroid apart from its violent peers is that it is truly civilized in its warrior-ness. Located between war-hungry Mars and philosophical Jupiter, Pallas employs elements of each planet's qualities in order to create a unique brand of intellect-focused fierceness. You can think of Pallas as the *evolved* warrior. Instead of using brute force, Pallas encourages the use of ingenuity, intelligence, critical thinking, fair reasoning, and even compassion in its methods of doing battle. Pallas is civilized, not animalistic—it's not an inherently violent or destructive force (in the way that fellow warrior planet Mars can be, at times), and actually attempts to strategically use intelligence and mental power to avoid such primitive behavior. Pallas rules *prudent* warfare, remember? That said, Pallas is a warrior just the same, so while defense rather than offense is the name of its game, it will still strike when necessary—and when it does, it can be lethal. Pallas is incredibly skilled in the art of killing and defense, so crossing its path is not advisable (although it's thoughtful enough to give you a chance to explain yourself first, at least).

Clearly, a sharp and rational mind carries an important emphasis when it comes to Pallas's rule. But what's unique about Pallas (and what sets it apart from intellect-focused Mercury, deep-thinking Jupiter, or idea-generating Uranus) is the *feminine* aspects of her intelligence. Rather than eschewing intuition in favor of dry rationality, Pallas welcomes intuition into her line of thinking, consciously choosing to trust it like a sixth sense, blending her sensory perception into rationality to create perhaps an even more wise and insightful form of intelligence. Pallas also represents fairness. This asteroid is naturally justice-oriented and reminds us to consider all sides before lashing out or chaining ourselves to a detrimental or an unfair opinion. Additionally, Pallas represents creativity in thinking—the ability to identify patterns and bring together an eclectic combination of thoughts and ideas to form new ones. This is one of Pallas's great skills as a thinker.

As a feminine asteroid, there's also an element of nurturing here, but it comes in the form of healing. Pallas's strength, as well as her intelligence, is seen as having the power to heal. In our birth chart, Pallas shows us where our creativity, intelligence, wit, and strengths have the potential to really sparkle. Our Pallas sign reveals how we express our most evolved ideas, whether they're intellectual thoughts or opinions about what's right or wrong. Our Pallas sign can also reveal insights into our relationship with our father (due to Pallas's relationship to Zeus in mythology) or with masculine energies in general.

Your Pallas placement might also indicate an area where your gifts and talents are being undervalued or underutilized—perhaps due to self-consciousness, self-doubt, or a feeling of rejection. Just as our imbalanced patriarchal society has taught us to reject our natural intuition and has placed less value on or respect toward traditionally "feminine" energies, we may also feel that our naturally "feminine" gifts don't have quite the value that other talents and abilities might. Allow Pallas's warrior spirit in that area of your chart to revitalize you and remind you that your talents *are* worthy, and that you have a feminine warrior spirit inside of you, too, ensuring your independence and individuality.

✳ Instead of rejecting traditionally "feminine" aspects such as intuition, fluidity, kindness, or creativity when it comes to intellect (or battle, for that matter), Pallas encourages us to embrace these parts of ourselves, and reminds us that they can be helpful tools in allowing us to evolve in our thinking and maintain our independence. ✳

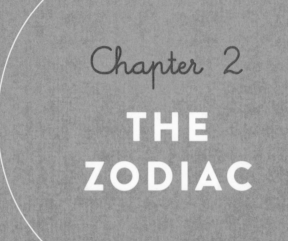

Chapter 2

THE ZODIAC

LIKE VINTAGE YEARS OF WINE, WE HAVE
THE QUALITIES OF THE YEAR AND OF
THE SEASON OF WHICH WE ARE BORN.

—Carl Jung

So you've met the planets (and a few asteroids, too!), and now it's time to meet the next set of powerful players in astrology: the twelve signs of the zodiac. The signs are perhaps the most talked about and well-known aspect of mainstream astrology and a massively important component in the art of astrology. For many people who haven't looked deeper into astrology, the nominal "What's your sign?" is essentially the be-all and end-all question. But as you're probably beginning to figure out, this is just the tip of the astro iceberg (although, not gonna lie, that's still a *very* important question to ask anyone, in my book!).

Zodiac Fundamentals

When a planet travels through a sign's territory of the sky, that sign serves as a sort of filter for the planet's expression. If each planet represents a different chunk of a whole person, then we're all the sum of these planetary parts. But that's a grand generalization, and even if we're talking about things and qualities that *everyone* does or experiences or possesses, we all *express* energy differently. We love differently, work differently, think differently, communicate differently, and dream differently—and *that's* where the signs come in. Zodiac signs are *vibes*. They are powerful and influential, and they dictate the style in which the planets do their thing.

But what are signs? And what is the zodiac? The twelve signs that comprise the zodiac correspond to twelve theoretical chunks of the sky that were mapped out by astrologers and astronomers centuries ago. The twelve sections of the sky (aka the zodiac) were named for different constellations that fell within their region of the heavens. Thus, the twelve signs of the zodiac were born.

> Together, the planets collide and interact to create the whole of a person. We are *all* affected by the placement of each of these planets on a daily basis, and understanding their influence can help us feel more connected to the cosmos and ourselves.

During the course of the year, the Sun appears to slowly move through the sky—and as it does, it passes through each constellation's domain. So when we say that people with an Aries Sun are born between about March 20 and April 19, that refers to the dates of the year during which the Sun is passing through the area of the sky in which the constellation "Aries" appeared at the time the zodiac was created. So when we say that a planet is "in" a certain sign, this refers to its placement in the heavens as perceived from Earth.

Planets embody different parts of *ourselves*, such as how we think, value, act, learn, love, communicate, discern, and beyond. Signs, on the other hand, embody the *style* in which we do those things.

The zodiac isn't just an astrological concept, though: It's acknowledged in astronomy, too! These are real constellations and real stars, after all. These signs just carry a particularly important significance in astrology. You can think of the signs as the ~vibes~ that describe how a certain type of energy is expressed.

The Signs and Their Energy

The signs represent the *way* in which that energy is expressed. As a planet transits through a particular sign, its energy is expressed differently. The planet still has the same goal, the same focus, the same essence, but the way it goes about its business will change from sign to sign. The signs also affect how capable a planet is of doing its work, how well it's able to express its qualities, and the manner in which it will do these things (we see this in the form of planetary dignities). The signs color a planet's energy.

If you'd like a nice, relatable metaphor to help clarify things, let's think in terms of social media content. Imagine the planets as social media users. Each planet has its own unique identity, so the nature and content of its posted photos would reflect that. For example, Mars's photos would probably be intense action shots, with stereotypically masculine themes, whereas the emotional Moon might have more creative, simple, gentle shots that would likely be more modest, feminine, and personal in nature. Now, the *signs* represent the filters that get slapped over the planets' content. So the Moon might take a vulnerable little still life of their morning breakfast spread. But if the Moon enters impulsive Aries, the photo would likely be posted immediately, without a filter, and with a wild and spontaneous caption— because Aries is too busy taking charge to think about what other people will think! Or consider one of Mars's action shots—perhaps a quick selfie of themselves weightlifting at the gym, covered in sweat. When Mars enters Libra (the sign of its detriment), its energy is likely to filter the impulsively taken selfies through at least *six* photo-editing apps to give them a soft and uniform aesthetic and then maybe add a list of well-planned hashtags—you know, 'cause Libra is social like that. Obviously, such fluffy filters and social media self-

Back when *astrology* was a budding field, people were still under the impression that the Earth was fixed in the sky and that the Sun did the orbiting. Now, of course, we know that Earth-centric view is not accurate— but in astrology, we do still track the Sun's (and others planets') apparent movement through the sky. A lot of astrology is about where the planets are (and how they move) from our perspective here on Earth. Keep that in mind as we talk about Sun seasons and other concepts!

awareness makes Mars frustrated, as that's not at *all* his vibe and it makes it hard to get his point across. Such is the power of a sign's influence on a planet's ability to do its *thing*.

The planets are always influencing us differently, because they're always moving through the zodiac. The signs, however, are fixed. Zodiac sign energy can be activated for us when we have planets traveling through them, which inherently influences the way we experience things. We have each and every one of the twelve zodiac signs somewhere in our personal birth charts, so the whole spectrum of signs affects our unique astrological makeup, too.

While we can easily personify planets and give them emotions as they move through the sky (e.g., Venus is happy in Taurus and frustrated in Virgo), the energy of a zodiac sign just *is*. Signs don't move; *we* move in relation to them. *We're* the ones living on a constantly spinning space rock that's orbiting a star! The sky, however, is fixed, and thus, so is the zodiac. This means that a sign is itself no matter *what*. And because each sign represents a fixed space in the sky (and not a location-changing object like our ever-orbiting planets), they don't ever find themselves in a place where they're "happy" or "sad." They just simply *are*.

While the sign that most people typically identify with correlates to the Sun's place in the zodiac at the time they were born, we actually have different signs for each and every planet (because they were all floating around *somewhere* in the sky when you were born!). Keep in mind that all twelve signs are incorporated into every person's birth chart.

While I won't blame you for a second if you immediately jump into reading about your own Sun sign or the Sun sign of your crush/partner/BFF and call it a day, it can be really helpful to get to know the energy of *all* twelve zodiac signs, because all of these signs are influencing you all the time, in so many different ways. Getting familiar with them will help you understand your own astrology much better, and put you more in sync with the natural cycle of planets moving through the signs. So get out your trusty birth chart and check out which planets you have in which signs. All of those signs' energies are going to be particularly important to you, and they'll help you sort through the ways in which you may naturally express certain aspects of yourself or your personality.

Additionally, as our luminaries—the Sun and Moon—and other planets move through the zodiac, we can all tap into and feel the energy of these transits, whether or not we have any planets of our own in each sign. For example, we might feel more inclined to indulge our emotions and get a bit daydreamy and weepy when the Sun is in Pisces, or we may feel extra motivated to start new things during Aries season. Because of this, the more you know about each sign, the better. This way, you can better embrace the qualities and strengths of each sign as major planets transit through them, or at least know what to expect when they do!

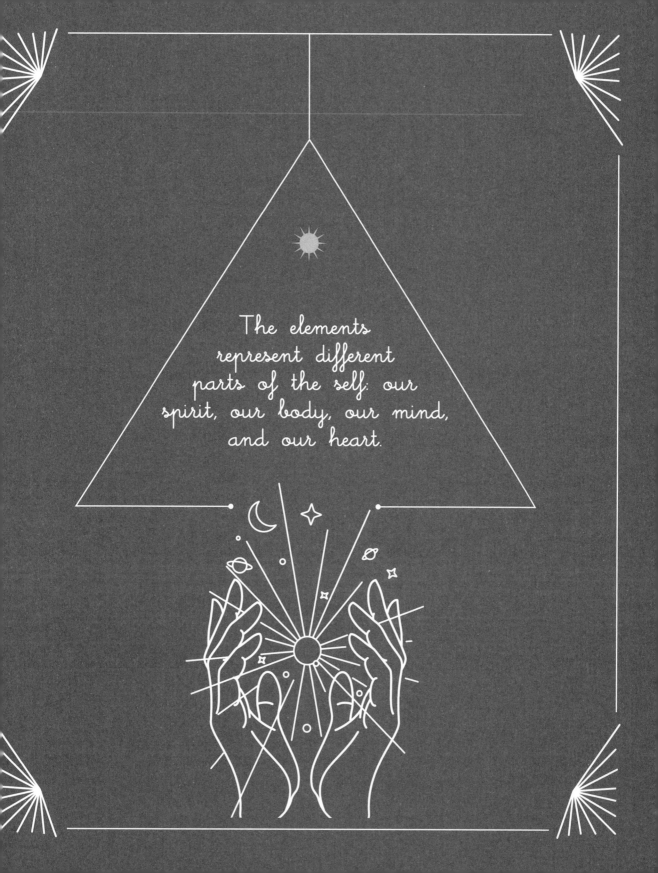

The elements
represent different
parts of the self: our
spirit, our body, our mind,
and our heart.

Elements, Modalities, and Polarities

Before we introduce you to each of the signs, let's break down some of the main ways that the signs are categorized. The four elements, three modalities, and two polarities comprise the fundamental concepts that identify similarities and differences among the signs' energies. These categorizations indicate how different groupings of signs serve different purposes, have different focuses, and possess different strengths. And they all work in tandem with each other to create a perfectly symbiotic system of energies.

Getting to know these categories can give you the upper hand when it comes to understanding signs in general, and can actually be used as a little cheat sheet on how to understand the energy of each zodiac sign, without actually memorizing all their details. For example, without knowing any of the nuances of Capricorn energy, if you know that it's a cardinal earth sign, then you can assume that it's gifted when it comes to taking initiative in practical matters, which is completely true!

Here's how it's all broken down.

ELEMENTS

Elements are perhaps the most fundamental force when it comes to breaking down the signs in astrology. **There are four elements in astrology: fire, earth, air, and water.** Each of the four elements is associated with three signs of the zodiac, and thus the elements are also sometimes called *triplicities*. The concept of assigning unique, archetypal energies to certain elements isn't unique to astrology—it's actually an ancient concept, and these four elements were believed to comprise the basic foundation for all life and matter on Earth. Everything from tarot cards to the four directions use the symbolism of the four elements.

Each of the elements have different qualities, strengths, and focuses, and the strengths of the signs within one element symbiotically balance out the weaknesses of the others, and vice versa. Fire is about our bright-burning inner spirit; earth is about our physical bodies and material senses; air is about our intellect and mental capacity; and water is about our emotional selves.

We can use the elemental energy to help guide us. For example, when the Sun moves through fire signs, we know that it's time to take action and get "fired" up. In earth sign territory, we know it's a good time to get grounded and focus on practicality. With the air signs, it's time to focus our energy outward and be social and open to learning and thinking. And with water signs, it's time to get introspective and deal with our emotions and feelings. We can find the elements working together and synthesizing in *so* many different things that we do. So if you're only going to get familiar with one of these categories, let it be elements.

FIRE

The Spirit

SIGNS   Aries, Leo, Sagittarius

KEY WORDS   Dynamic, energy, passion, drive, desire

Fire signs are as fiery and fierce as the element they're named for. Like the hearth fire that used to burn in the center of the home, fire signs represent our will and life force energy. They correspond with our spirit, our drive, and our passions. They lead with their spirit, and allow their desire and will to drive them.

What do we think of when we think of fire? Heat, danger, warmth, life, and *action*. These signs are perhaps the most *driven* of the bunch; it's as if they have a fire under their feet, constantly motivating and inspiring them to get things done, take action, and make moves.

So what defines a fire sign? Burning desire. Flames of passion. Trailblazing. These signs are truly made up of firepower. Their focus is outward and action-oriented: Aries wants to *do*, Leo wants to *create*, and Sagittarius wants to *grow*. Fire signs want to bring things forth into the world. Just like a fire is apt to spread through a forest, fire signs want to expand and cover more ground. They'd certainly rather burn out brightly than fade away. Fading away simply isn't a fire sign's style—but causing an attention-grabbing explosion of passion, feeling, drive? That's more like it. These signs aren't afraid of stepping into the spotlight. After all, they can take the brightness *and* the heat.

Of course, fire signs can easily burn out if they go *too* hard. All fire signs are prone to burning the candle at both ends, and while they certainly have the energy to withstand this more than most, they sometimes lack the sensibility, logic, and self-awareness to know when they've reached a limit.

We love fire signs, as they're essentially the hype people of the zodiac. With their excess energy and heat, these signs tend to be warm and giving with their passion and have a gift when it comes to putting a fire under everyone else. They tend to be spontaneous in their actions, always more concerned about following their impulses in the moment than they are with the consequences that might come of them. But be careful, because we all know that if we play with fire, we could get burned. Fire signs feel things with hot, burning intensity; anger, passion, rage, desire, and excitement are their emotional languages. They experience their feelings with *zeal*.

EARTH

The Body

SIGNS   Taurus, Virgo, Capricorn
KEY WORDS   Stable, grounded, sensual, physical

Earth sign energy is associated with the physical and tangible matters and needs of a human being—the earthly realms. Like the earth itself, these signs tend to be grounded, with deep roots that keep them tethered to reality and focused on practical responsibilities. They're not up in the clouds like an air sign or drowning in feelings like water signs, nor are they blazing forth like a fireball in a fit of desire like the fire signs. They're reliable, sturdy spirits, like the ground beneath us.

What do we think of when we think of the earth? Grounded, lush, stable, providing. Earth signs have got both feet on the ground. They're generally reliable and predictable. As babies of the earth, they are deeply in touch with their physical senses and practical matters of responsibility and security. Our physical reality, like the roots of a tree, keep the earth signs' feet firmly planted on the ground. They're not typically big risk takers, and would prefer to stick to the cycles that they're familiar and comfortable with—patterns as reliable as the seasons and natural cycles of the earth.

Because their pragmatism takes the driver's seat, they're incredibly efficient when it comes to getting things done, staying organized, and providing stability. But they may often find themselves trying to rationalize *everything*—including their emotions, their passions, and their ideas, too—which obviously isn't always useful. Their desire to keep their feet on the safety of the ground can sometimes limit them from exploring the deep seas of emotion, blazing flames of passion, and open sky of creative thoughts.

The element of earth also corresponds with tangible, earthy, material things, which includes money and material wealth, too. Earth signs appreciate the practical, functional, sensible, and comfortable. Taurus loves luxury, Virgo loves efficiency, and Capricorn loves financial security. Together, these are an expensive and highly efficient crew when it comes to taking care of business and keeping their wits about them.

Earth signs can also run themselves into the ground by being overly focused on practicality, hard work, stability, and the maintenance of their own comfort zones, but conversely, they're adept at being able to bring *others* back down to earth, and we love them for it. The grounding, reliable, and stable force of earth energy can be soberingly useful when it comes to injecting reality into a situation that's getting blown out of proportion or carried away.

Earth signs tend to view matters through a lens of rationality. They sense their way through the world using practicality and are gifted with the ability to stay present, in tune with their bodies, and focus on their most practical and basic needs.

AIR

The Mind

 Air signs are as light and elusive as the element they're named after. Like a cool breeze or a sudden gust of wind, air signs represent the buoyant and airy energy of thought and intellect. They correspond with our mental energy, ideas, and thinking.

When I say that air signs characteristically have their "heads in the clouds," that simply means that they tend to *think* a lot. They spend a lot of time inside their brains, and they relate to the world by conceptualizing things, forming ideas and theories, and figuring out ways to apply logic to the way the world (and everyone on it) works. They tend to ponder life's many possibilities from a more concept-driven angle, and can easily get carried away with their creative narratives.

But they also have a great ability to be objective observers. They're gifted at taking in the details of the world around them and then forming opinions, without letting those opinions be marred by their own passions, perceived limitations, or feelings. For example, Gemini is information-seeking, Libra is balance-seeking, and Aquarius is change-seeking. All air signs have the ability to stand back from a situation and be impartial. On the other side of the same coin, this gives air signs a reputation for being a bit cool and detached. Like air itself, air sign energy can be elusive, slippery, and hard to pin down.

Air signs are quick and perceptive, and this also associates them with communication. They tend to be social and enjoy sharing ideas, learning new things, and collaborating. They play off of the energy of others and easily express their thoughts (as well as comprehend others'). They tend to be imaginative and creative people; because they spend so much time with their ideas, we'd hope so! These creative and thoughtful spirits are the thinkers of the zodiac.

 Air signs lead with their minds, and allow their thoughts and perception to drive them.

WATER

The Heart

SIGNS   Cancer, Scorpio, Pisces

KEY WORDS   Emotional, spiritual, sensitive, intuitive, feelings-driven

Water signs are as fluid, changeable, and free-flowing as the element they're named for. Water signs represent our emotions, corresponding with our vulnerable side, our sentimentality, our deepest feelings, and our intuitive senses.

Because of their intuitive, feelings-driven nature, the water signs are often thought to be the most spiritual in nature of all the signs, and the most connected to the occult. This is even apparent in looking at the planets that rule over them: the emotional Moon, transformative Pluto, and dreamy Neptune. All of these planets have an otherworldly and spiritual nature to their power and rule.

Water signs possess a more inward focus. They relate to their world through their emotions, and rely more on their sixth sense of intuition than they do on their physical senses. They favor their feelings over facts or logic or just about anything else.

The downside of being a water baby? They are at risk of totally drowning in their tears and feelings. Water signs are often so caught up in emotions that it can bring out negative aspects. For example, if they're feeling oversensitive, Cancer can get moody and hold a grudge, Scorpio can get jealous and vindictive, and Pisces can get sad and dissociative.

That said, water signs have a deep capacity for feeling and spirituality, and if you're able to get them to open up, they can show you a whole new, beautiful, nurturing, intense, and dreamy world under their seas.

Water signs lead with their hearts rather than their brains, and they allow their feelings and intuition to guide them.

MODALITIES

There are three modalities in astrology: cardinal, fixed, and mutable. These are also sometimes referred to as *qualities*, and because there are four signs in each modality, they're also sometimes called *quadruplicities*.

Within each elemental group, there is one sign that's assigned to each modality (meaning there's one cardinal fire sign, one fixed fire sign, and one mutable fire sign, and so on through the other elements). The modalities also reflect the Sun's movement through the sky during the three stages of a season—spring, summer, autumn, and winter each begin with the Sun entering a cardinal sign, following along on its journey through a fixed sign, and then ending with a jaunt through a mutable sign.

Symbolically, modalities tell us about the nature in which a sign's elemental qualities are expressed. **Cardinal signs build a foundation, fixed signs provide follow-through, and mutable signs embrace change in that they end cycles and prepare us for the transition into the next ones.**

So while all earth signs are practical and pragmatic, a cardinal Capricorn is going to be better at planning and beginning a project than a fixed sign like Taurus, which is stronger at being stable and sustaining energy. Got it? Now let's get to know these three types.

CARDINAL

The Initiators

Ready to get started on a project or begin something new? If anyone knows where and how and when to start, it's a cardinal sign. These signs are naturally able to see a big-picture structure and instinctively know where to begin to create a foundation. Cardinal energy is all about building things from the ground up, taking control and feeling sure of one's ability to handle a task. Cardinal signs easily come up with new ideas and rarely struggle to start something from scratch. They feel comfortable taking the lead on projects and embodying a directorial role with confidence. They are the initiators of the zodiac—if you hand them a blank canvas, they'll return it to you with the outline you need to get started.

Cardinal means "important" or "foundational," and cardinal energy is certainly both of those things. The start of the Sun season of each of the cardinal signs corresponds to important dates, too: the solstices and equinoxes that herald in the four meteorological seasons. Cardinal Sun energy begins our journey into each of the seasons ahead and helps us come up with fresh ideas, lay out our plans, and lay out the blocks upon which we can build our goals ahead.

Although cardinal energy is motivated and energetic when it comes to getting things off the ground, each of the cardinal signs shows this strength in a different arena, depending on their element. Aries are amazing at taking action. Cancers are the initiating force of giving and nurturing. Libras are magic-workers when it comes to inspiring clear and balanced thinking and communication. And Capricorns are the leaders when it comes to creating material stability and success.

FIXED

The Sustainers

Need someone to bring forth the energy it takes to keep something afloat and sustain a project? Look no further than a fixed sign. Fixed energy is about stability, hard work, and perseverance. While cardinal energy cranks out ideas and outlines, fixed energy comes through with an unbeatable work ethic and the ability to carry out what's been started with focus. They're the taskmasters of the zodiac; if you hand them a plan, they can run with it. They are comfortably able to deliver a consistent and stable energy.

If something is fixed, it means it's not liable to move or change—and this sort of reliability is important when it comes to the energy of the fixed signs. Because the Sun season of each of these signs falls in the middle of each season, right in the heart of it, it's got a big job to do: It must sustain us through the thickest, heaviest part of the season, when the freshness of change has worn off but the excitement of a new beginning is still too far off to take note of. It must also be consistent, as we rely on it to get us through. This energy is diligent, focused, and perhaps even a little stubborn—fixed energy is resistant to change and appreciates routine, security, and solidness (as this is the only one of the three modalities that doesn't deal with the beginning or end of a seasonal transition).

Although the fixed signs excel at *doing* and *achieving*, they each embody this energy differently, based on their elements. Taurus's wonderfully grounding presence is all about stability and physical comfort. Leo's incredible stamina helps us maintain the passion and fire once we've kicked something off. Scorpio possesses an intense ability to persevere through the deepest of emotional storms. And Aquarius bring consistency and reliability to thinking and the collective.

MUTABLE

The Changers

Looking to put the final touches on a job and then, inevitably, prepare to bid the finished project adieu as you embark on your next journey? The flexibility and openness of the mutable signs are at your service. Mutable energy is all about the ability to bring things to their natural conclusions and embrace change. While cardinal energy kick-starts something and fixed energy puts in the work to make it real, mutable energy steps in when it's time to wrap things up, practice letting go, and prepare for whatever might come next. It's here for change, adjustment, movement, and total transformation. Mutable signs have an incredible ability to shapeshift and accept things as they are.

Mutable energy is comfortable embracing the ever-changing nature of existence, and therefore tries to not get too attached to any one single way of being. Mutable means "changeable"—and this sort of flexibility and adaptability is essential to a mutable sign's nature. The Sun moves through a mutable sign during the final month of every season, making these the signs that conclude whatever we started at the beginning of the season and prepare us for the changes ahead as we embark on the next season. In that sense, the mutable signs are doing double duty—they must be flexible enough to assist us through endings as well as hold our hands as we usher in new beginnings.

Although mutable energy excels at going with the inevitable flow and accepting whatever hands they've been dealt (in the direction of the cardinal energy's plans and the fixed energy's work), each sign shows this strength in a different way, depending on their element. Gemini is gifted when it comes to changing opinions and remaining open to new information and communication styles. Virgo swoops in to make adjustments to the practical issues in any plan with its incredible eye for detail. Sagittarius's free spirit is amazing at going with the flow and spontaneously changing course. And Pisces has the gift of being able to travel between realms, blending the emotional with the spiritual.

POLARITIES

The last of the sign categorizations that I'll leave you with are the polarities, **masculine and feminine**. These are also known as *binaries*. It's easy to remember which signs fall under which polarity, as all fire and air signs are considered masculine, while all earth and water signs are considered feminine. But remember, when we talk about masculine and feminine energies, we're not actually referring to any sort of stereotypical gender roles. The symbolism of masculine energy is simply embodied by a more active role, while feminine is considered more passive. Masculine is outwardly focused, and feminine is inwardly focused.

There is a beautiful balance of masculine and feminine energy in every person and every thing. In astrology, these words describe specific energies rather than gender or sex.

MASCULINE

ELEMENTS	Fire and air
SIGNS	Aries, Leo, Sagittarius, Gemini, Libra, Aquarius
OTHER ASSOCIATIONS	Day, yang, active, outward-focused

The masculine signs are considered to be more active and outgoing in nature. Their energy is focused outward. They're interested in objectively observing the world around them, conceptualizing it, then taking action. This half of the zodiac tends to move more quickly than the other half, and we see a greater emphasis on action, initiative, and thinking.

With the three fire signs, we see this in their focus on *doing* things—following passions, taking action, creating energy. With air signs, we see this in their focus on *conceptualizing* things—gaining knowledge, communicating with others, making mental connections. These signs expand outward into the world and generate measurable forms of energy.

FEMININE

ELEMENTS	Earth and water
SIGNS	Taurus, Virgo, Capricorn, Cancer, Scorpio, Pisces
OTHER ASSOCIATIONS	Night, yin, passive, inward-focused

The feminine signs are considered to be more passive and receptive in their nature. Their energy is focused inward. These signs are known to move a bit slower, allowing themselves time to feel into and sense their surroundings, paying close attention to the way that affects them and the world around them. There's a greater emphasis on sensing, feeling, and gentleness with this half of the zodiac.

With the earth signs, we see this in their focus on the *senses*; they're in touch with their bodies and the tangible world around them, paying heed to the sensations of their bodies and using that to help them move forward. With water signs, we see a focus on *feelings*; they're connected to the emotional landscape of their inner worlds and maintain a connection with their personal intuition. These signs direct their energy inward and open up to the invisible forces of emotion and experience.

The Ascension of the Zodiac

The zodiac signs aren't randomly ordered—there is a clear designation to the signs, one through twelve, and each planet's journey through the full twelve-sign cycle of the zodiac represents an evolution of the spirit and self.

The first sign of the zodiac is Aries, which means the first day of Aries's Sun season also marks the first day of the solar astrological year (and yes, this *fully* gives you astrology babies permission to celebrate New Year's for a second time in March, because who *doesn't* love a second chance to set goals and start fresh?). **Thinking about a year as not an arbitrary chunk of time, but rather a full evolutionary journey through the zodiac signs, adds a *cosmic* significance to this new beginning.** From Aries, the zodiac progresses through the remaining succession of signs, all the way up through the twelfth and final sign, watery Pisces. The completion of this cycle serves as a marker of our growth and our experiences through each of these different energies. And this is true of *any* planet moving into Aries, not just the Sun. This transit indicates that a planet has completed yet another full cycle through the zodiac, and is beginning a brand-new one.

The first sign, Aries, represents our most basic foundation: our will to *live* and *do*. From there, we move into Taurus, which provides us with earthly stability and sensory observation. Next up is Gemini, which offers us *intellectual* observation and helps us process information, communicate, and objectively interact with the world around us. We continue through the signs, gaining more wisdom and insight, until we finally reach Pisces, the ethereal and otherworldly twelfth sign of spiritual awakening and transcendence. None of these signs is better or more important than another. They all work in tandem with each other to create a whole *evolution*, each one simultaneously building upon the energy of the last and relying on the symbiotically powerful energy of the next.

PERSONAL SIGNS VS. TRANSCENDENT SIGNS

Just as there are the inner, personal planets and the outer, transpersonal planets, there are more personal and more transcendent signs, too. The first six signs of the zodiac (Aries through Virgo) deal with *personal* matters of the self: our life force, our security, our minds, our homes, our pleasures, and our routines. All six of these

> As you move through the zodiac, you also move through a personal evolution—you can think of it almost like traveling from the base of your needs pyramid to the very top of it, becoming a new version of yourself.

signs' energies are focused on interacting with the environment that is tangibly and directly around them. They deal with matters that are personal and integral to our basic needs. Here we see a focus on our physical health, vitality, day-to-day functioning, conscious mind, and financial security, as well as an exploration of our closest familial relationships, habits, and hobbies. You'll also notice that none of these six signs is naturally ruled by any of the three outer generational planets (Uranus, Neptune, and Pluto). In fact, these six signs are the domiciles to the luminaries and the three closest planets to the Sun exclusively—not even the so-called "social planets" (Jupiter and Saturn) have domiciles among this personal grouping. This is a reflection of the way these first six signs make up the *foundation* of our needs pyramid. They provide us with the solid sense of self and awareness necessary for us to build upon toward further evolution.

The latter six signs of the zodiac (Libra through Pisces) deal with *interpersonal* and more *transcendental* matters: our subconscious, relationships with others, personal growth, life's purpose, place in the community, and spiritual awareness. Here's where the focus of each sign's energy begins to shift *outward* and *upward* and even *inward* instead of focusing on the direct environment around us—we're dealing with slightly more complex and less tangible sides of life, and delving into the realms of our subconscious and unconscious mind, too. These six signs deal more with abstract concepts, as well as our role in relation to other people and forces. Here we see outside relationships and perspectives coming into focus, as well as higher-minded spiritual and philosophical concepts. All three of the transcendental outer planets have their domiciles among these final six zodiac signs, as do the later-discovered "social" planets, Jupiter and Saturn (in fact, the only one of the five original personal planets to have a domicile in this group is Venus, which rules Libra in addition to Taurus).

What's the Deal with Cusps?

There are twelve different signs, which means they all border each other, which means there are going to be people born on the first or last day of a sign's season. But just because you are born *near* a cusp doesn't mean that your sign becomes a blurry combination of the two adjacent signs. I'm sorry to tell you that there is no such thing as a "cusp sign"—a planet is either in one sign or another. It simply can't be in both. Of course, you can be born *near* the cusp of two signs. You could even be born within the last *minute* of the Sun being in a certain sign! But even then, a planet can only be in one sign or another, and it doesn't take on a blend of two different signs' energies just because it falls within the first or final degrees of one.

For example, one of my best friends was born with the Sun in the very first degree of Aries (in fact, during most years, her birth time and day actually falls officially into Pisces territory!). She was mere *hours* from being born a Pisces Sun. That said, this doesn't make her any less an Aries. Her Sun's Aries-like expression isn't any fuzzier or less defined or less pure because of this. She's still an Aries Sun, through and through. Even if she'd only been born one measly *minute* after the Sun moved out of Pisces, she'd still be just as much an Aries.

That said, if someone is born near a cusp and swears by their "cusp sign" because they don't fully identify with their Sun sign, there are a zillion reasons why that might be. Perhaps they have several major planets clustered together in a different sign, or perhaps their Sun is being eclipsed by other planets in their chart. I was born just before Scorpio season, and I know if I had subscribed to the cusp myth growing up, I could have easily found a lot of Scorpio influence in my personality and called myself a "cusp sign." But now that I know more about my chart, I realize that the Scorpio influence *wouldn't* be because I was born near its cusp. It would be because I happen to have multiple planets and points in Scorpio in my birth chart!

If you *are* born on the cusp, it's very important to check your birth time (grab your birth certificate ASAP) and either pull up your birth chart via an online calculator or consult a professional astrologer who can do it for you. This is because the planets don't follow a nice, clean twenty-four-hour clock that matches the measurement of our days, meanings planets don't typically switch signs at midnight. It could happen at 11:11 a.m., or 8:18 p.m., or 4:29 p.m., which makes it super important for cuspers to double-check.

Houses in Astrology

In addition to signs and planets, there is one more system that you'll be introduced to in Chapter 3, and those are called *houses*. There are twelve houses, and each one represents a different area of our life and our experiences. Houses are used in the realm of astrology charts, like a birth chart, and they divide the round chart into twelve slices. These houses roughly correspond with the themes of the twelve zodiac signs: Each zodiac sign is considered the "natural ruler" of one house.

I suggest you take your time getting to know the energy of each zodiac sign, just as you should take your time getting to know the energy of each planet. Once you have a working knowledge of these various forms of energy, you'll start making your own connections, seeing your own patterns, and creating your own interpretations, which will make astrology much more real and *much* more fun. Even if you can't read your own birth chart and get a complex, detailed analysis going, you *can* get an idea of what it means when an online article or a random person mentions that Venus is in Leo. You'll know that we all might be feeling a little more dramatic, flamboyant, and showy (Leo) about the way we love (Venus), and we'll probably be drawn to creatively expressive (Leo) forms of art (Venus).

That said, it's time to learn about the signs—yours, mine, and everyone else's—and get to know these incredibly diverse, powerful, and fascinating energies in the world of astrology.

MEET
the
ZODIAC
SIGNS

ARIES

Welcome to the very first sign of the zodiac! It's no coincidence that Aries leads the zodiac brigade as zodiac sign number one, ruler of the house of self, and torchbearer of the new astrological year. This fire sign is self-motivated, confident, and full of energy, making it the perfect zealous leader to ring the astrological new year bells and set us off on our journey with enthusiasm, excitement, and fearlessness.

Aries is symbolically represented by the ram. These animals are foolhardy, energetic, and pretty much unstoppable—all of which Aries energy embodies to the max. Rams are known for their iconic set of horns, and those babies serve a purpose: They'll use 'em to get what they want and to go where they're going, even if it means butting them up against (and maybe, just possibly full-on *demolishing*) whatever obstacle has found its misfortunate self in their way. Such is true for an Aries, too. Rams are headstrong with their sturdy horns, and Aries are headstrong in every other sense of the word (which, yes, certainly lends itself to stubbornness and hardheadedness at times). As the leaders of the zodiac, Aries *need* to possess that kind of bold strength, energy, zeal, and confidence. How else can you get something off the ground?

As a cardinal fire sign, Aries energy is all about *making it happen*, and they epitomize large-and-in-charge energy. They're fantastic initiators, full of passion, and single-minded in their mission to take the wheel. Aries shine and sparkle when they're able to command the ship, and they absolutely *love* to lead (so even if the Aries in your life aren't top dogs at their day jobs, you can probably see them thriving, taking initiative, and being a boss at whatever it is they do). Aries are leaders of the pack, and they're totally comfortable in that role—a burning torch feels *reeeeal* good in their powerful hands.

Aries is self-starting, self-motivating, and self-confident, so it's no surprise that this sign naturally rules the first house, which is known as the house of—you guessed it—the *self*. Aries's self-assuredness comes from the fact that they're so confident in who they are. Aries takes orders from *itself*, from its own will. Aries energy allows its

Aries energy is like an astrological energy drink.

> Acting on our *impulses* feels good sometimes, as does honoring our physical desires, and Aries helps us tap into our energy reserves and start making things happen.

desires, needs, and wants to triumph over anything that might stand in the way. It teaches us to courageously summon our inner badass, the one who doesn't care what anyone else thinks, the one who trusts their impulses and isn't worried about failure.

Ruled by Mars, planet of war and passion, Aries knows damn well that there's a warrior inside of them. They are immensely brave, tenacious, and generally unwilling to back down. You can often catch them impulsively diving headfirst into any situation without thinking too deeply about the consequences (or considering them at all, for that matter!). When I'm feeling unsure or overly obsessive about a decision, I often ask myself, "What would an Aries do?" Because an Aries, my friends, wouldn't waste their precious time agonizing over the pros and cons. They'd listen to the feeling in their gut, the physical desire and impulse that they easily sense in their body, and then they'd just *DO*.

Why We Need Aries Energy

Aries season follows Pisces season, which is dreamy, emotional, and spiritual. Aries, however, is very rooted in its primal instincts, relying on its base desires and physical energy to guide it, and this is actually a refreshing shift following the deep, soul-soaking intensity of Pisces season. Boy oh boy, do we need that buzzy spiritual energy drink after the emotional drain of Pisces season!

The day that the Sun moves into the sign of Aries also marks an important seasonal transition: the spring equinox, or the first day of spring. The zodiac wheel coincides perfectly with the Earth's seasons, so when the Sun hits 0 degrees Aries each year, that'll always be the time of the spring equinox. This also happens to be the beginning of the astrological new year, so we always celebrate a new rotation through the zodiac cycle with Aries's keyed up, fresh-start energy.

How We Can Work with the Energy of Aries Season

We all need a lil' Aries energy from time to time because sometimes we do simply need to *act*—not *think* or *conceptualize* or *feel* or even *plan* our way through a situation—but just *act*. Aries is jumping in headfirst to its next idea or passion without allowing myriad thoughts, feelings, and rationales that so often govern our decision-making abilities to cloud up their will. Those considerations have their place, of course, but when you want to dive headfirst into a new situation/project/life, call on the power of Aries. Aries will pop you in a cannon and shoot you out toward your destination.

TAURUS

SUN SEASON	April 20–May 20 (approximately)
ELEMENT	Earth
MODALITY	Fixed
RULING PLANET	Venus
HOUSE	Second House of Value
SYMBOL	The Bull
STUFF TO ♥	Reliable, patient, devoted
STUFF TO LOOK OUT FOR	Stubborn, bossy, resistant

Welcome to Taurus: the grounded, stable, and sensual force of the earthly realm. This fixed earth sign is all about good food, good sex, and hard work. It simultaneously encourages us to slow down and smell the roses, but also to put in the work necessary to continue moving forward with our goals. Taurus is deliberate, loyal, and really wants us to pamper our senses *just* as intensely as we cherish our personal goals. Taurus works slowly but surely in all facets of its energy.

In the zodiac's symbolism, Taurus is represented by the bull. And what do we know about bulls? Well, they're notoriously hard to conquer. They're large, robust, powerful creatures, and Taurus energy is equally sturdy and robust. Bulls are known for their *stamina*, and this is something that Taurus has got in spades. Once Taurus gets going, it really devotes itself to the job. It knows exactly how to put in the work and sustain something, moving slowly and deliberately toward a goal. And while we often think of barbaric bullfights when we think of bulls, these animals can actually be quite gentle and quiet in nature when they're not being provoked. The same is true for Taurus energy. Taurus is patient, caring, and enjoys leisurely experiencing life's pleasures, but it will charge at an enemy in order to protect its comfort zone and ensure its security if threatened.

But all work and no play would make Taurus a dull boy, so it has a fun-loving side to explore. Ruled by romantic, sensual, luxury-lovin' Venus, Taurus is all about the indulgence and activation of the physical senses.

As the second sign of the zodiac, Taurus still represents a very physical, grounded, foundational part of our being, as Aries does. But while Aries *expresses* energy

Being the grounded earth sign that it is, Taurus energy is all about taking in life's most sensual pleasures— delicious tastes, beautiful sights, fragrant scents, gentle caresses, and sweet sounds.

physically (as a masculine sign), Taurus *receives* energy physically (as a feminine sign). And because Taurus moves through the world in such a sensually focused way, this sign's energy really loves to feel comfortable and secure, both physically and emotionally.

The tendency to indulge the senses is part of why Taurus gets a reputation for being the *hungriest* sign of the zodiac (although, let's be honest, Taurus *does* love to snack, and they're usually the first to say yes to or suggest going out to eat!), as well as the sign most likely to give in to its lazy side (but that's not totally accurate, either—Taurus is an extremely hard worker!). That said, there's nothing this energy loves more than relaxing and basking in the pleasure of doing *nothing* while feeling *pleasure*. Taurus wants to wine and dine. It wants fluffy comforters, rich foods, juicy-smelling flowers, and expensive chocolates. Under the influence of its ruling planet Venus, Taurus absolutely *loves* luxury and is notoriously good at self-care. You can catch Taurus with its phone on DND, sporting a face mask, enjoying breakfast in bed, and admiring a bouquet of roses on the nightstand.

As a fixed earth sign, Taurus is also stable and quite financially responsible (who else can they rely on so steadily to uphold their fancy, luxurious lifestyle?). This sign appreciates feeling secure and enjoys a sense of predictability in their lives; they aren't into being caught off guard or having to do things quickly or spontaneously. For Taurus, it's all about being slow, steady, and sure of themselves. It hates to be rushed, and wants plenty of time to think through its next move. It also wants plenty of time to gently and leisurely take in the many sensory pleasures the world has to offer.

Why We Need Taurus Energy

Taurus's Sun season falls right in the middle of spring, spanning from April through May, and its stable, grounding energy holds our hand as we work to get through the April showers until we can finally enjoy the beauty of the May flowers. Taurus is a highly sensual sign, and its symbolic bull is a symbol of fertility (apparently, a single bull can impregnate an entire herd of cows!), so it's no coincidence that this sign's reign falls during perhaps the most fertile period of the solar year.

How We Can Work with the Energy of Taurus Season

Taurus energy helps us stick diligently to our plans and tend steadfastly to our needs without being swayed by distractions. Taurus's stubbornness gives us the tunnel vision, don't-care-what-you-think attitude and perseverance that is absolutely *necessary* when we're trying to make major headway on a project or a personal goal. In that sense, the stubborn nature of the bull is actually one of Taurus's secret weapons.

GEMINI

SUN SEASON	May 21–June 20 (approximately)
ELEMENT	Air
MODALITY	Mutable
RULING PLANET	Mercury
HOUSE	Third House of Communication
SYMBOL	The Twins
STUFF TO ♥	Curious, talkative, witty
STUFF TO LOOK OUT FOR	Easily distracted, flighty, righteous

The third sign of the zodiac is chatty, witty, quick-thinking, sharp-tongued Gemini. Represented by the sign of the twins, Gemini is the energetic embodiment of duality. It feels comfortable bouncing between the extreme ends of any given spectrum, exploring the nuances and thought processes that define one viewpoint or experience from another.

But twins aren't actually two halves of a whole. Instead, they're two individual energies that are connected and sometimes functioning as one. The same could be said for Gemini's ability to do the work of two while being only one. The twin symbolism speaks to this sign's incredibly quick and high-functioning brain, which is able to sort, dissect, process, question, and share information at a rate that feels like twice the speed of any other.

Gemini's ability to so easily embody two opinions, feelings, or states of being at once is what gives its energy the reputation of being "two-faced" and untrustworthy, although that's an unfair label to place on this witty, social, and information-loving sign. While Gemini's ability to think on its toes and change its opinions could in theory allow it to lie and cheat more easily than another sign, that doesn't mean it will use its energy that way. This sign is merely naturally paradoxical in nature, and it can't help it if it happens to be quick-thinking, convincing, and gifted at the art of conversation.

You're likely to see your Gemini friend texting, tinkering with their laptop, checking their reflection in a mirror, *and* eating lunch—all while somehow still holding down a conversation with you. This is because Gemini truly is a multitasker extraordinaire, just like its ruling planet, Mercury. Mercury rules over everything, from communication, learning, and objective thinking to scheduling, short trips, and technology, and it takes an

Gemini energy is like a web browser with three dozen open tabs, each from different websites and on different topics. It's a little chaotic (and would drive any earth sign up the wall), but in Gemini's world, this is the norm.

equally hyper, busybody zodiac sign to serve as the planet's domicile. Gemini lives, experiences, and processes information by absorbing all of it, all at once, all the time.

Just like Taurus (its preceding sign), Gemini is a keen observer of the world around it. But instead of using its physical senses to interact with its environment, as Taurus does, Gemini uses its *mind*. This sign possesses an exceptional mental power. It gets a kick out of quirky details and loves to ponder things like hypothetical situations and riddles. And clever Gemini enjoys a good *mind* game just as heartily as it enjoys a good *word* game. Its quizzical outlook views all things like a puzzle that's waiting to be solved, and this sign simply can't say no to a mental challenge.

Speaking of games, this sign is also very playful, enthusiastic, and witty, and bestowed with a fun and sharp sense of humor. This is part of why you can catch Gemini asking so many questions, whether it's during class or simply during a conversation with a stranger at a bar. These curious conversationalists are always hungry for fun and interesting facts. Essentially, Gemini has never grown out of the phase that most children go through that involves asking "But *why?*" after anything anyone says.

That said, Gemini is also perhaps the quintessential sign of communication. Gemini is highly social and absolutely *loves* to talk. At length. About *any* topic under the sun. Gemini loves sharing its opinions, and hearing yours, too—but watch out, because their views are subject to change at a moment's notice.

Geminis don't feel any need or desire to align themselves with any one single way of being or thinking—in fact, these independent creatures crave the freedom to think and say whatever they please and to change their minds at the drop of a hat. As a mutable air sign, they are intellectually driven and see the world through a more abstract lens, and their mutable nature enables them to seamlessly flit from thought to thought, like a humming-bird sipping nectar from a field full of flowers. The adaptable, shapeshifting, duality-embracing form of the twins is mutable in every sense.

The quickly moving pace of the Gemini brain can also make this sign easily distracted, flighty, and noncommittal. These air signs are *not* blessed with a sustained attention span; it's notoriously difficult to keep Gemini's focus on just one thing for any extended period of time (or in general, as they're usually juggling multiple thoughts, tasks, and conversations at once). Gemini won't hesitate for a second to change a plan long after it's been set, or change its mind long after it's taken a stance; while this might drive others crazy, Gemini doesn't see the issue, as last-minute changes only give this air sign the opportunity to flex their mental prowess and show off their incredible, chameleon-like ability to adapt in any landscape or situation.

The sign of the twins has double the energy to work with, so it truly is the chameleon of the zodiac. Given Gemini's mutable-sign ability to shapeshift and adapt quickly to any situation, this sign could be the best cheater, liar, and scammer around on a bad day, with its intense ability to process information quickly, pick up on and store details about the people and things around them, and pull a fast one on any unknowing victim. But on a good day, Gemini is the ultimate gift to our ability to communicate: witty, hilarious, sharp, sarcastic, endlessly curious, interested, and fun.

Gemini rules over the third house of the zodiac, which represents communication, thinking, and learning, and it brings an energy, wit, and sharpness to these important functions of our day-to-day life. While this part of the chart might seem somewhat mundane (as it has to do with regular daily tasks, thoughts, and relationships), the presence of lively and versatile Gemini in the house helps keep things interesting, fresh, and exciting. Gemini genuinely loves learning new things, and tends to be physically hyper (although this stems from its highly active mental energy, rather than an excess of physical vitality), which, when combined, makes it great at taking on many different projects at once (although perhaps not the most adept at finishing them all).

Gemini energy is easily amused, able to generate seemingly endless amounts of entertainment from even the most mundane of situations, and blessed with a knack for catching the most fascinating little details of a story, scene, or situation. That said, Gemini energy is just as easily bored, ready to move on to the next person, place, or thing once its interest has waned and it's caught wind of the next cyclone of information it can throw itself into. Such is the *mercurial* nature of this sign, which genuinely loves to think and conceptualize.

Why We Need Gemini Energy

Gemini's Sun season transitions us from the lushness of spring into the warmth of summer, and is the perfect mental wake-up call to open our eyes and enjoy the power of our minds and our consciousness. While Taurus (Gemini's preceding sign) works slowly and with lots of deliberate focus, Gemini helps us loosen up, step out of our bodies, and pick up the pace mentally as we prepare ourselves for the sunshiny summertime. It's also great for moving us into a more social headspace as we enjoy perhaps the most temperate months of the year—late spring.

How We Can Work with the Energy of Gemini Season

Gemini's adaptability, sharp mind, and insatiable curiosity about the world is exactly the type of energy we need to take us out of our own bodies and get us to pay attention to how endlessly interesting and fascinating the people, places, things, and *ideas* all around us really are. Let your mind lead during Gemini season instead of your body! While Gemini's attention deficit can certainly make it harder for us to focus, we'll also be busy gathering up *lots* of useful information, so the hyperactivity is worth it.

CANCER

SUN SEASON	June 21–July 22 (approximately)
ELEMENT	Water
MODALITY	Cardinal
RULING PLANET	The Moon
HOUSE	Fourth House of Home
SYMBOL	Crab
STUFF TO ♥	Nurturing, patient, empathetic
STUFF TO LOOK OUT FOR	Moody, sensitive, needy

Welcome to the emotional shores of cardinal water sign Cancer, the zodiac's loving nurturer.

Cancer is the ultimate maternal sign. On a good day, Cancer is the sweet, sensitive, loving second mom we always wanted: It's protective of our feelings, sensitive, and warm. But on a bad day, Cancer can be as crabby as the crab it's named for, expressing as needy, oversensitive, or passive-aggressive. But these qualities are merely defense mechanisms to protect the incredibly empathic, caring, and gentle Cancerian soul that resides beneath the crab's outer shell—and it's this soul that makes Cancers so special.

The crab is a very fitting symbol for Cancer energy. These ocean dwellers coast on and off the shores, following the ebb and flow of the Moon-ruled tides and ocean waves. Crabs, just like Cancers, have a hard shell of an exterior that protects the softness that lies beneath. Similarly, Cancers—who are arguably the most emotionally sensitive and sentimental of the zodiac signs—are known to put up a protective shield to lower the risk of their vulnerable inner selves being penetrated by cruelty, heartbreak, betrayal, judgment, or misunderstanding. For being so naturally emotion-oriented, Cancers really dislike feeling emotionally exposed, which is why they take steps to avoid feeling so defenseless.

Upon meeting a Cancer, they'll likely seem much more distant and surface level than they truly are, but an incredible depth emerges once Cancer builds trust. This is simply how it protects its very sensitive inner self.

And just as the waves that a crab floats through are ruled by the lovely Moon, so is the sign of Cancer itself, making it one of only two signs in the zodiac ruled by a luminary. It's no surprise that the sensitive and emotionally focused Moon would choose Cancer as its home. Cancer's qualities are *perfectly* suited to this sentimental planet's needs and wants. Also, well, Cancer happens to possess the ideal qualities and energies of a good and welcoming homemaker. Cancer energy shines and sparkles when it's nurturing others, whether by cooking you nourishing foods, offering you a warm and cuddly place to rest, or making you feel safe and protected, both physically and emotionally. Intrinsically caring and dedicated to creating safe and secure spaces, Cancer can't help but make someone feel like they can kick off their shoes, take off the masks they wear in their daily lives, and relax into themselves in Cancer's presence. It's no wonder the Moon loves her domicile.

Because it is in Cancer's nature to care for others, this sign has become synonymous as a sort of mother figure for the rest of the zodiac, so it makes sense that it rules the domestic fourth house, which represents the realm of home and family. This house deals with our childhoods, parental figures, and nostalgic memories, as well as our *current* homes and families. It's a house that deeply appreciates safety and privacy, both things that Cancer energy appreciates, too. This sign's energy requires a safe, private, comfortable retreat where it can be itself and let its emotions bask freely in the moonlight. Cancers love to retreat from the harshness and insensitivity of the world around them, and they'll get crabby if they don't. They need their naps and they *don't* want to be disturbed. They're motherly and parental, but these signs can become as cranky as a baby if they aren't given the space they need to relax, unwind, and shut off the constant flow of distractions from the outside world.

Cancer may be the matriarch of the zodiac, but none of this is to imply that Cancers are just home-bodies who want to cook, clean, and raise the kids (although they *do* have a well-earned reputation for being homebodies!). Cancerian talents span far beyond the realm of the domestic. This energy is sensitive, highly empathic, and can easily pick up on the nuances and feelings of those around them. Cancer's natural nurturing ability is also useful outside of the home, because it isn't just Cancer's own children who need its particularly coddling brand of TLC: The whole *world* needs the motherly love that Cancer energy offers.

Cancer energy is the type of energy that's so warm, inviting, and compassionate that even a perfect stranger is likely to feel comfortable opening up and sharing their deepest secrets and vulnerabilities. But Cancer's deep sensitivity goes both ways, and also makes this sign supremely touchy when it comes to other people's opinions of and actions toward *them*. Cancers can often pick up on the tiniest of microaggressions (or even *misperceive* them if they're feeling overly sensitive!), and can end up feeling hurt quite easily.

Because of the Cancerian aversion to becoming too vulnerable, it has a tendency to quickly retreat into its shell on reflex, which can result in it handling conflict in a childlike and avoidant way. Think silent treatments or passive-aggressive drama. But don't fault Cancer too hard on this, as we must remember that this sign's ruling planet, the Moon, moves *very* quickly through the zodiac (faster than any other planet!), meaning that its influence on Cancer's watery moods is ever-changing. This manifests in Cancer as full-blown moodiness. This emotional sign is prone to hurt feelings, and finds itself easily disappointed, offended, and inclined to hold a grudge. On the plus side? Grudges only exist where feelings still exist, too, so there's always a chance of rekindling things if you've found yourself suddenly pushed outside of Cancer's inner circle. There's likely still love there somewhere.

Cancers are clearly fantastic at tending to the needs of others, but what about when Cancer needs taking care of? If Cancer doesn't feel loved and deeply appreciated for their nurturing efforts, they'll become cranky and crabby and very needy, very fast. When you have to be a "mom" all the time, you need to balance things out by acting like a baby once in a while, right? When Cancer is feeling unloved or underappreciated, expect the retaliation to be immature. Cancer can get possessive, and even codependent.

Cancers are deeply sentimental. They'll hold on to a crush for just as long as they'll hold on to a grudge—and in both cases, we're talking a *very* long time, if not forever. This emotionally committed energy illustrates the way in which Cancer doesn't want to let go of things, whether that thing is a mistake someone made or the love someone gave them. But we mustn't forget that this is a *cardinal* water sign we're dealing with here, so Cancer is one of the *creators*. Cancers have the power to initiate when it comes to the emotional element of water. By creating a safe, nurturing environment, they are able to coax the feelings and sentimentalities out of the cracks in which they were hiding, serving as the catalyst for the entire emotional process to come.

Why We Need Cancer Energy

After the hyper-social and slightly chaotic energy of Gemini season, Cancer season serves as a well-earned hibernation of sorts. It gives us a chance to turn our energy inward; instead of focusing on the information, people, thoughts, and ideas that float all around us, as Gemini does, Cancer focuses on nurturing the inner self and focusing on emotions.

As a water sign, Cancer energy has a free-flowing nature and obviously an immense sensitivity and desire to nurture. This is why Cancerian souls, male or female, are often described as maternal. But again, we mustn't forget that Cancer is indeed a cardinal sign, one of the major initiators and action takers of the zodiac. So while we think of them as very gentle, we must also remember that Cancers, like mothers, are *warriors*. Being a caretaker or mother figure takes emotional power and strength of *all* kinds, and there's a deep sense of responsibility attached to this type of role. Cancer's subtle, gentle strength reminds us of the sheer power of being vulnerable. We can retreat into our shells when needed, yes, but that doesn't mean we should take on the persona of the shell altogether. Beneath a crab's shell are still its gushy, defenseless insides. It's important to stay soft, even when the waters get choppy.

How We Can Work with the Energy of Cancer Season

Cancer has a tendency to dwell in the past, and while this can cause them some melancholy, it also gives them the secret power of *compassion*. We can and should call on Cancer energy any time we need to nurture or be nurtured. This cardinal sign is actually the initiator of deeply important personal processes—the processing of our inner emotional landscape.

Cancer is gifted at helping us create a cozy little nook where we can safely lay out our feelings for further exploration and analysis.

LEO

SUN SEASON	July 23–August 22 (approximately)
ELEMENT	Fire
MODALITY	Fixed
RULING PLANET	The Sun
HOUSE	Fifth House of Pleasure
SYMBOL	The Lion
STUFF TO ♥	Confident, generous, warm, loyal
STUFF TO LOOK OUT FOR	Egotistical, demanding, selfish

Powered by the Sun, their ruling planet, Leo energy exudes confidence, vitality, creative power, and a clearly defined sense of self. Whether a Leo is quiet or outgoing, they tend to have at least a subtle brand of confidence about the way they present themselves (although usually it's less subtle and more in-your-face!), but this self-assuredness and warmth also make them one of the most positive and supportive signs of the zodiac.

Regal, proud, and powerful, Leo, unsurprisingly, is represented by the lion. The lion is known as the "king of the jungle," which makes sense, because Leo is sort of the king (and queen) of the zodiac, too! Perhaps this is why this sign is often likened to royalty. Leo seeks fame and notoriety. It wants to express itself, and it lives for little ego boosts. Leo expects to have the prestigious accommodations, amenities, and devout loyalty bestowed upon them in their everyday life that would be shown to *actual* royalty. Of course, in exchange, you have the honor of . . . being in the presence of a Leo! This sign is proud and powerful, with a larger-than-life ego that must be stroked, fluffed, and petted on a near-constant basis. Oh, and fun fact—Leo Suns have a reputation for having a great mane of hair. Think through the Leos you know and report back.

Leos are starlets, and they know it. They feel comfortable and very much themselves when the spotlight is on them. The feeling of having eyes and ears and minds focused in their direction doesn't make them nervous, but rather offers them a deep sense of satisfaction and confidence. It's a source of power. This is because Leos know exactly what messages they'd like to get across; they understand the power of presentation. Self-expression is deeply meaningful to them, so even if the Leo you know isn't an extroverted, star-of-the-show, life-of-the-party type, they likely have *other* hobbies or interests that are based on their personal brand of self-expression.

The Leonian need to share its vision with the world is why so many Leos tend to get into creative fields and take up artistic hobbies.

Leo energy reminds us to live big, wild, creative, and proud.

Leo may have a *big* ego, but you'll be hard-pressed to find a sign that has a bigger heart. Their capacity for passion runs large and deep.

Take a look at a list of famous Leos and compare it to that of other signs—there's a *reason* so many actors, performers, musicians, and other entertainers are born with their Sun in Leo. Creative energy is plentiful with this fire sign, so expressing themselves through visual, performative, or otherwise creative means comes very naturally.

The downside of being so damn Hollywood all the time? Leos tend to possess a flair for the *dramatic*. Yep, that's right. If the lion isn't being given enough attention, then you can expect to hear a roar soon enough—and it'll last just long enough to ensure everyone's focus shifts back to its rightful place! Sometimes Leo energy can attract drama without even wanting or meaning to; it just comes naturally with the passion of the fire sign. You know the phrase "Any press is good press"? That's true for Leo. They're not overly concerned with *what* people think of them, as long as people are thinking of them. Leos love to be loved, of course, but they don't need to be loved as much as they need to be *known*. Because, ultimately, Leos really don't want to be forgotten.

Leos tend to walk, talk, and otherwise exude the vibe that they're *special*. And *important*. And you know what? In a lot of ways, they really are. How can you *not* feel like the center of the universe when you happen to be the singular sign that the one and only Sun has chosen as its domicile, and one of only two signs ruled by a luminary in all of astrology? Just like its ruling planet, the Sun, Leo energy just wants to *shine*. It's vital, bright, creative, fiery, passionate, and generous, just like the life-giving Sun around which all the other planets circle. The Sun is the planet that rules our ego, and similarly, the Leo ego is important, too. Leo energy is large, bright, and in charge. It's the energy of the Sun itself, built to express, create, and give.

But it's not just about the Sun's ego. Leo energy brings a warm and sunny disposition. With Leo, it's always summer, and it's always daytime. It's a beautiful thing. When you're ruled by the Sun, provider of all life, you know you have a *lot* to give, so there's very little scarcity mentality when dealing with Leo energy; this sign is naturally gregarious, abundant, and full of love and passion to spare. While Leo can be self-centered, it's not necessarily *selfish*. In fact, Leo energy is filled to the brim with genuine warmth, kindness, and generosity. They may love the glow of the spotlight, but they'll gas *you* up just as much as they gas themselves up, and their sunshiny attitude toward life is unbeatable in its positivity and optimism. To be loved and supported by a Leo is one of the greatest gifts, and it will make *you* feel like the center of the universe, too. Leo is the zodiac's number-one hype person. This energy is ready to cheer you on, support you, and blast you out on social media until the day is done.

You're likely to catch Leo admiring their reflection and posting daily glammed-out selfies as often as you'll find them telling their friends/partners/coworkers how incredibly amazing they are. They dish out compliments as often as they fish for them.

As a fire sign, Leos are made of pure passion, and as you know, their will is motivated by the need to express who they are inside. As a fixed sign, their gift is in putting in the work and getting things done. They're one of the zodiac's top *doers*. They're the kings and queens who expect royal treatment, 'tis true, but they're simultaneously deeply loyal and dedicated, both to people *and* to projects. Once they start working on a creative endeavor, getting into a hobby, or kicking off a passion project that's close to their heart, they can easily become full-blown workaholics!

When it comes to communication, Leos can be performative, expressive, and flamboyant, even intense! It's definitely *not* a good idea to ignore or interrupt Leo; otherwise, expect the roaring lion inside of it to come forward. These lions are typically bubbling over with confidence (or at least appear to be), and it shows.

Why We Need Leo Energy

The Sun's journey through its home sign of Leo takes place during the dead center of the summer season, when the days are longest and the temperature is hottest. While Cancer season is all about tending to our emotions, Leo takes us out of that watery and moonlit hibernation and drags us directly out into the sunshine without skipping a beat. This is a time to embrace the heat and intensity of midsummer energy. Soon, the days will start getting shorter, and Leo wants you to show off who you are with confidence and zeal!

How We Can Work with the Energy of Leo Season

If you're feeling shy about sharing your artwork or passion, putting yourself out there for a lover or job, or feeling stuck in the throes of imposter syndrome, ask yourself, "What would Leo do?" Well, I'll tell you: Leo would primp up the best parts of themselves, and then *shine*, just like the Sun itself. Leos have confidence, but that doesn't mean this sign's energy isn't also riddled with (and sometimes crippled by) insecurities. The downside of having such a large ego is that its sheer size makes it a bit fragile at time, and it needs twice the stroking and gassing up. The difference, though, is that at the end of the day, Leo energy knows what it is. It knows how strong, vital, bright, and important it is. So the next time you're feeling less than confident about something, channel your inner Leo to *rawr* your way through and grab the spotlight that's rightfully yours.

VIRGO

SUN SEASON	August 23–September 22 (approximately)
ELEMENT	Earth
MODALITY	Mutable
RULING PLANET	Mercury
HOUSE	Sixth House of Wellness
SYMBOL	The Maiden
STUFF TO ♥	Organized, service-oriented, orderly
STUFF TO LOOK OUT FOR	Nitpicky, critical, perfectionist

Welcome to the clean, pristine, and impeccably organized castle that is the zodiac sign of Virgo. Virgo energy relates to the world through its down-to-earth and pragmatic sense of orderliness and duty. It knows exactly what should go where, and it wants to clean house to ensure life runs as smoothly as it possibly can. This sign is the zodiacal equivalent of the organization expert we all wish we could hire to reorganize our closets, clean out our junk drawers, and completely revamp our to-do lists from the ground up.

Virgo is ruled by the planet Mercury, and it's easy to see why the planet that's named after the messenger of the gods would choose the immaculate Virgo as one of its two domiciles. There is no sign more organized, detail-oriented, practical, and helpful as Virgo. Mercury rules over things like scheduling and timing, and these are areas in which Virgo energy absolutely excels. This sign hates sloppiness and messiness. It feels uneasy when things are up in the air or out of its control, and perhaps this is because it's so damn good at being *in* control. Virgo energy sensibly grasps timing and scheduling quickly and easily, like a lil' energetic calculator. Through Virgo, Mercury is able to function and complete its many tasks with grace, efficiency, and absolute thoroughness.

Virgo energy is *insanely* thorough—it doesn't leave a single corner undusted or stone unturned. If you want to ensure a job is well-done and guarantee that every *i* has been dotted and *t* crossed, hire a Virgo to do your dirty work. This sign is *definitely* the zodiac's perfectionist, for better or worse. Virgo simply can't *help* but notice every

The phrase "Cleanliness is next to godliness" often comes to mind when I think of Virgo energy, because for Virgo, keeping things neat, tidy, and pristine is one of this sign's greatest contributions.

single tiny detail, nor can it resist its urge to fix and improve. Virgo derives glee from cleanliness and organization, and is subsequently driven up the wall by carelessness and negligence. Even if a Virgo-heavy person *isn't* a totally type-A, hyper-organized pragmatist who is glued to their calendar, it's likely that their perfectionist tendencies still manifest in some other way, perhaps in their infallible work ethic, need to have details mapped out, or just by being super particular about the way things are done in their daily routine.

Speaking of routines, they're a big deal for Virgos. As you may have guessed given the Virgoan knack for organization and efficiency, this is a sign that deeply appreciates a well-managed schedule and regular routine. While *too* much routine can box you in, Virgo knows that the right amount of regularity and reliability can allow you to be freer, as well as more efficient. That said, it's no surprise to learn that Virgo rules the sixth house of the zodiac, which represents—you guessed it—routines, as well as wellness and work. This area of the chart is all about how we take care of ourselves and manage our ability to function and get things done, and Virgo has a natural gift for identifying areas that need improvement and implementing healthy solutions.

Represented by the maiden, or the virgin, Virgo is a sign often associated with purity. It loves any space, energetic or physical, that's free of debris and clutter. It wants things to be as uncomplicated, simple, and pure as possible. This is why Virgo is so skilled in the arts of decluttering, organizing, and streamlining. Purity is the natural state for Virgo.

Uptight and straitlaced Virgo may not have a reputation for being free-spirited, but we mustn't forget that it is, in fact, a mutable sign. Virgo energy is absolutely adaptable and willing to flow with change. In fact, this is where its talents can best shine. Like a cosmic editor, Virgo energy jumps into any situation and helps us cut and paste (and probably cut some more) until things are in order. As is always the case with the mutable signs, it sends us into the season to come, and Virgo gives us the gentle and subtle confidence that's needed to do just that.

Of course, while being a perfectionist might put you at the top of the class and ensure you execute your tasks with precision and excellence, it's not always a good thing. On a bad day, Virgo energy is critical and nitpicky, with a tendency to nag and find faults in just about everything. It can be exhausting to deal with an energy that spots mistakes and minor slips with the precision of a supercomputer, but Virgo simply can't help that they're natural-born fault detectors. Virgo never criticizes to be cruel. This sign genuinely and truly wants to *help* others. Virgo is a perfectionist because it wants to make the world a better, purer, more efficient place for all of us.

On that note, I'd be remiss to discuss Virgo without expanding further on the incredibly altruistic and humanitarian nature of this sign. Virgo can be critical, yes—it can't help that it's thoroughly absorbed by earthly and practical matters—but Virgo is also defined by its service-oriented nature. This sign is inherently helpful. Virgo energy is unique in the fact that it's deeply pragmatic, rational, and sensible, as well as genuinely helpful, giving, and altruistic. Virgos want what's best for the world and the people in their lives. We all have that aunt, grandparent, or even parent who always seems to find fault in everything we do. While that can sting, at the end of the day, we know it's because they believe in us, and they want us to do our best. They want to offer constructive criticism because they care. Virgo energy is exactly that: constructive criticism.

Why We Need Virgo Energy

The Sun travels through Virgo during the final weeks of the summer season and leads up to the autumnal equinox, or the first day of fall. Thus, the maiden prepares us for the time of the harvest. While we party hard with Leo's glitzy and glamorous energy through the dog days of summer, we wrap up the season with Virgo's pragmatic and down-to-earth organization skills. This earth sign centers our energy and grounds us back into ourselves, reminding us of the work that lies ahead as the days get cooler and the season of the harvest approaches. In other words, Virgo energy helps us get our lives together. It's good to spend some summer fun in the Sun—and sunshiny Leo makes sure we do exactly that—but Virgo gives us a gentle dose of reality and encourages us to start preparing for the new season ahead.

How We Can Work with the Energy of Virgo Season

The powerhouse of Sun-ruled Leo season, which precedes Virgo season, is as flashy as they come. Virgo energy, however, is much more subtle, though equally powerful. Leo season asks us how we can more passionately express ourselves, but Virgo asks us to self-reflect instead of self-express.

In truth, Virgo simply wants to be of service and make our lives as well managed as they can possibly be. Because if we take care of our wellness and leave room in our schedule for growth, that's when we can *truly* thrive.

Virgo energy is the perfect combination of gentle and kind, plus a dash of let's-get-shit-done. It makes staying organized and being practical look easy, fun, and sexy. Spend a lot of time around a Virgo, and you'll start to see the beauty in paying your bills on time, organizing your bookshelf alphabetically or by color, and actually updating your Google calendar on the regular. In a world that's so insanely and inherently messy, Virgo brings us down to earth and reminds us of the little details that we *do* have control over. Deep breaths. One step at a time. This is the gift that Virgo energy gives us.

LIBRA

SUN SEASON	September 23–October 22 (approximately)
ELEMENT	Air
MODALITY	Cardinal
RULING PLANET	Venus
HOUSE	Seventh House of Partnerships
SYMBOL	The Scales
STUFF TO ♥	Diplomatic, social, balanced
STUFF TO LOOK OUT FOR	Flaky, shallow, indecisive

We've now officially entered the latter half of the zodiac, which comprises the more interpersonal— and transpersonal-focused signs—and Libra is the perfect diplomatic leader to hold our hands as we make this slight thematic shift. Libra is the official sign of partnerships; social, diplomatic, charming, and popular, Libra is gifted when it comes to maintaining a solidly cheerful social equilibrium and keeping the peace.

Represented by the symbol of the scales, Libran energy is inherently focused on balance. Think about a scale—it's an inanimate object, and *balancing* is its sole function. To weigh one thing against another is this object's entire purpose. Thus, this is inherently how Libras function and relate to the world as well. This sign is constantly weighing one option, opinion, person, place, thing, or decision against another. That said, it comes as no surprise that Libras are naturally indecisive. It's not that Libras don't have opinions; it's simply that they have the gift (or the curse) of being able to see the pros and cons of many *different* decisions all at once, making it difficult for them to commit to one over another. And you know what else uses the scales as its symbol? The law. The "scales of justice" represent our legal systems being upheld in a fair and unbiased manner. Libras, too, are very concerned with justice and fairness, which is often what drives their almost obsessive need to weigh the pros and cons of every option, as well as their very intellectual ability to step back from a situation and see it from multiple perspectives.

Libra rules the seventh house of commitments and partnerships, and this house could have no more well-suited ruler. Libra energy truly comes alive and sparkles when it's in a symbiotic partnership with another. This sign absolutely *loves* to be in love. Of course, Libra energy has many beautiful and notable qualities all on its own, as an independent party, but it seems that this sign

> The Libran need for attention stems from a desire to be not known, but *loved*.

> The Libra constantly strives for *equality* in and fair treatment of all people and situations, and painstakingly takes the time and effort to objectively consider all sides of the coin (or in some cases, the polyhedron).

is able to maximize its beauty and strength best when it is paired up. This is why Libras get a reputation for being serial monogamists—they do truly adore the energy, excitement, hope, mental stimulation, and beauty of relationships and love, as it makes them feel alive and even more themselves than when they're alone. Additionally, this is why Libra people tend to be popular and have lots of friends and romantic partners.

Of course, this can manifest as Libras not giving themselves enough alone time, or any at all. Because Libras are naturally partnership-oriented, constantly seeking to balance out their thoughts (and perhaps their entire *existence*) with thoughts, company, and validation of another, they might struggle to prioritize their own needs over anyone else's. Remember how indecisive Libra energy can be? Because Libras are inherently social creatures, they struggle to make any decision that might dominate over the will of someone else. The Libran ability to see things from all perspectives, while making them incredibly diplomatic, fair, and pleasant, can *also* make them overly accommodating people pleasers. This is rooted in the deep-seated need to avoid conflict, as Libras deeply loathe and fear confrontation, disagreements, or anything else that disrupts the harmonious equilibrium that they seek to maintain in all facets of their existence (but especially in relationships!).

Libra loves attention more than just about any sign of the zodiac (other than Leo, of course). But while Leo loves attention simply for attention's sake, Libra only wants attention of the *adoring* variety. And when we dig below the surface and get to the root of Libra's desire to be loved? There simply lies the desire to have peace and balance. Where there is love and adoration, there is often harmony, and this harmony is the environment in which Libra can truly blossom. No sign despises discord, conflict, and confrontation more than Libra. This is why, rather than run from it, Libra energy often takes on the role of the peacemaker and mediator.

This diplomatic ability to step outside of the emotions of a situation and conceptually understand both sides of an argument gives Libra a unique ability to make people feel *understood* and validated, but it can give Libra a reputation for being fake, as this behavior can easily be construed as playing both sides of the field. Their true intention, though, is just to keep things running smoothly and maintain the peace.

Libras are so good at being diplomatic that this can sometimes be interpreted as flirtiness. Their Venusian influence means they can't help but be quite charming and aesthetically aware. But Libras don't just flirt with people they're attracted to—their charismatic nature could manifest with the old lady at the coffee shop, or their dogs. They simply express themselves in a unique way, which, combined with their airy, intellectual nature, makes them very easy and pleasant conversationalists.

Let's also talk about Libra's ruling planet Venus and the influence the planet of love, beauty, and romance has on this sign's energy. Libra seeks balance when it comes to beauty and aesthetics *just* as it seeks balance energetically in partnerships and in every other area, too. Because this sign is ruled by Venus, it naturally seeks and appreciates beauty. For Libra, balance equals beauty: Think about the fact that symmetrical features on a face read as attractive to the human brain. Libras understand this concept, and this gives them a sharp and refined aesthetic sense (which often leads Libras to creative fields or artistic endeavors).

While Taurus, which also shares Venus as its ruler, appreciates luxury because it brings them comfort and sensory pleasure, Libra, on the other hand, is just as committed to living a luxurious lifestyle, but Libra cares much less about the comforts of luxury than it does the sheer elevated aesthetic. Libra will choose beauty over function any day. You know that adorable vintage sweater in the back of your closet that's insanely itchy but looks great on you? Or that pair of shoes that's slightly too small but matches tonight's outfit *perfectly*? Wearing those items anyway is *such* a Libra vibe. Beauty is pain, and Libra is fine with that. Because of the Libran attitude toward beauty combined with their absolute obsession with being loved and adored, Libras get a reputation for being a little bit vain and shallow. But Venus-ruled as they are, they simply love beauty for beauty's sake and appreciate the occasional need to keep things surface level in order to maintain a peaceful status quo for everyone.

Libra is the social butterfly who does us all the great service of making sure social functions are not only pristinely decorated and well-stocked with punch and macarons, but also that the social and energetic flow is balanced, fun, light, and beautiful. Libra can serve as a world-class matchmaker when it comes to both lovers and friends, given their knack for finding balance and symbiosis in all different energies. And no one will make you feel as special as a Libra can—even if it's only for five minutes, before they're whisked off to their next conversation (or potential crush). On a good day, you'll catch Libra bringing a refined sense of class and sparkle to every space it graces while simultaneously making every single person in the room feel special and understood. On a bad day, you'll catch Libra sacrificing their own needs to desperately please everyone around them, and overbooking themselves by about six too many social engagements. Either way, charming Libra energy is light, sparkly, and fun. It's the bubbly glass of Champagne of the zodiac.

Why We Need Libra Energy

As a cardinal sign, Libra helps us ring in the beginning of fall; the first day of this sign's Sun season is the same day as the autumnal equinox. Libra helps us begin the fruitful and celebratory season of the harvest with a social and partnership-focused bang. As we enter the latter half of the astrological year, during which the weather gets colder and the resources become scarcer, Libra energy encourages us to connect with one another, enjoy the company of friends and lovers, and appreciate the simple beauty of the autumnal harvest.

How We Can Work with the Energy of Libra Season

Libra is able to take the initiative in building communication and partnerships with others, laying out the foundation on which we're able to build all future relationships, and refine our ability to judge and discern in a fair and objective manner. Libra energy ups our social intelligence (and intelligence in general!) by analyzing the complexities within the relationships all around us, encouraging us to pick up on social cues, read emotions and factor them into our thinking, observe basic etiquette, and consider what other people are thinking.

SCORPIO

Welcome to the dark, intense, and brilliantly transformational chambers of Scorpio's lair.

Scorpio may be a water sign, but it stands apart in that its waters are made from pure blood, sweat, and tears. Keenly perceptive with an incredible ability to see through the surface level of things, Scorpio energy is as drawn to mystery as it is mysterious in and of itself.

The intense and passionate water sign Scorpio is, interestingly, ruled by the scorpion, a traditionally desert-dwelling arachnid, which is a far cry from the water-dwelling crab and fish that represent that other two water signs, Cancer and Pisces. Positioned far from the free-flowing emotional landscape of the sea and instead left to fend for itself in the harsh and unforgiving drought of the desert, the scorpion symbolizes the very Scorpio need to maintain a strict and severe control over its image, deep feelings, and life in general.

If provoked, a scorpion won't hesitate to strike with its sharp vessel of poison. It's advisable to tread lightly if you're near an agitated Scorpio, and avoid attempts to cross, control, or crack its shell, lest you want to risk getting stung yourself.

But Scorpio wouldn't feel the need to protect itself with such destructive and venomous force if it didn't have something extraordinarily delicate and valuable to keep safe. In this case, it is the sign's deep, vast, and endless well of emotion. Scorpio can arguably feel, love, and transform energy on a level deeper than any other sign: It is unmatched in the fierceness of its emotions and its capacity for loyalty and devotion (Scorpio is a fixed sign, after all, meaning devotion comes easier to it than most).

While emotional Cancer's crab shell certainly serves as a protective force over its soft and sensitive inner core, Scorpio protects its emotions with even *more* intensity—this baby has an exoskeleton *plus* the lethal force of its stinger.

146

Scorpio feels things in its soul on a cosmically deep level. Everything from pain to love can be used as ingredients in Scorpio's emotional alchemy.

Once someone has passed Scorpio's exhausting trust-detector test and is allowed to proceed in gaining its affections, it would be wise to not break that impossibly hard-earned invitation into Scorpio's complexly beautiful yet dangerous inner world. Because, as you can imagine, this emotional depth goes both ways: Scorpio energy can also harbor hatred and feel betrayal more deeply than any other sign. When trust is broken, Scorpio can become vindictive, jealous, obsessive, and fixated on revenge, and can hold a grudge that lasts far beyond the likes of any other sign. The terror of vulnerability and even the *potential* for betrayal can make Scorpio energy paranoid and possessive, wielding its stinger and preparing to strike even before there's a real chance of danger.

While Scorpio's stinger-wielding habits may occasionally seem preemptive, they may not be, as this sign is actually the zodiac's undercover detective and absolute truth seeker. Scorpio possesses a sort of emotional x-ray vision—it's able to see people's true feelings, motives, weaknesses, strengths, and truths quite easily. This sign is obsessive, highly perceptive, occasionally paranoid, and inexorable when it comes to meeting its goals or finding out what lies beneath the surface. It can be manipulative and highly strategic when it comes to getting what it wants, but at the end of the day, its mission is noble: It seeks to face the mysteries of life with strength and an immense trust in the transformation process of truth. Scorpio cares nothing for surface-level matters like keeping up appearances or partaking in social niceties (we leave that behind with its preceding sign, the small-talk master Libra). Anything fake or artificial simply won't cut it. Scorpio cares only about slicing straight into the heart of the matter, and at the heart of every matter, of course, is truth.

Transformational and *emotionally* attuned Scorpio is the perfect energy to call upon when embracing issues that fall along such transformational spectrums as life and death, creation and destruction, growth and decay.

This means Scorpio wants the truth and nothing but the truth, so help them god. Truth at *all* and *any* cost. Sometimes the truth hurts, but Scorpio doesn't run from pain. It would rather be shattered, broken, and alone than live in a lie. Rather, Scorpio energy runs *toward* the pain if they determine that such pain brings an opportunity to see the truth and lead them to a transformation. On a good day, you'll catch Scorpio using its intensity and nearly psychic ability to read the emotions in the room to create intimacy, realness, and an embrace of the truth. On a bad day, you'll find that intensity and perceptiveness channeled into rageful jealousy, paranoia, manipulation, and possessiveness over others. In either case, the Scorpio presence is an austere, notable, and effective one.

Scorpio is perhaps the most reserved (on the surface) and private of all the zodiac signs, so it makes sense that it's ruled by the most distant planet in the zodiac, Pluto, which is named for the god of the underworld. Distant Pluto deals in matters of transformation and hidden realms, much like the sign of its domicile. Scorpio's cavernously deep waters are the perfect subterranean setting for the intense planet of death, destruction, transformation, evolution, and rebirth to do its dirty work—the work that no other planet has the stomach or strength to oversee. This singular determination and intensity to do the work that other planets won't is mirrored in Scorpio's uniquely deep and driven qualities. This sign will face painful truths, collecting them like coins, like no other sign. It will feel emotions like no other sign. It will burn itself alive only to emerge from the ashes, completely reborn, with an intensity that nothing else in the zodiac could quite compete with. Scorpio energy wants to fire-walk and free-fall—not for the thrill of it, but simply to see what's on the other side of the intensity.

"Intensity" is a key word when it comes to Scorpio energy. The ability to persevere in the face of even the most dire threats is what makes this fixed water sign one of the zodiac's doers. The fixed signs are steady, reliable workers, and the water and emotional realm is where Scorpio does its work. Scorpio has the ability to maintain its emotional intensity and intimacy in relationships and all matters, and this ability to steadily *maintain* is what sets it apart. The emotional endurance of Scorpio is unparalleled. No matter *how* intense a feeling or situation gets, Scorpio isn't willing to sugarcoat it or run the other way. It is ruthless in its drive to bring us to the transformational breaking points of all matters.

We can't possibly talk about Scorpio without noting the sign's affiliation with sex and darkness. What could be more transformational than sex? An act filled with passion and emotion, that also serves as the catalyst for the alchemical reaction that, in some cases, results in the creation of life itself? This is quintessential Scorpio territory. Scorpio isn't squeamish in the least when it comes to dark emotional themes, taboos, or death and destruction because Scorpio understands the process of transformation: From birth comes death and then comes rebirth again. Destruction makes room for creation. This is why the sign has a reputation for being a "dark horse" and gravitating toward the darker and more morbid parts of life and culture (although no, not all Scorpios are black-lipstick-wearing, goth-dressing witches, as stereotypes would have you believe). It also makes sense that transformation-focused Scorpio would be the natural ruler of the most mysterious and least understood house in astrology: the eighth house. This house rules over a very strange and intense smorgasbord of concepts, including sex, death, taxes, inheritance, and the occult.

It makes sense why Scorpio was also originally ruled by Mars. This sign cares deeply about power and constantly employs a strategic, even manipulative way of thinking in order to maintain control over its intense waterfalls of emotion. Like Mars, Scorpio energy can be vitriolic and competitive, too. And similar to fiery Aries, which is the only sign ruled by Mars in modern-day astrology, Scorpio is deeply passionate and driven. But the Scorpio sense of power and competitiveness stems from its internal self, rather than the external factors that drive Aries's behavior. Scorpio energy seeks deep and emotional introspection. It's constantly challenging itself to shed the layers of its exoskeleton and compete with *itself* to be better—to transcend the bullsh*t and transform into the most powerful version of itself. Scorpio derives its power not from conquering others, but from conquering *itself*, proving its strength and ability to persevere. It's resourceful, determined, and strategic. And while Scorpio is most commonly symbolized by the scorpion, it is also affiliated with the firebird phoenix, the mythical bird that combusts into flames at the end of its life, only to be reborn from its own ashes. This represents the true transformational nature of the sign and harkens back to its Mars-ruled roots.

Why We Need Scorpio Energy

The Sun enters Scorpio after the first month of autumn, meaning this sign's energy carries us through the middle of the season. While Libra season is all about balance and aesthetics, Scorpio season blows a tidal wave over the whole thing and reminds us all that we better do some soul-searching before winter comes and freezes over everything in sight.

How to Work with the Energy of Scorpio Season

Scorpio energy is the freaky, intense, enduring, and real vibe that we *all* need to lean into once in a while when we want to get deep. Don't you ever find yourself pondering life's great mysteries, wondering what transformations of your soul and spirit lie ahead? Scorpio energy teaches us to embrace these inevitable transformative moments instead of trying to fruitlessly avoid them. It teaches us that we can persevere.

Scorpio energy teaches us to tear ourselves open and let the pain of reality destroy us—and to trust that, like the phoenix, we will be reborn from the ashes, even if it doesn't feel like it.

SAGITTARIUS

SUN SEASON	November 22–December 21 (approximately)
ELEMENT	Fire
MODALITY	Mutable
RULING PLANET	Jupiter
HOUSE	Ninth House of Expansion
SYMBOL	The Archer
STUFF TO ♥	Free-spirited, happy-go-lucky, optimistic
STUFF TO LOOK OUT FOR	Restless, reckless, blunt

Welcome to the nonstop party that is the sign of Sagittarius. This passionate, excitement-seeking fire sign is truly shining and sparkling when it's able to party on its own schedule, stay out all night talking to people from every walk of life, travel the world, and freely jump from one plan and mind-opening conversation to another without restriction. This sign wants freedom, and it brings a happy-go-lucky, charmed energy with it as it travels through the world. It also leads the charge in our meeting the final sign from each zodiacal element. Sagittarius is the final fire sign of the bunch.

Sagittarius is represented by the centaur archer (although often, it's just thought of as the archer). Centaurs are half man, half beast: The upper half is a man's body, while the bottom half is a horse's body. Because the Sagittarian centaur is an archer, always wielding a bow and arrow, it perfectly represents the Sagittarian need to pull back the bow on life and shoot for the stars. This is a constant desire in the life of Sagittarius.

Limits and restrictions are the antithesis of what Sag energy is about. This sign's optimistic energy believes anything is possible, and it brings its endlessly idealistic fire-sign passion to every lofty, exciting, through-the-roof adventure. That said, Sag can be idealistic and optimistic to a fault. It is not very receptive to anyone or anything that it interprets as trying to dampen the flames of its fire or limit its sense of adventure.

Some astrologers also note the significance of the centaur symbol as speaking to the Sagittarian's flaming desire for growth and expansion—it wants to transcend its animalistic instincts to find a higher purpose. Fellow fire sign Aries leads the charge in embracing its basic

As soon as Sag energy senses stagnation and routine, it tends to immediately begin putting out feelers for its next move.

sense of self and energetic instincts, Leo comes next and introduces a deeper awareness of the self and a need to express it, and Sagittarius follows and wants to take that sheer energy and need for self-expression to a new and higher level. Sagittarius energy is likely the most philosophical and intellectual of the fire signs, as it has a deep interest in knowledge, learning, and experimenting with different schools of thought.

Like an arrow set loose from an archer's bow, shooting through the skies, Sagittarian energy has a need to feel free and stay in motion at all times. They're rolling stones—they need movement, excitement, and new stimuli. They're constantly picking up tidbits of wisdom, knowledge, culture, and experience everywhere they go, and subsequently feeling *immediately* restless if they're forced to stay in one place. They absolutely detest feeling held back or stagnant—mentally, physically, sexually, or otherwise. Movement and excitement are musts, as these restless souls are on a constant quest for new ideas and experiences. This unfortunately means that Sagittarius can become very quickly bored and disinterested, and will begin to move on to the next endeavor without much thought as to what it might be leaving behind (and often, without tying up any of the loose ends, leaving that task to others). This can, of course, be inconsiderate to the needs of others. The Sagittarian ability to flit from one thing to the next can sometimes make people around it feel expendable, dismissed, or forgotten.

Even if the Sagittarius person you know isn't booking an excess of exotic vacations or enrolling in a new trade school every six months, you'll likely see this need for change, movement, and fresh experience manifest in other endeavors in their life—perhaps in the rotating door of diverse romantic partners in their love life, or a voracious appetite for knowledge and mental stimuli that shows through its constantly reading of new books, listening to new music, and appreciating new art. You're also likely to see this in Sagittarius's taste in people and things: Sag energy loves an eclectic vibe, so they tend to keep friends from all different social groups, backgrounds, and walks of life, as well as gravitate toward food, art, and music from all over the world.

Sagittarius brings its own personal brand of fiery and passionate *joie de vivre* to every situation it encounters. You can often catch Sagittarius booking last-minute plane tickets to Thailand, eloping with a recent lover, or taking up a totally random and unexpected hobby. On a bad day, you'll catch Sag quitting its job without notice, ditching plans with friends at the last minute if something more exciting comes along, or being overly blunt, righteous, and tactless in the way they express their thoughts and feelings to others (Sag doesn't *mean* to be so harsh—it simply moves so fast that it doesn't always give itself enough time to consider the feelings of others!). It's easy to forgive Sagittarius for its overconfidence and brashness in communication, though, as its energy is also fair and honest. Sag is such an idealistic, comedic, and fun entertainer that it'll break your frown into a smile in no time. It's hard to stay mad at such a free spirit.

Why We Need Sagittarius Energy

The Sun moves through Sagittarius from November to December, which carries us directly into the winter season, as well as the winter holidays. It follows up Scorpio season with a similar theme of growth, but while Scorpio season directed our growth *inward*, pulling us into the depths of our souls and the core of our emotions, Sagittarius season is here to counterbalance that by directing our growth *outward*. It encourages us to expand our awareness into the great beyond, just as Scorpio asks us to do that on an internal level.

It's also no coincidence that such a bright and fiery sign would be given its solar reign during what is perhaps the darkest part of the year. Sagittarius energy is there to pump us up and light up the late autumn skies with fireworks of passion and mental stimulation. It reminds us that this is a time of celebration, and that we should focus on *abundance* rather than scarcity. The longer and darker the night, the more hours Sagittarius says we can party.

How to Work with the Energy of Sagittarius Season

This fiery energy is gifted at the art of living in the present—it neither dwells on the past nor overanalyzes the future. Of course, this lack of regard for past lessons or the potential consequences that lie in the future can make Sagittarius come off as brash, abrasive, and reckless, but such is life for the archer who shoots for the stars and thinks not of yesterday or tomorrow. And honestly, couldn't we *all* use a little bit of that kind of fiery, passionate optimism? Couldn't we benefit from being so invested in our growth, in collecting as many experiences as we can during our stint on this planet as human beings, that we simply follow our excitement as our personal compass? Embrace the free-spirited Sagittarian in you when you need to break out of the day-to-day routine and say yes to *expansion*.

CAPRICORN

SUN SEASON	December 22–January 19 (approximately)
ELEMENT	Earth
MODALITY	Cardinal
RULING PLANET	Saturn
HOUSE	Tenth House of Public Recognition
SYMBOL	The Sea Goat
STUFF TO ♥	Hardworking, disciplined, prudent
STUFF TO LOOK OUT FOR	Pessimistic, restrictive, overly traditional

Welcome to the last installment of element earth, where we meet Capricorn, the disciplined, hardworking, and masterful builder who knows how to get things done efficiently. Capricorn won't settle for less than the best, and its pragmatism combined with its tenacity and ambition guarantees this sign reaches the loftiest and most successful heights.

Capricorn is BBE—big boss energy. It's as wise as it is sure-footed, as patient as it is calculated. Unlike Aries, another big boss sign, which embodies more of the eager, hyper tenacity of a tech-bro startup CEO, Capricorn's brand of BBE is more that of the longtime CEO of a decades-old and highly successful company. It's not that they love to lead, the way Aries energy does. It's simply that they're incredibly efficient at getting things done, conquering their goals, and being successful. Capricorn almost begrudgingly takes on a leadership role. Because it knows, like everyone else, that it's the best energy for the job.

Capricorn energy is slower and more deliberate in its choices and never, ever impulsive. This isn't because Capricorn *likes* to move cautiously, but simply because it has figured out that taking calculated steps and moving slowly will give them a higher rate of success. This sign is loyal to tradition, but always in the favor of efficiency (meaning they certainly won't stubbornly refuse an alternative if they have examined it and deduced that it is the more practical choice even if it occasionally takes them out of their slightly more conservative comfort zone). That said, these traditionalists usually have trial and error on their side, so they have no need to take a risky approach. They stick with the tried-and-true methods of success, and—while it may take them longer and look less glorious on the way up—it almost always gets them to where they aim to be, landing them at the top.

This judicious sign is represented symbolically by the sea goat, a mythical hybrid creature with the upper body of a goat and the fins and lower half of a sea creature. While Capricorn is represented by a sea goat and not a mountain goat, I'd be remiss not to make a comparison to the latter, as its sure-footed path to the

> ♑
>
> Capricorn's dogged determination drives them steadily and surely toward their goals, no matter how many windy mountain roads it must traverse to get to the top.

> Capricorn energy doesn't let *loose* often, but that just means there's a lot of pent-up earth-sign sensuality inside that needs to come out and play.

top guarantees success. The wise and deeply pragmatic Capricorn brain easily calculates the safest and most assured route and overcomes obstacles to make it up the steepest climbs without tumbling down. Another sign might try to race to the top of the mountain in some less effective way, or would simply choose to conquer a small hill instead. But not Capricorn. Purpose, patience, and discipline ensure that Capricorn will reach the mountain's peak without setback. This is why it's so difficult to stop Capricorn from reaching success.

As a cardinal sign, Capricorn is one of the zodiac's builders, and as an earth sign, what it builds is financial security and stability. Security is deeply important to Capricorn. It appreciates riches and life's finer things, just like its sister earth signs, but it's not satisfied when it reaches a goal. The cardinal energy of this sign motivates it to press on, never getting too comfortable with success. This sign isn't trying to ride on anyone's coattails. While the other cardinal signs get busy building personal passions, emotional landscapes, and social lives, Capricorn comes in to help build the material realm.

This is a sign of lasting power and endurance. As a builder with a shrewd eye for business and numbers, Capricorn knows how to create something that's made to *last*. It's not looking for fifteen minutes of fame, but rather a whole lifetime of success. Nothing irks Capricorn like a shaky foundation; this sign is in it to win it, and it's patient and willing to sit things out for a slow and steady burn rather than a firecracker-like explosion. Capricorn knows the slow-burning fire, while less flashy, will keep them warm and thriving for so much longer.

Capricorn thinks in terms of having security for the future in all of its endeavors. It's wary of anything that claims to be a quick fix or an easy way up to the top. Capricorn's secret power lies in the fact that it knows with total certainty that hard work leads to success. It sounds simple enough, right? You might argue that *everyone* knows this. But truthfully, having an unshakable faith in your own work ethic paired with the diligence, patience, and endurance it takes to keep truckin' when the goin' gets tough is actually an incredible and rare gift.

As an earth sign, Capricorn's idea of success concerns tangible security—money, finances, wealth—and this is why we see Capricorns with such a high ambition in work and a focus on careers. It's simply because it is through our work that we can obtain financial security and material success. Just like sensual Taurus, Capricorns *love* their earthly pleasures, but they won't allow themselves to indulge in them the way Taurus does. And just like down-to-earth Virgo, Capricorn is extraordinarily practical and talented when it comes to the tools of getting work done, but they aren't satisfied with the simple things the way Virgo is. Capricorn wants it all: money, glory, power. It wants an empire, but this sign isn't looking for free handouts or shortcuts.

Saturn, the greater malefic and planet of boundaries, restriction, and tough love, is the ruling planet of Capricorn. In traditional and disciplined Capricorn, Saturn is able to smoothly execute its role as boundary-setter. Some might say Capricorns have "old souls," and it's because they do tend to have a sort of conservative, reserved, and old-school quality to the way they do things. This energy has a reputation for being serious.

Some astrologers note that the under-the-sea tail of the sea goat symbolizes the sensitive emotional side that lurks beneath the practicality-minded exterior of Capricorn. And while Capricorns may be serious, they're also known for their dry, witty, and sometimes dark senses of humor. Capricorns take themselves as seriously as the day is long, but they're also willing to laugh at themselves and can be self-effacing in their manner of joking.

While they won't often show it, Capricorns want to feel acknowledged for their hard work. Capricorn rules the tenth house of career and public recognition, so while they're incredibly humble and comfortable building their success without accolades, they do want to be appreciated for their efforts, whether it's knowing that they've left behind a small fortune for their family or simply that their boss respects and trusts them as an employee. They're not so comfortable in the spotlight and would prefer to work in the background being quietly in charge rather than the front-and-center face of something.

Why We Need Capricorn Energy

Capricorn's Sun season brings us its work-focused energy at an ideal time. The Sun moves through this sign starting in December and goes on through January, so Capricorn season always coincides with the beginning of the new Gregorian calendar, aka New Year's Day. And what almost always goes hand in hand with the New Year? Well, New Year's resolutions, of course. Capricorn's incredible self-discipline helps whip us into shape and kicks off our yearly set of self-improvement goals with a whole lot of confidence and cardinal energy.

How We Can Work with the Energy of Capricorn Season

Capricorn energy will motivate you like there's no tomorrow. Their tenacity and ambition is palpable—but only if you look ahead. Otherwise, these humble and grounded earth signs could fly right under your radar, as they forego the flashy displays of competition exhibited by fire signs. You can catch Capricorn working and studying harder than anyone you know (and refusing to be tempted by the prospect of fun social activities), and lovingly dishing out reality checks to all their closest friends. When it comes to work, career, and money, Capricorn energy is the catalyst you need to start forming a stable, solid, and practical plan.

 Call on Capricorn energy when you're ready to start building your empire in a serious way.

AQUARIUS

SUN SEASON	January 20–February 18 (approximately)
ELEMENT	Air
MODALITY	Fixed
RULING PLANET	Uranus (traditionally Saturn)
HOUSE	Eleventh House of Community
SYMBOL	The Water-Bearer
STUFF TO ♥	Progressive, innovative, unique
STUFF TO LOOK OUT FOR	Detached, impractical, rebellious, condescending

Aquarius is the zodiac's oddball. Its energy is a little bit out there and eccentric—it's highly unique, and it *enjoys* being unique. The Aquarian soul appears to have traveled here directly from the future, and this sign is the zodiac's forward-thinking maverick. Originality is a big deal for Aquarius! Aquarians might come off immediately as quirky and out-of-the-box, or they may be hard to read until you notice their vast and strange variety of interests, penchant for spouting off about conspiracy theories, or impressive ability to think about things on a grandiose scale. Aquarius's far-out ideas and opinions are always fresh, interesting, unconventional, and avant-garde.

In fact, they will challenge the status quo just for the fun of it! Aquarius detests rules and routine, and isn't afraid to do things differently. It values none of the comforts of tradition, and would much prefer to pave its own way, even if (and *preferably* if) that way is entirely uncharted territory. In fact, you could think of this sign as a rebellious, future-embracing anti-traditionalist. No matter how old and "set in its ways" an Aquarius may be, it will likely somehow maintain a solid grip on new technologies and remain progressive in its viewpoints. Because the status quo is *always* Aquarius's enemy, it has no interest in sticking to the ways of the past. If something feels outdated, it's *out*, as far as Aquarius is concerned. Of course, this rebellious streak can occasionally get the best of Aquarius, and can result in its acting like an overly angsty teen, railing passionately against any and every form of authority or rules, even the ones that might make sense.

Aquarius has a *need* to be unique, an itch to be original, and a drive to destroy the status quo.

Aquarians may be rebels, but they most certainly have a cause. Aquarius energy *loves* a good cause. Aquarius is represented by the symbol of the water-bearer, which is typically depicted as a person carrying or pouring a jug of water. Some astrologers note the symbolism of the water jug as a representation of the collective world's emotions, and the cool Aquarian ability to observe and consider them while maintaining an objective stance that allows them to make decisions for humanity. Because even though Aquarius is a mentally focused air sign, it's also a true humanitarian. In order to care about the state of the world, you also have to consider the feelings of the living beings in it. As the water-bearer, Aquarius bestows its visionary worldview on the masses, just as its symbol offers up a life-giving liquid for all to drink from and submerge themselves in.

Aquarius thinks in terms of the collective—it's the ultimate socially transcendent sign. It's still an air sign, so we know it excels in communication and intellectual matters, but the Aquarian vision is *much* different than any other. While Libra analyzes relationships and dynamics between people, and Gemini analyzes the details of the world around it, Aquarius analyzes the potential in *all* things. It looks beyond what *is* and straight toward what *could be*. It looks beyond personal relationships and into the relationships of one community or collective to another.

Ruled by the revolutionary planet Uranus, Aquarius brings the winds of unexpected changes and innovation. It makes sense that this planet would choose the Aquarian airs as the domicile in which it feels most at home. Uranus seeks to disrupt the status quo, strike brilliant new ideas into the collective consciousness like a bolt of lightning, and abruptly change course without a shred of self-doubt; the planet feels right at home in rebellious Aquarius. Aquarius energy will never settle into the mundane or allow a restrictive routine to rule its nature, and freedom-loving Uranus appreciates this. Uranus is the planetary weirdo, and it partners with an equally unique and originality-seeking zodiac sign in order to properly express itself.

What's interesting is that, in spite of Aquarius's Uranus-ruled penchant for unexpected twists, sudden changes, and dramatic rebellions, this is actually a *fixed* air sign, which means it's one of the zodiac's stabilizing forces. The sustainable, reliable, hardworking nature of fixed signs doesn't seem to fit Aquarius's freedom-loving, eccentric energy at first glance, but as soon as Aquarius taps into one of its wind tunnels of passion, you'll find that this sign can bring the focus, determination, and steady hard work like no other. Aquarius seeks to find new ways of doing things and will be endlessly experimental in its quest to utilize new technology, schools of thought, and ways of doing things, but once it finds something that resonates, it brings the stamina and focus necessary to see it through. In Aquarius's eyes, the well-being of the collective and the strength of the future rides on it, so it doesn't take its work lightly!

Of course, this all speaks to the extremely paradoxical nature of Aquarius. Aquarius is ruled by change-seeking disrupter Uranus, yet is also one of the stability-obsessed fixed signs. It also, ironically, was traditionally ruled by Saturn—the most restrictive, rule-obsessed, tradition-upholding planet of them all. It carries and considers the emotions of humanity as a whole, but struggles to show up for the emotions of any one individual (or even acknowledge its own). Aquarius energy also hates tradition and prides itself on being endlessly open-minded, but can easily get preachy and self-righteous about its own views and be highly opinionated—even judgmental—toward others.

Because Aquarius energy is gifted when it comes to zooming out its magnifying glass and seeing a global picture, it can, of course, more easily spot areas of injustice, and this tends to make Aquarius energy quite altruistic and humanitarian.

Of course, this hyper-focus on the collective means that Aquarius energy can sometimes struggle in the realm of personal emotions. Aquarius has a reputation for being a bit cold and emotionally detached. While it's easy for them to feel the sting of global injustices, they sometimes struggle to see eye to eye when it comes to being compassionate toward individual problems. Aquarius energy might easily work itself into tears over a human rights issue, but may come off as distant or even condescending if you're looking to discuss your recent breakup with them. That's just Aquarius: It's hard for them to see things from a single perspective. Aquarius takes fellow air sign Libra's need to see both sides of a story to a new level—it sees *all* the stories, from *all* sides.

This doesn't stop Aquarius from being highly social and involved, though. Aquarius rules the eleventh house of community, groups, and friendships, and is one of the most friendship-oriented signs out there. It believes in the power of teamwork, the power of the collective, the power of cooperation.

Why We Need Aquarius Energy

The Sun sails through Aquarius during the middle chunk of the winter. The Sun in Capricorn helps us get our act together and lay out a solid foundation for work, career, and other tangible, materially focused goals. But then, just as we're finding ourselves overworked, the winds of Aquarius blow through, bestowing us with unique, brilliant, and innovative ideas that can carry our hard work to new heights.

How We Can Work with the Energy of Aquarius Season

Aquarius energy helps us evolve by opening our minds to new ways of thinking and doing and seeing; by teaching us to step back and see the big picture instead of staying so focused on our insular, singular experience as an individual; and by helping us detach from mindless rules and traditions and think about the future.

PISCES

SUN SEASON	February 19–March 19 (approximately)
ELEMENT	Water
MODALITY	Mutable
RULING PLANET	Neptune (traditionally Jupiter)
HOUSE	Twelfth House of the Subconscious
SYMBOL	The Fish
STUFF TO ♥	Empathic, spiritual, creative
STUFF TO LOOK OUT FOR	Unrealistic, oversensitive, dissociative

We've finally reached the last of the zodiac signs, water sign Pisces. As the only sign of the zodiac that lives fully submerged under the sea, Pisces represents a whole other world—a world where we feel instead of think, where we intuit instead of observe, where we speak in poetry and music and ritual instead of regular ol' words. As the final sign of the zodiac, Pisces represents the dissolution of boundaries and the embrace of a spiritually awakened, all-one energy.

Represented by the fish, Pisces is the only zodiac sign whose symbol lives entirely underwater—fish dwell in a different world from us entirely. They swim instead of walk. They don't just drink from and bathe in the sea of emotions, they *live* in it, fully submerged. They breathe underwater, and will *die* if they're forced to spend too much time on the shores of our world. This is all incredibly symbolic of the uniquely sensitive, otherworldly nature of Pisces. As a water sign, it's inherently oriented to emotions, feeling them deeply and with intensity. Emotions are the force that perhaps wields the greatest influence on Pisces's energy.

This focus on and sensitivity to the invisible forces that affect all of us—energy, emotions, "vibes"—also make Pisces a very naturally spiritual sign. Pisces often feel a natural connection to a divine source or some other form of higher power, and are often drawn to the mystical arts or divination practices (think tarot, crystal healing, or witchcraft). As the twelfth and most "elevated" sign of the zodiac, it represents

Pisces is the living embodiment of *feeling*—it feels its own emotions, the emotions of others, and intuitively feels the energy around it, making this sign prone to some extrasensory perception. So yes, your Pisces friends may have a higher potential to be psychic!

leaving behind the physical realm and entering the etheric, spiritual realm. Pisces is about cosmic spiritual awakening. You can think of it as the crown chakra of the zodiac signs—it transcends the physical and leads us to ultimate oneness, a connection to the divine.

Pisces's ruling planet Neptune is an equally spiritual, dreamy, and intuitive illusion-dweller. Neptune favors feelings over facts, intuition over objective observation, so it's able to express its fantasy-like flavor with ease in the waters of Pisces's sea. Neptune, prone to escapism and with a focus on the invisible unconscious mind, finds an otherworldly refuge in Pisces's boundary-dissolving realm and is able to float as far or sink as deep as it pleases. It's no wonder that this planet would take over Pisces as its trusty domicile. Interestingly, Pisces's traditional ruler was Jupiter, planet of luck and abundance. In idealistic Pisces, Jupiter is able to be its positive, optimistic self. Pisces's endless spiritual openness and fluidity serves as a lovely playground for Jupiter's expansion-focused, philosophical, growth-oriented energy to dance and flourish.

Unlike its water sign sisters, Cancer and Scorpio, Pisces has no hard, protective exterior to protect its delicate and emotional self. Covered only in scales and its soft skin, the fish is completely vulnerable. This is part of what makes Pisces so special: It wears its bleeding heart on its sleeve, and is completely present in its emotions. It gives everyone access to its gentle, spiritual, feelings-focused inner world, empathically, even *psychically* picking up on the emotions, feelings, and energies of everyone around it. This gives Pisces the incredible gift of compassion and emotional depth.

But such vulnerability and lack of emotional boundaries is, of course, quite dangerous at times. Pisces energy is easily victimized and wounded, and at risk of being taken advantage of. This energy is built for a world that is *evolved* in its thinking and feeling abilities, which is, unfortunately, not the world we live in. Because Pisces energy wants to *dissolve* boundaries in an effort to attain spiritual oneness, it's difficult for it to maintain boundaries in everyday life, which means that it's prone to getting sucked dry by energy vampires who are seeking a sympathetic victim. All of this lends to the Piscean desire to escape from the confines of reality by checking out and immersing itself in an escapist fantasy life, whether that be through healthy means, like channeling feelings into art, or by focusing on spiritual acts like meditation or astral projection, or by less-healthy means, like dissociation and isolation, drugs and alcohol, or constant daydreaming and sleeping for prolonged periods. This is why Pisces energy can sometimes find it so difficult to exist and function in everyday life.

This sign is the ruler of the ethereal and esoteric twelfth house, which relates to hidden realms, secrets, dreams, and all things invisible (aka Pisces's cup of tea!). The twelfth house is largely about *healing*: healing karmic debts and healing the wounds of our subconscious minds. It's about secrets, yes, but also about *revelations*—bringing shadows into the light so that they can no longer scare us. This perfectly illustrates Pisces's role as the zodiac's healer; Pisces can absorb and validate your darkest emotions, carry you into a deep and spiritual journey, and connect you with your higher self by leading through example.

You could say that there's a childlike, even babyish, quality to Pisces energy. It's highly sensitive, detached from reality, and sometimes struggles to take care of rational matters (things like paying bills on time and managing a calendar aren't typically Pisces's strong suit). But it's interesting that for all these baby-like qualities, this sign's energy is considered to be the most *evolved*. This is because Pisces energy *transcends* worldly matters. Our society hasn't yet come to a mass spiritual awakening, nor has it embraced its emotional needs or creative instincts. But it is within *these* realms that Pisces is magnificently strong. In these realms, where many of us would feel naked, vulnerable, lost, and exposed, Pisces feels perfectly at home. But in the earthly, day-to-day grind, Pisces can quite feel like a fish out of water. They'd rather lose themselves in the watery dream world of their thoughts, feelings, and illusions.

On a good day, you'll catch Pisces writing beautifully emotional poetry and music, radiating with an incredible interconnectedness with all beings, and being the unofficial therapist and spiritual advisor of their social circle. On a bad day, you might catch Pisces paralyzed and overwhelmed by their own emotions, falling dreadfully behind on their day-to-day responsibilities, or totally dissociating instead of dealing with a toxic situation. But no matter what, you can count on Pisces energy to be emotionally insightful, spiritually evolved, and deeply transcendental.

Why We Need Pisces Energy

As the sign of the zodiac that wraps up the winter (and the astrological year!) and prepares us for the fruitful joys of spring, Pisces has an inherent hope and optimism. Pisces season follows Aquarius season and plunges us from the high-altitude reach of the final air sign straight into the depths of the last water sign. While Aquarius energy seeks to escape the current confines of reality by coming up with new ones, Pisces energy seeks to transcend it altogether. With Pisces, we are all one.

How We Can Work with the Energy of Pisces Season

Pisces is a highly spiritual energy. The existence of Pisces energy reminds us that we absolutely *must* live in accordance with our highest, most spiritual self. We *must* make safe spaces for our feelings (as well as the feelings of others) to exist and flourish. And we *must* pay attention to mystical symbols, energies, and secret clues that the universe shares with us to let us know we're all part of the same magical mystery.

Chapter 3

The
ANATOMY
of an
ASTROLOGY
CHART

ASTROLOGY IS A LANGUAGE. IF
YOU UNDERSTAND THIS LANGUAGE,
THE SKY SPEAKS TO YOU.

—Dane Rudhyar

Congratulations: You've officially been introduced to the major planets, asteroids, *and* the twelve signs of the zodiac, so hopefully you're feeling a little more at home in our corner of the universe. By now, you should have an idea about how to make the most of each Sun season. And you have a jumping-off point to explore what it might mean when any given planet transits through any given sign, thanks to your newfound understanding of the planets' personalities and the way each sign affects their expressions. These are the building blocks of astrology, and from here, you can begin making connections and growing from these roots.

But these planets don't just exist in a vacuum as they float through the zodiac of the sky—they're constantly interacting with each other and being influenced by each other's presence. Whether you're simply analyzing the astrology of today *or* looking at the astrology of *your life* based on the minute you were born, you have to consider how all these signs and planets work together and how they are related.

In order to see this, we must look at the symbolic castle in which all of these planets and signs live, and that is within a pie-chart-lookin' circle called an ***astrology chart***. This circular map essentially takes the sky above and forms it into a nice, compact visual representation of all the planets within the zodiac at any given time. Astrology charts are incredible tools, rich with layers upon layers of information about how the cosmos influences our lives, personalities, tendencies, and more. It's like an astrological map.

There are basic layers to each chart, and they overlap each other: First, there are the twelve houses. Then, there are the twelve zodiac signs. The planets are placed atop those overlapping layers and form relationships to each other. The base of this map is a ring or pie chart of **twelve houses** (which divide the circle into twelve equal parts), and these are fixed in place. The ring of twelve signs overlap the houses (these are not fixed, and rotate depending on what time you were born), and the planets live within them. **While planets represent different parts of our energy and signs represent the way that energy gets expressed, the houses each represent a different area of our life and experience.** These cosmic ingredients are rich in meaning on their own, but like I said earlier, they don't exist in a vacuum.

There is lots to take into account when looking at your chart. You have to consider which sign each planet and house falls into, as well as which house each planet falls into. And then, you must also identify how the planets *interact* with each other (which requires you to note the degree of each sign in which the planets are located). It's complex! This is why analyzing your birth chart with the help of a professional astrologer is highly advisable, as they can help identify layers of information that may be harder to spot at first glance.

But that doesn't mean you can't start exploring the nooks and crannies of an astrology chart yourself. Each element of a chart (planets, signs, houses, and much more) has an incredible energy force. Think of the gravitational pull of each of the planets if you want a *literal* interpretation of this! In this chapter, we'll explore how these moving parts interact and work together within an astrology chart to give you a full picture of the way the cosmos influences you.

Birth Charts

When you talk about *your* sign (like saying that you're a Pisces, or that your Moon is in Taurus, etc.), you're referencing what was going on in the skies at the exact minute you were born. You could theoretically create a chart for *any* situation, not just someone's birth! But when you *do* create an astrology chart for the time you were born, it's called a **birth chart** or a **natal chart**.

In this sample birth chart, the circled numbers on the outer layer of the chart designate the twelve houses, while the symbols within the next layer represent the twelve zodiac signs. The smaller symbols within the innermost ring represent the planets, while the lines and symbols within the inner circle represent planetary aspects (or the relationships between the planets based on their placement in the signs/houses).

When an astrologer creates a birth chart for someone, they need not only their birth *date*, but also the birth *time*. This is because, as you know, planets are all moving at different speeds and changing signs all the time, so if you happen to be born on a day when a planet switches signs, a birth time is pertinent for accuracy.

But this is also necessary because of the way the twelve houses are laid out on a birth chart. The twelve houses actually represent a progression of what appears to be the Sun's twenty-four-hour rotation around the Earth. The cusp of the first house begins at the exact degree of whatever zodiac sign was on the eastern horizon line at the time of your birth (in other words, the place where the Sun rises), and this is also called your ascendant (or your rising sign). This is a must-know point because, as the cusp of the first house, it dictates the placement of everything else on your birth chart. Your ascendant has a degree within a sign—just like each of the planets do—except this is a *point* and not a celestial body. More on that later. Thus, in order to identify the sign and placement of the ascendant (and thus where each of the subsequent houses are located), an astrologer needs the exact minute of your birth.

What Makes an Astrology Chart?

Within an astrology chart lives all twelve signs and every single planet, as well as the twelve *houses*. As mentioned, each house represents a different part of your life, and they don't just exist on the chart—they actually align with the conceptual space or path that the Sun appears to follow around the Earth over the course of a single day. This apparent path is called the *ecliptic*. I say "apparent" path because this is the path that the Sun *appears* to follow, from our vantage point here on Earth. Of course, we know that the Sun doesn't *actually* orbit the Earth—it's the other way around! But from an Earth-centric view, because we're spinning, it looks as though the Sun is moving across our sky through the course of the day. That path is the ecliptic, and it's an important concept to keep in mind when studying the anatomy of an astrology chart and some of the angles and points that we'll discuss in this chapter.

We'll get more into the meaning of each house shortly, but here's how things are laid out:

First Layer: Houses and Angles. You've got your zodiac pie, sliced up into twelve parts—the twelve houses. The lines that divide each house are called cusps, and the cusp of the first house is always directly left of the center, then the houses are numbered counterclockwise from there. That first house cusp (located at exactly 9 o'clock) is also known as the *ascendant*, or the place of your *rising sign*, and it represents the point in the ecliptic that the eastern horizon line was at the time when you were born. From ascendant, the houses are then labeled in order counterclockwise from there, with each proceeding cusp designating the beginning of each house.

Like the ascendant, the cusps of the other three houses on the X and Y axis of the wheel (representing 9, 6, 3, and 12 o'clock) all have specific names and extra significant meanings, too. These are known as *angles* or *points* and are labeled as ASC, IC, DSC, and MC on the chart to the right. They function similarly to planets in the way they represent parts of ourselves and can be activated and aspected, but they are simply points in space rather than celestial bodies.

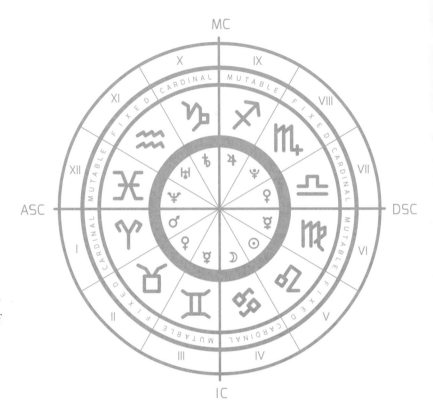

Second Layer: Zodiac Signs and Degrees. Now, we're going to add a ring around the pie chart; you can think of it as a crust, if you're really into the pie analogy, or as a second set of overlapping slices. This layer is made up of the twelve signs of the zodiac. Within each of the twelve signs' slices are 30 degrees (0 through 29), which of course form a 360-degree circle in full. As planets move through the zodiac of the sky, they move through each sign's degrees, starting at 0, so degrees measure where in the zodiac sign a planet or point is located.

Note that the cusps of each zodiac sign don't need to align with the cusps of the houses. In fact, in real life, they almost never do. Like the houses, the signs always go in order counterclockwise (from Aries through Pisces for the signs, and one through twelve for the houses), but unlike the houses, the signs are *not* fixed in any one given position. The zodiac wheel rotates to align with the placement of the ascendant.

Third Layer: Planets. Then there are the planets. As you know, at any given time, a planet will be within one of the twelve zodiac signs, and that means it will be within one of the twelve *houses*, too. This means an astrology chart can show you how the planet expresses its energy (by depicting which zodiac sign it's in) and the part of your life where that planet's energy has the heaviest influence (which is dictated by the *house* it's in). You'll want to look at two things on your birth chart: which *sign* a planet is in, and which *house* a planet is in.

Fourth Layer: Planetary Aspects. The relationships between the planets as interpreted through an astrology chart are known as *aspects*. Interestingly, these are based on simple geometry. An astrology chart will often identify these aspects by using lines to show the geometric relationships or aspects between planets in the circle. The aspects in the chart below are depicted using the straight, intersecting lines within the center of the circle.

There are many different ingredients, measurements, and other elements to an astrological birth chart, some of which we've lightly touched on, others that are new. There are also many different schools of thought in astrology and different systems of breaking down the houses, reading planetary aspects, and more—this is just *one* way, and it's just a start! If you like the taste, then I recommend you continue spending time in the astrological kitchen.

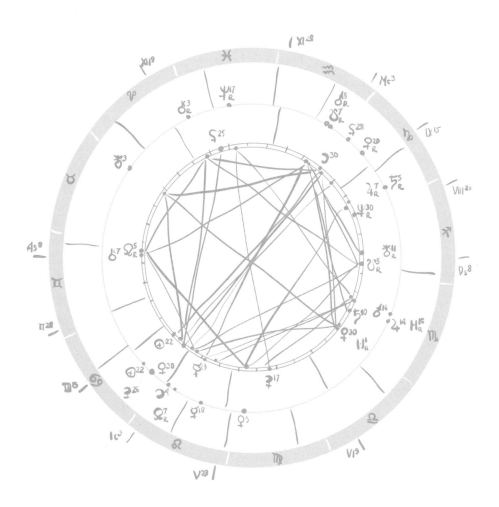

The Houses

Okay, you've heard the basics, but now it's time to actually *meet* the aforementioned twelve houses of an astrology chart!

The houses overlap with the zodiac signs, and whichever zodiac sign the cusp of a house falls in is considered to be the sign that rules the house in any given chart. Then, of course, the planets are sprinkled over that, set to the exact degree of each sign (in other words, the places they were in at the exact time that's set for the birth chart). **While signs represent *how* a planet's energy is expressed, houses dictate *where* in our lives the planets' and signs' energy expresses most.**

As planets transit through the zodiac, they can activate different houses in your birth chart. So if the Moon is in Taurus today and you want to know how that might affect you, you could look at your birth chart and find whichever house you have in Taurus in order to see what part of your life the Moon is currently activating. Even if you don't have any natal planets in a single house in your chart, the house still matters for you personally because you can gain insight into how that part of your life might look or feel based on the sign that it's in, *and* that part of your house can still be activated as planets cycle through the zodiac.

Natural Rulers of the Houses

Each of the houses are also naturally affiliated with a different zodiac sign and planet. As you may have guessed, the houses' affiliations move in order of the zodiac, beginning with Aries as the natural ruler of the first house, all the way up through Pisces as the natural ruler over the twelfth house. When you note the areas of your life that each house rules, you'll see that their natural rulers align quite clearly, and it makes sense why each sign would be matched up with its corresponding house. Each of the houses also naturally correspond to a different planet, which also corresponds with its ruling sign. Each of these energies is different.

However, note that there's a difference between a house's *natural* sign ruler and the sign that will rule it in any individual birth chart. It is most likely that the ruler of each of your houses will differ from their natural rulers. That gives us individuality!

> Houses represent different areas of our lives, experiences, and selves. It is within these spaces that our natal planets (meaning the placement of the planets at the time we were born) live and express their energies through the zodiac signs.

Domains of the Houses

The first six houses in astrology (like their naturally corresponding zodiac signs) deal with very personal parts of life—yourself, your basic values, your routines, your day-to-day relationships and activities, your family and home life, and more. The latter half of the houses in astrology deal with more outward-focused parts of your life—your relationships and commitments to others, your career, your higher goals, your spiritual life, your community, and more. You can also glean insight into the areas of our life that each house rules by looking to the qualities of the opposite house, because the qualities will be opposing in nature.

What's a Stellium?

It's important to look at which planets you have in which houses, as it shows you which areas of your life have the most action happening within them, as well as where in your life certain energies are more likely to manifest. **If you have three or more natal planets or significant points in one house, you have what is called a *stellium*.** A stellium is a cluster of planets that are close to the same degree in the chart, or at least within the same sign or house. Stelliums indicate a large amount of energy being focused on and expressed within the area of your life represented by the house that it's in, as well as a heavy lean on the expressive qualities of the sign that it's in. For example, if you have a stellium of planets clustered in your first house (which represents the self), you're likely to focus a lot of energy on yourself and have a highly expressive and visible personality. If you have a lot of planets in your tenth house of public image, you're likely to focus a lot of energy on your career and reputation. Stelliums can be helpful, but they can also cause a little imbalance. That said, people with a stellium should look to the opposite house and sign to see energy that may be lacking in their life and make sure they're not neglecting those areas and ways of expressing.

Let's quickly meet the houses and find out about the unique parts of your life they represent.

FIRST HOUSE

Self • Personality • Identity • Initiative

NATURAL SIGN RULER Aries
NATURAL PLANET RULER Mars

Welcome to the first house! The first house is often referred to as the "house of self" because it represents you and your awareness of yourself at the most basic level. This house is about your *identity*. It's your ego and your sense of self; it's both how you perceive yourself *and* how others perceive you. It even governs your appearance. Beyond that, it rules over self-driven qualities such as your leadership style, the way you take initiative, and new beginnings.

The first house is also a house of general firsts. It governs your first responses (like your impulse-based, off-the-cuff reaction to something) as well as the first impression you make on other people. It even represents the first impressions made *upon* you, as it covers formative experiences early in life that have contributed to your sense of self.

The cusp of the first house is a special point known as the ascendant, also known as your rising sign (a term we get into more fully below), and thus there's a lot of overlap when it comes to what your rising sign represents and the things that your first house rules. If you have planets in your first house, expect them to show up in your personality in big ways—a first house planet is usually a very visible and showy one! For example, if you have Venus in your first house, you'll exude the planet's natural Venusian charms (sensuality, sweetness, romance) in a very up-front and easy-to-read way. Whatever sign your first house cusp falls in indicates the way you express yourself on the surface.

SECOND HOUSE

Values • Worth • Money • Possessions

NATURAL SIGN RULER   Taurus
NATURAL PLANET RULER   Venus

Next we have the second house, which rules over value of all types. First, let's talk about value at the most tangible level: that's your money and your possessions. The second house rules over your personal finances, assets, and belongings, specifically those that are worth something or are valuable to you. This house also rules over your physical senses, and how you see, hear, smell, taste, and feel the world around you.

The second house also rules over less-tangible values, like the values that you hold close to you personally as well as the ways in which you value *yourself*. Thus, things like your self-esteem and self-worth are affiliated with the second house. This house also deals in your own values system: what you believe is worthy, prized, and important.

When planets are in your second house, expect to see the effects manifest in your relationship to money and physical wealth, as well as your self-worth. Your attitude toward money and finances will be expressed through the sign that your second house cusp falls into. Trouble in the second house could mean financial stresses and low self-esteem.

THIRD HOUSE

Communication • Thinking Patterns • Environment • Transportation

NATURAL SIGN RULER Gemini
NATURAL PLANET RULER Mercury

The third house governs all sorts of information processing and task management at a basic level. It is within this house that we begin relating to things outside of ourselves and our earthly possessions, such as our immediate surroundings, the people and places we come into contact with on a daily basis (like neighbors and siblings, both of which are ruled by this house), and observations of everything around us.

The third house governs the way we think about and learn things, the way we relate to the tangible and immediate environment around us, and the way we communicate basic information and thoughts (this includes texting, talking on the phone, gossiping, small talk, writing letters, and more). The third house is also associated with day-to-day travel (like getting from place to place or taking a short trip), as well as basic education (so anything pre-college).

As you may notice, the third house themes have lots of overlap with its naturally ruling planet Mercury! The way you interact with your immediate surroundings will be reflected through the sign that your third house cusp falls into. Having planets in the third house puts an emphasis on our communication skills and style, the way we learn and our quest for knowledge, and our natural curiosity about our surroundings. Difficulties in the third house could put a strain on clear communication and thinking about everyday tasks.

FOURTH HOUSE

Family • Home • Memories • Roots

NATURAL SIGN RULER	Cancer
NATURAL PLANET RULER	The Moon

This house is more than a house—it's our *home*. The fourth house governs our most private, foundational, and close-to-home affairs. This includes our family life, our comfort zones, our parents, our memories and nostalgia, our childhood experiences, our emotions, and the places we call home. "Home" can be taken literally, in the sense of real estate and your actual place of dwelling, but it also indicates everything that makes you *feel* at home—the people and places that make you feel safe, nurtured, comfortable, and most yourself. It's the most sentimental of the houses.

Because the fourth house cusp is also one of the significant angles of the zodiac (called the imum coeli, or IC) and is located at the very bottom point of the chart, it's known as being the base of our chart, representing our *roots*. It's all about our foundations. This is why it's known to relate to our early childhood memories, as well as our parents or caretakers.

Because this house represents midnight on the birth chart, it also symbolizes our more private sides—the sides that are hidden and shrouded in the shadows, like our most intimate emotional self and our inner child. Having planets in the fourth house can create an added focus on family issues and affect the way we relate to our safe spaces and places we call home, and troublesome planets or aspects here can add turbulence to our home lives or even show up in our childhoods. The sign that your fourth house cusp falls into can tell you a lot about the way you approach family affairs and handle deep-rooted issues.

FIFTH HOUSE

Romance • Pleasure • Creativity • Leisure

NATURAL SIGN RULER Leo
NATURAL PLANET RULER The Sun

This lovely house is all about fun, pleasure, and creative energy. Anything we do for fun, simply because it brings us joy and helps us to express ourselves, relates to fifth house themes. Think hobbies, passion projects, leisure activities, and pleasure-seeking endeavors. It's about letting your true self shine, but also having fun while you're doing it.

Because of the pleasure aspect of this house, love is a big one here! All types of pleasure (whether it's the butterflies-in-your-stomach feeling of falling in love or orgasmic sexual pleasure with a casual fling) fall under this umbrella. While more formal and committed partnerships fall into seventh house jurisdiction, the purest form of romance falls here. It's an important distinction! This means dating, casual sex, crushes, falling in love, and all sorts of romantic gestures are ruled by the fifth house. Of course, the creative act of sex can also sometimes lead to children, so it's no surprise that they fall into this house, too. They are, after all, a result of the most innate creative force within us: reproduction!

We can also think of this association as bringing a childlike joy to our endeavors, and an encouragement to follow our excitement, passion, and imagination, like a child would. Planets in the fifth house bring an emphasis to matters of the heart, and can highlight the way you creatively express yourself and pursue your personal interests. Difficulties in the fifth house could result in some creativity blockages or a struggle to access free-flowing energy in love and pleasure. The sign that your fifth house cusp falls into in your birth chart can point to how you express your creative side.

SIXTH HOUSE
Routine • Health • Wellness • Service

NATURAL SIGN RULER Virgo
NATURAL PLANET RULER Mercury

The sixth house rules our day-to-day routines and habits. It's sort of the "maintenance" house. Health, wellness, hygiene, diet, and exercise all fall into this house, as well as things that tie in directly with our daily habits of eating, sleeping, and taking care of ourselves—our overall wellness. You can think of this as a house of self-care.

Why is it important that we maintain our wellness? Well, so we can do our jobs and do the things we want to do, of course. In that sense, this house is also about service and work, but rather than ruling your career (which is more tenth house territory), it's about our ability to *be* of service and *perform* the work that we're expected to do. This ties in with maintenance. If you think of our bodies as machines, like a car, then we know we must perform "maintenance" on it in order to keep the parts running properly (after all, a car can't drive if its parts aren't being kept in working order and being regularly cared for). Such is the case for the sixth house: This house doesn't dictate your career, but rather your ability to be of service to others and do your job. This, of course, requires self-care.

Planets here can affect the way you take care of yourself. Depending on the planet, it could either make you naturally health-conscious and self-care oriented, or it could make it so you struggle to care for yourself or break bad habits. The sign that your sixth house cusp falls into can point to the style in which you manage your wellness practices and approach your day-to-day routine.

SEVENTH HOUSE

Partnerships • Commitments • Relationships • Cooperation

NATURAL SIGN RULER Libra

NATURAL PLANET RULER Venus

This house is all about our relationships and commitments to other people. When we think about relationships and partnerships, we may think of love—but this house isn't really about love or romance (that's all the fifth house). Rather, this house is about *commitments*. While this can certainly overlap with love when it comes to marriage and more long-term and devoted relationships, it's not inherently about a hearts-and-flowers type of love. This means that when a romantic relationship goes from casual to committed, it moves from a solely fifth house affair to a seventh house affair. Of course, love is involved in those relationships, but the seventh house is about the symbiosis and mutual benefit of partnerships.

In this sense, the seventh house also rules over things like business partnerships, creative collaborations, and strong friendships. Any time there's a one-on-one commitment that involves working with someone else, creating a contract between two people, or balancing two different energies (whether they're opposing or in sync), we have a seventh house concept. Conversely, this house also rules over less positive partnership issues—things like divorces, enemies, and feuds. This is the dark side of one-on-one relationships, or the directions relationships can turn when commitments are broken or go awry.

The cusp of the seventh house is directly opposite the first house and is known as the descendant. The sign that the descendant falls into in your birth chart represents the qualities of ourselves that come out in relationships, or that we relate to within relationships—as well as the types of people we're generally attracted to. Having planets in the seventh house highlights the way we operate in one-on-one partnerships and the importance these relations play in our lives.

EIGHTH HOUSE

Sex • Transformation • Death • Taboo

NATURAL SIGN RULER	Scorpio
NATURAL PLANET RULER	Pluto

Sex. Taxes. Death. The occult. These are just a few of the mysterious areas that the eighth house governs. Strange, right? In short, the eighth house rules over transformations and surrendering (especially as pertaining to relationships) as well as things that lie beneath the surface. This is officially the house of death, which is an undoubtedly transformative experience that we have no choice but to surrender to. From death comes rebirth, and from creation comes destruction. These kinds of extreme give-and-take exchanges are a major part of what makes this house unique. By surrendering to the powerful and inevitable eighth house forces, we're able to overcome crises, deepen our relationships, and transform into a new version of ourselves.

To aid in making sense of the seemingly random assortment of eighth house governances, it can help to think of the eighth house in terms of its themes being opposite to those of the second house. While the second house rules over your *own* money and possessions, the eighth house rules over your relationship to *other* people's valuables—hence the affiliation with things like taxes, debts, wills, inheritances, and alimony (some of which also has to do with death). And while the second house teaches us to find the value beneath the surface of our outward-facing self, the eighth house teaches us to look below the surface of our *inward*-facing self and our *relationships*, including things like intimacy, taboos, secrets, occult workings, alchemical rituals, and clairvoyant abilities.

This is also the official house of sex. While the fifth house rules over sex as an act of heart-fluttery pleasure, the eighth house rules over sex for its intimacy and power to be an alchemical force of regeneration and rebirth. It's the transformational energetic exchange—and the intense intimacy that goes along with it—that puts sex under the eighth house umbrella.

Planets in this house indicate an emphasis on deep, meaningful, and spiritual relationships, as well as a potential preoccupation with power or surrender—and depending on the planet, this could either be a deeply challenging existential journey or a smoother descent toward growth and transformation. The sign that the eight house cusp falls into tells you a lot about how you relate to power dynamics and set boundaries.

NINTH HOUSE

Big Ideas • Growth • World Travel • Knowledge

NATURAL SIGN RULER Sagittarius
NATURAL PLANET RULER Jupiter

The ninth house is all about big ideas, even bigger dreams, and perhaps an even *bigger* thirst for growth and knowledge of the philosophical and spiritual sort. This house rules over our belief systems (which include our morality, ethical views, life philosophy, and relationship to religion), as well as pursuits of knowledge. That's why higher education and learning (basically college-level and beyond) fall under this house's jurisdiction.

This is also the house of adventure; it rules over world travel, long trips and journeying, explorations of all sorts, trying new things, taking risks, and conceptualizing things on a larger scale. Foreign cultures, places, and languages fall under this category, as do books (which can bring us adventure without even leaving our bed) and publishing in general.

It's easy to see how these ninth house governances are extensions of its opposing third house's themes. While the third house focuses on observing its environment, the ninth house focus is much wider and deeper. It's about thinking big, observing the whole *world* rather than our immediate surroundings, and forming a deeper understanding of things. The ninth house is about wisdom, whereas the third house is simply about information.

Having planets in the ninth house highlights parts of your life that take up a lot of space and energy, inspire you to dream big, and could signify areas where you're unafraid to take risks and be adventurous. The way you seek knowledge and choose to expand your mind is influenced by the sign in which the ninth house cusp falls into.

TENTH HOUSE

Career • Public Image • Reputation • Status

NATURAL SIGN RULER	Capricorn
NATURAL PLANET RULER	Saturn

The tenth house is a showy house indeed, as it governs career life, professional aspirations, fame, social status, and overall life path. Your tenth house is all about your public image. It's about your professional life rather than your personal life, and it's more of your "persona" rather than your actual identity. The tenth house doesn't only govern the career path that you choose (although that's certainly a big part of it), but it's also about the impact you make through your work and the mark that you leave on the world. It's your contribution to society. This also means that it's not simply about your social status and public image, either; it's also about your legacy, your long-term reputation, and the impression that you leave behind.

The cusp of the tenth house is a very significant point in the chart known as the midheaven (which we'll get into more below), which represents similar themes regarding your reputation, career aspirations, and life purpose. This is the highest point in your chart. The tenth house always falls to the left of the uppermost point and is therefore the most "visible," as it's closest to the Sun in the sky. This part of your chart is about being seen through the public eye. It's also the house of fame (or infamy, depending on the circumstances).

The tenth house is opposite the fourth house and is its perfect counterpart. The fourth house rules your home and private life, whereas the tenth house rules your career and public life. Some astrologers feel the tenth house also represents the more paternal and authoritative forces of parents and caretakers (converse to the fourth house's maternal energy).

The cusp of the tenth house is also known as your midheaven, and the sign that this point falls into in your birth chart indicates the energy that's aligned with your purpose and higher calling, or the impression you leave on the world—whether that's through your job or some other publicly visible part of your life. Having planets in the tenth house can affect your career and public life, bringing extra energy to your work and notoriety.

ELEVENTH HOUSE

Community • Friendships • Humanitarianism • Collective Consciousness

NATURAL SIGN RULER Aquarius
NATURAL PLANET RULER Uranus

The eleventh house governs our place within a social group, club, community, or society. It's essentially our place in the circle, whether that circle is your tight-knit group of friends, your community, or even society at large. This house represents our relationship to the collective, the collaboration and cooperation between multiple parties, and anything that involves teamwork. If it has to do with working together as a group to accomplish something, then it's likely an eleventh house matter.

Friendship and social groups also fall into this house, so while the seventh house rules over partnerships, the eleventh house focuses on *groups*. It transcends a one-on-one interpersonal relationship and focuses more on the parts of our lives that involve a blending and cooperation of more people, energies, and causes.

It also governs over the parts of our lives that *affect* the collective, so things like humanitarian causes, social justice issues, societal ideals, and our hopes and goals for the collective future are ruled by this house, too. Having planets in the eleventh house puts a major focus on our social lives and our ability to work within a group setting or for a worldly cause, and troublesome planets or aspects here can put a strain on these areas. The sign that the cusp of the eleventh house falls into shows you the type of energy you bring into your social life, group activities, and any sort of collectives.

TWELFTH HOUSE
Secrets • Subconscious • Karma • Healing

NATURAL SIGN RULER Pisces
NATURAL PLANET RULER Neptune

Welcome to the mystical twelfth house, the final abode in this astrological succession. The twelfth house is where we delve into our subconscious mind and all the secrets that it holds and symbolic dreams that it generates (this house literally rules sleep!). While there is much hidden within our subconscious (all of which is governed by this house), there is also much room for healing, and that's the ultimate goal here. Our healing, spiritual evolution, and transcendence are ruled by this house. Thus, it's no surprise that this house is considered to be quite spiritual in nature despite all that lurks within its shadows.

There's also a sense of loss, suffering, escapism, and restriction within this house, as it rules things like mental illness and addiction. It also governs over institutions such as hospitals and prisons, which remove people from their everyday routines (an area that is governed by this house's opposite, the sixth house) and put them into a more "hidden" realm. While the sixth house deals with the maintenance of our bodies, the twelfth house deals with the maintenance of our souls, which is a much more complicated and less concrete bag. Thus, things like our karmic debts, past lives and past life trauma, shadow selves, and subconscious habits are ruled here, too.

Planets in the twelfth house indicate that there's a lot going on beneath the surface, and there may be wounds that need tending to and secrets that you must work to keep out in the open. The sign that your twelfth house cusp falls into shows us the way we navigate the more hidden and subconscious elements of our being.

Degrees

When I say astrology gets complex and mathematical, I'm quite serious, and learning about degrees in the circle of the astrology chart is likely a vivid reminder of this fact. You've already heard a bit about degrees (and likely remember them from any bit of geometry you may have learned in the past), but let's make sure you're crystal clear on the concept. Each of the twelve zodiac signs in astrology is made up of 30 degrees (0 through 29), which makes 360 degrees total in a circular birth chart. Makes sense, right? As a planets transits through the sky (and subsequently, through the zodiac signs), it will consecutively ascend through each sign's degrees as well.

Degrees are important for several reasons. First, degrees are integral when it comes to identifying *aspects* between planets (which we'll discuss more below). Aspects are essentially angles formed in the astrology chart between the planets. They represent the *relationships* between the planets at any given time. Some aspects are harmonious (which means the planets are functioning well and giving us good vibes), but other aspects are strained (which can make things a struggle for us in the areas governed by said planets). But this all gets rather mathematical: The angles (or aspects) have to be exact, or pretty damn close to exact, in order to have an influence, and this is measured by a planet's degree in any given sign.

Degrees are also important when it comes to identifying *decans* in astrology. We'll talk more about decans and how they affect us in the next chapter but think of them for now as subdivisions within each sign that slightly change the way a sign's energy is expressed. There are three decans within each sign, each with a unique set of qualities, and these are separated by degrees as well (0 to 9, 10 to 19, and 20 to 29). It's believed that the energy of each sign slightly changes and shifts as a planet moves through its degrees. This is one way to explain why some Aries Sun people may seem so different than other Aries Sun people!

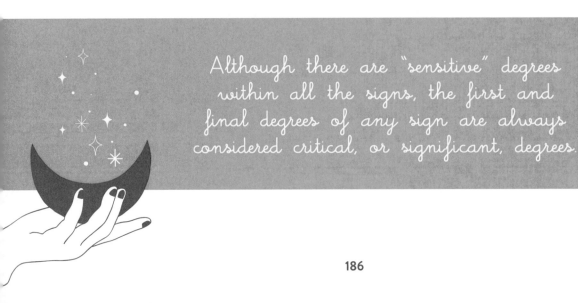

Although there are "sensitive" degrees within all the signs, the first and final degrees of any sign are always considered critical, or significant, degrees.

Critical Degrees

While degrees designate which decan a planet is in within a sign at any given time, there are also a couple of **critical degrees** to take note of.

The 29th degree (which is the final degree) is also known as the *anaretic* degree. If you were born with any planet at 29 degrees (or if a planet in transit hits the 29th degree), expect to feel constantly impulsive in that area of your life. The 29th degree is *just* at the edge of the next sign. The planet is eager to complete the evolution at hand, and it has *almost*, just *almost*, hit completion and mastery of its current sign—but it hasn't just yet. This makes it anxious and hasty in nature, always sensing that it's on the precipice of something new. This can make the planet's energy indecisive, wily, and hard to contain. It's certainly an energetic degree, though, which brings a lot of spontaneity and excitement.

Then, of course, if a planet moves one degree forward and into the next sign, it'll be at 0 degrees, which is another critical degree in astrology. The energy of a planet at 0 degrees is all about a new beginning. A planet at 0 degrees is starting a whole new journey through that particular zodiac sign—it signifies the beginning of a brand-new cycle, ripe with possibility. The hope, wonder, excitement, and even fear of the great unknown are recognizable qualities of this fresh-start degree. But still, like the 29th degree, the 0 degree planet has some trouble with impulse control. While the 29th degree is anxiously eager to move forward, knowing that it's at the edge of something entirely new, the 0 degree planet is impulsive due to being naive: It's a baby, starting a journey from the very beginning again.

Angles/Points

Remember how I mentioned that the cusp of the first house is always directly left of center? That cusp is actually one of four very important *angles* (also known as points) in your zodiac chart: the ascendant, descendant, midheaven, and imum coeli. Each of these four points falls on an X-Y axis of the birth chart and marks the cusp of the first, fourth, seventh, and tenth houses.

Angles and points function similarly to planets in that they can be activated, aspected, and have different

meanings, motives, and things that they represent about you. Their expressions change depending on which sign they fall into (so you have an ascendant sign, aka a rising sign, as well as a midheaven sign, and so on).

But *unlike* planets, these angles aren't actual celestial objects—they're just conceptual points in space that correspond to actual points on your birth chart. These points are constantly shifting through the wheel of the zodiac (cycling through all twelve signs in a single twenty-four-hour period), which is why you really need a birth time to calculate an accurate chart.

Ascendant (ASC or AC)—aka Your Rising Sign

The first and most well-known angle in astrology is the *ascendant*, and is also commonly known as your rising sign. Your ascendant is indicated by the exact place in the zodiac that the horizon line was on in the east (or the side of the rising Sun) at the exact time that you were born, or where the first light of the day would have appeared had the Sun just ascended over the horizon line (this rising Sun analogy is exactly why this angle is also known as your rising sign).

Everyone's ascendant is located in the same place on a birth chart. If it were a clock, this would appear at exactly 9 o'clock, or on the left side of the wheel's horizontal axis. The reason everyone's rising signs are different is because the zodiac wheel twists to meet the ascendant, and that's what makes this point imperative to the creation of an accurate chart.

As you work your way deeper into the land of astrology and how it affects you personally by analyzing your birth chart, knowing your rising sign is actually *massively* important. This is because of the houses on the zodiac wheel that we just discussed. As noted, your ascendant always indicates the cusp of house numero uno, so it determines the exact placement of the zodiac wheel (as well as the placement of each of your subsequent houses) in your birth chart. For example, if your rising sign is Sagittarius, that means your first house is *also* in Sagittarius, which means your second house would likely be in Capricorn, your third house in Aquarius, and so on. *Très* important!

Because the ascendant marks the cusp of the first house, its significance corresponds heavily to the themes of the first house in general and matters of the *self*. This means that when planets pass through or near your ascendant, you'll likely *identify* with them, taking in their qualities as your own. Similarly, whatever sign your ascendant falls in is probably quite prominent in your personality, because while it may not represent who you are at your core, it certainly represents a recognizable part of your social identity, image, and self.

As the point at the cusp of the first house, your ascendant also corresponds to a lot of *firsts* in your life and personality. For example, you can think of your rising sign as being indicative of the first impression you make on others, as well as the first instincts you have when reacting to situations off-the-cuff. Your rising sign rules over your external self; things like your appearance and your surface-level personality are indicated by your rising sign. It's very common for someone to guess your sign as your rising sign if they haven't gotten to know you well, as your ascendant is believed to influence the way you *present* yourself, and subsequently, how you're perceived by others.

Because the rising sign is actually one of the most important personal signs in astrology, we're going to explore each ascendant placement sign by sign in the next chapter, so look there if you want more information on *your* rising sign specifically.

As the kick-off to the succession of the first six "personal" houses of your astrology chart, the ascendant is all about your *identity*—it's a quick, catchall sign that represents your image, sense of self, and surface-level personality.

Descendant (DSC or DC)

Since we're dealing with an axis here, let's slide to the right, straight on to the point that is directly opposite to the ascendant: the *descendant*. The descendant is the point of the cusp of the seventh house. As the ascendant's opposite in both space and meaning, this point kicks us into the latter half of the twelve houses in astrology (seven through twelve), bringing us into the area of the birth chart that corresponds with our more outward-focused energies. Together, the ascendant and descendant work in tandem to blend these two opposing halves of the zodiac together. When a planet moves through or near your descendant, you will likely find yourself relating to *others* through that planet's qualities.

As the cusp of the seventh house, the descendant corresponds specifically with seventh house themes, meaning it relates to partnerships and committed relationships of all sorts. The descendant is a mirror to your ascendant, which represents *your* image, so it's believed that the sign of your descendant can illustrate the qualities in *others* that you often find yourself attracted to. It's the point that shows us what kind of people we're into. They say opposites attract, and that law is definitely at work when it comes to the ASC and DSC! For example, if your descendant is in Leo, it doesn't mean you'll only want to date Leos—it just means that you may be attracted to people with some surface-level Leonian qualities and behaviors, like being confident, gregarious, and maybe even a little egotistical.

Conversely, this point can also represent the qualities in *ourselves* that manifest in our closest and most committed partnerships. Your descendant will be in the opposite sign of your ascendant, which means it will embody qualities that are essentially the *opposite* of what you view and project yourself as. You may find yourself overtly admiring these qualities in others *because* they're qualities you struggle to embrace in yourself; it creates balance. But that balance could also come from *you*, rather than a partner, so your closest relationships might be the place where you can let your descendant's qualities come out to play. You know how different sides of your personality come through when you're in love? You can think of it that way. So while your outer self (the ascendant) may project one side of you, we mustn't forget about the power of duality and balance, which pushes the opposite of those qualities to come forth in your closest relationships.

You can look to your midheaven sign to see the qualities to embrace in order to reach your highest point of success and recognition.

Midheaven

Let's move to the tippy-top of the astrology chart, where we have the tip of the Y axis and the cusp of the tenth house: **the midheaven**. Midheaven is a nickname for medium coeli (or MC), which translates literally to "middle of the sky." This is the midpoint between the ascension of the ecliptic from the eastern horizon (the ascendant) toward the western horizon (the descendant), or the top of your chart. And as the highest point of the heavens, it represents the most public, notorious, and chart-topping version of you.

As the angle of the tenth house cusp, the midheaven represents all sorts of tenth house subject matter, such as public recognition, fame, and legacy. While the ascendant might represent the first light of you on the eastern horizon—or your face to the world—the midheaven is basically high noon. It's you at your most successful. It's more than your outward-facing self (like the ascendant); it's actually your *public* self, both the impression people have of you *before* they meet you (your reputation) and the impression that stays with people based on your achievements and contributions. The tenth house is the house of fame and reputation, after all, so it makes sense that this is what the midheaven sign would represent in your chart, too.

Many people consider the midheaven to be the angle that signifies your life path and career path. This is the unique angle that shows all you have to offer to the world—it's the lasting public impression you make through your contributions in life and your legacy. It's also associated with your social standing, reputation, and lifetime achievements.

If you need help clarifying your career goals, look no further than your midheaven. This sign can help you see some of the successful career paths that are most fluidly achievable based on your skill set. Even if you already have a career trajectory (in mind or embarked upon), the midheaven tells you the parts of yourself that you should hone, focus on, and embrace in order to *achieve* your goals. These are qualities that are most visibly strong; they stand out to others and come naturally when achieving your goals. While your ascendant is in charge of your first impression, your midheaven sign leaves a *longer-lasting* impression, much like the way the noontime Sun can leave a pool of water warm long after it has peaked.

Imum Coeli (IC)

Now let's slide straight down to the opposite angle in the chart from the midheaven, known as the imum coeli (or IC), which means "the bottom of the sky." The IC may represent the bottom of the sky, but it's also found at the bottom of our zodiac charts, at the 6 o'clock point of the circle. As the entrance to the fourth house (this angle, like the others, is the house's cusp), this point deals in issues of family, beginnings, and private matters of the home.

As the base of the astrological chart, the IC can be considered the roots and foundation of ourselves. These are the qualities that represent our beginnings: the private space where we learned about who we were, before we had reputations to worry about. The IC is not looking for recognition, like the midheaven—quite the opposite, actually. The IC seeks safety, nurturing, privacy, and retreat.

If the midheaven is high noon, then the IC is midnight. This angle deals with issues of the unconscious mind, such as early memories, formative experiences that we may have repressed, and anything related to our inner child who needs nurturing and emotional safety. This is the underworld of our chart, which simply means that it can be associated with the shadow sides of ourselves— parts of us that we're still grappling with and working to form a better understanding of.

Because the midheaven and IC angles are on the same axis, we must ideally make peace between their opposing qualities—one without the other simply won't do. If you want to be able to embrace your midheaven and achieve your highest potential, you must also leave room to nurture your inner child and provide yourself with a reprieve from the public eye by embracing your IC sign's qualities.

> Many astrologers believe the IC may even represent one of your caretakers, likely a parent or another guardian, who nurtured you in your youth.

The Lunar Nodes

In addition to the four angles on an astrology chart, there are some additional *points* in astrology that are highly significant. Just like angles, these represent conceptual points in space and *not* physical celestial bodies (like planets or asteroids). But unlike the angles, these aren't fixed onto the angles of a house system in an astrology chart. Instead, they function more like planets, moving through the signs of the zodiac in a very similar fashion. They can be activated and aspected just like planets and angles can.

There are a number of significant points in astrology, but the two that are most widely incorporated into a chart reading are the two we'll discuss, which are the lunar nodes, made up of the north node and the south node. These points move more slowly than the angles, more like a planet would, and they move in a retrograde motion (so they travel backward in the zodiac instead of forward).

The lunar nodes are also known as the Nodes of Fate or the Nodes of the Moon. These two points represent the exact spots where the path of the Moon's orbit intersects with the Sun's ecliptic at any given time (if you're doing your birth chart, then it would be the time of your birth). When the Moon *itself* intersects with the Sun's ecliptic, then we have an actual *eclipse*. We'll talk more about the astrological significance of these astronomical events later. But like the lunar nodes, they *also* have to do with fate.

The conceptual nature of the nodes as theoretical points on the ecliptic is mirrored in their spiritual, nontangible meaning in astrology, too. The north node and the south node represent our karmic life path in astrology. They're a bit more spiritual and "out there" than some of the other concepts in astrology (I know, some people feel that *all* of astrology is "out there," but I digress). While most of the planets and angles have to do with our journey through *this* life, the lunar nodes take into consideration the possibility of karma, energy, and even past lives that influenced us coming into our *current* journey as well as the karma, energy, and future lives that might await us *beyond* this journey. **The nodes represent the energy that we brought into this life (the south node) and the energy that we must grow into and embrace throughout the course of this life's journey (the north node).**

The nodes show us our potential—they are the duality between the lessons we've learned and the ones we still have to learn.

The south node is like your first language in this lifetime. These are the qualities that you naturally fall back on.

The north and south nodes are on opposite ends of the skies, meaning that they'll almost always be in sets of opposing zodiac signs (Aries/Libra, Taurus/Scorpio, and so on). They spend about a year and half traveling through any given sign, so people born within that approximate time frame from your birth date are likely to share lunar node signs. This is nice, given that the nodes concern our spiritual path. It means that your closest peers are also on a similar soul journey. While you may not necessarily have many surface things in common, you'll at least know that you share a common ultimate goal of embracing certain parts of yourself in order to spiritually evolve in this life. What a beautiful thing to share with those closest in age to you, despite any other surface-level differences! In that sense, and given the spiritual and karmic nature of these points, you can think of the nodes as mini-generations.

Let's dive in a little deeper to the meaning of each node, shall we?

THE SOUTH NODE

We're starting here, because the south node is our spiritual comfort zone. This point represents the past—not just the past like yesterday or last year, but also all the spiritual baggage, karma, and lessons that we may have brought with us into this lifetime from the last. If you believe in reincarnation or soul journeys (totally chill if you *don't*), then you can think of the south node as representative of the lives you've lived before this one. These are the lessons and experiences that have already been woven into your soul's fabric; they're the skills that you've mastered that come easily to you in this life. The south node made you who you are—it's a built-in *part* of who you are—and so its qualities are integral to both your personality and your soul.

The south node's qualities (which are dictated by the sign that this point falls into on your chart) are a karmic gift to you, no doubt. They're like having a conversation in your mother tongue. The problem arises when instead of using these gifts to propel you toward the destiny of your north node, you become overly complacent. The south node can be a curse if you refuse to leave the spiritual comfort zone that it provides to you.

Of course, this can be tough to do: Why *wouldn't* you want to rely on your old and faithful ways? It feels safe, secure, and sure-footed. The problem is, the south node is a set of skills you've already mastered, lessons you've already learned. Your job in this life is to embrace the *opposite* of that (which is your north node) to challenge yourself and to evolve. Only by tapping into your south node's qualities as your *foundation* and a *jumping-off point* for the risks and challenges you'll take in this life will you really utilize it for the gift that it is. It's the gift of a foundation of skills that you've already mastered. Your job isn't to stay in that realm, but to build on that and learn to embrace the other side in your soul's journey, too.

THE NORTH NODE

While the south node represents your spiritual and karmic past, the north node represents your future—not just the jobs you'll have or the people you'll fall in love with or the places you'll go, but the future of your *soul*. The north node is your spiritual calling; it's the path of your spiritual evolution in this lifetime. If you believe in such concepts, you can also think of the north node as your fate and your destiny in this life, too. It is the shining, sparkling, light-at-the-end-of-the-tunnel destination that your *soul* should be constantly working toward throughout your life. It's much more than a goal to be conquered. It is a lifelong journey that involves stepping outside of your comfort zone, embracing new sides of yourself, leaving behind what you know for the great *unknown*, and transforming your soul in ways that may feel foreign but that are *requisite* for your growth as a spirit.

Embracing the qualities of your north node (which are dictated by whatever sign the node falls into on your birth chart) is necessary for your growth, but that doesn't mean it comes easily. Leaning into your north node means embarking on a journey into yet-unchartered waters. It means abandoning what you know and leaving the comfort zone of your south node in order to try something totally new and different. This takes work, practice, frustration, and focus, but once you've gotten there, you'll find it opens up an entirely new world of possibilities.

Expect to find yourself resisting the qualities of your north node sign, much like an angsty teenager. Sometimes your spirit may simply feel lazy—you will *always* be tempted to cuddle up in the safety of your south node. But this makes you a big fish in a small pond, and you, little guppy, need space to grow. When it comes to day-to-day endeavors, you may not feel your nodes pushing you in any given direction, but if you look at the over- and undercurrents of your life, you'll see them there. The north node is ultimately your fate and your destiny, if you believe in such concepts. It is the energy that, at the end of your life's journey, you'll feel accomplished having embraced and integrated into yourself.

✷ **While the south node may be the language you've spoken since birth, the north node is the language you must learn throughout this lifetime.** ✷

Planetary Aspects

As the planets move through the zodiac, they're influenced by the energy of the signs that they move through, but they're also influenced by each other. This is because when planets form certain angles with one another in the sky, called *aspects*, they also form relationships with each other. Aspects are where the day-to-day drama of astrology can get ***really*** juicy. Each aspect has a different meaning that illustrates *how* two or more planets are relating to each other, such as whether the planets are fighting or getting along. Some aspects are harmonious and positive, bringing out the best sides of each planet, while other aspects are messy and stressful, creating tension and drama. Once you have the planets laid out in the map of an astrology chart, it's easier to see the aspects in action, as they are all based on mathematical angles between the planets in the chart.

"Orbs" of Aspects

Aspects are determined by identifying angles within the degrees of each sign in the chart, with the major aspects occurring when planets are 0, 60, 90, 120, and 180 degrees from each other. The tighter and closer the aspect (meaning the more exact they are to the degree), the stronger the aspect's effects will be. This is determined by the *orb* of an aspect, which tells us the allowable number of degrees away from an exact angle the planets can be while still causing that aspect to manifest. For example, a sextile aspect occurs when two planets are 60 degrees apart. However, if the number of degrees between the planets happens to be close to 60 but not *exactly*, like maybe 55 or 65, you could still consider it a sextile—it would just be a sextile with an *orb* of 5 degrees (or however many degrees away from a perfect 60 it may be). Most astrologers would say that an aspect with an orb of more than 6 to 10 degrees wouldn't be considered an aspect anymore, as it would simply be too weak. Other astrologers are even more strict, shrinking an acceptable orb to even *less* than 5 degrees in order to be considered. Usually, orbs on the larger allowable end are only granted to the more major planets, like the Sun and Moon, whereas the less impactful or more distant planets require a tighter orb in order for us to feel the effects.

But this is all relative. It's hard to speak definitively about aspects because they really do differ depending on which planets are involved, where the planets are in their orbits, and what else is taking place in the skies at the time. **When two or more planets are aspecting each other, we need to consider not only the influence of the individual planets *and* how they're interacting with one another, but also the energy of the sign they're in.** Different aspects between different planets activate different blended qualities and influence us in different ways; the energies of the involved planets can synergize, clash, or play off each other. Having Venus, for example, in Aries is going to affect us directly. But if Venus in Aries forms a *trine* to the Moon in Leo, we must consider how these energies work *together*. Planets in aspect combine to create a new, different, or more intense energy.

ASPECTS

♂	0°	□	90°
⚹	60°	△	120°
☍	180°	⚻	150°

Hard and Soft Aspects

As mentioned, the five **major aspects** occur when two (or more) planets are 0, 60, 90, 120, and 180 degrees apart. Of these aspects, there are some that are considered *hard aspects* (or difficult, complicated, and tense aspects), and others that are considered *soft aspects* (or more harmonious, positive, and easy aspects). I like that they're referred to as "hard" and "soft" rather than "bad" and "good" because that language feels more accurate to the nature of these aspects. This is to say that hard aspects aren't *bad*; they're just truly *hard*. They're challenging to work with, and require us to put in much more effort and struggle in order to get through them. Similarly, soft aspects aren't purely *good*; they are actually just *soft*. That means they are more gentle, easier to work with, and the benefits (or lack of challenges) feel effortless. It's the ease and softness with which these aspects flow that are what tend to make us think of them as positive.

While there are additional minor aspects considered in astrology, we'll just take a peek at the big five. Here's a rundown on the major aspects.

CONJUNCTION

A conjunction occurs between two or more planets that are within the same sign, sharing the same degree, 0 degrees apart (or within an allowable orb). Conjunctions are one of the more intense aspects of the bunch, almost always creating a visceral energy. In this aspect, planets are sharing very close quarters with one another, so their interactions are felt very strongly. This could be good or bad—if the conjunct planets are compatible, perhaps they'll throw a party and relish in each other's company. *Or,* if they're incompatible, they may feel cramped and throw a fit until they get some space. In either case, expect to really *feel* a conjunction, as it also brings a whole lot of energy to a particular zodiac sign *and* a specific house in your chart.

A conjunction is also the one major aspect that isn't considered inherently hard *or* soft, because it could *truly* go either way depending on the planets involved and the energy of the sign in which the conjunction is taking place. It could easily be either wonderful or immensely difficult (and while this is true of all aspects, the others tend to slant more one way than the other), but it will always be effective in creating change and action.

SEXTILE

A sextile occurs when planets are at a 60-degree angle from one another (or within an allowable orb). This is a soft aspect that's super benign and sweet in nature. Because a 60-degree angle in astrology indicates that the involved planets or points are two signs apart, sextiles almost always occur between signs of the same *polarity*, so the involved planets will always be in two masculine/yang signs or two feminine/yin signs. This inherently brings a sense of harmony to this aspect, as the signs that the planets are in already have some very basic things in common.

While this is undoubtedly a positive aspect, it's not very dynamic, meaning it may not inspire you to take action, nor is it likely to create much noticeable change in your life. It's characterized by its effortless, breezy easiness that feels good, but doesn't really energize or motivate us to *do* much. Of course, sometimes not rocking the boat is a *good* thing. Sextiles offer a smooth and pleasant meeting of planetary energies, and can be a nice reprieve during which we can sit back and enjoy a breezy and cool vibe. The planets are getting along and going about their business, and their interactions aren't set to disrupt your day.

SQUARE

A square occurs when planets are at a 90-degree angle from one another (or within an allowable orb of that angle). Like the hard lines and acute angles that make up the shape this aspect is named for, the energy of this aspect is definitively hard to work with. When planets meet in a square, expect to feel literally boxed in by their collective energy. It can be a real challenge to navigate the sharp corners of this aspect, as the planets involved aren't likely seeing eye to eye, and are operating within incompatible energies. It is tense, edgy, and feels uneasy.

When overcoming the challenges of a square aspect, we must work twice as much to climb over its hard angles, but once we do, we've *really* accomplished something. In this sense, a square can be a very helpful aspect (albeit a tough one) because it motivates us to problem-solve and think outside the (square-shaped) box to keep things moving under the influence of such a difficult and stubborn planetary conflict.

TRINE

A trine occurs when planets are at a 120-degree angle from one another (or within an allowable orb of that degree). This is by far the most powerfully

Some ingredients mix well, and others don't—and planets are no different.

197

positive soft aspect out there. Even the word seems to roll off the tongue with an almost musical, magical quality—*trine*. Because a 120-degree angle in astrology generally indicates that the involved planets or points are four signs apart, trines almost always occur between signs of the same *element*, which adds a beautiful harmony to the connection. The planets will be working with energies that express themselves in similar ways and with similar goals, so they're automatically able to work together with more synergy.

A trine has the potential to highlight the involved planets from all their best angles, as if they've stumbled into some cosmically good lighting. It immediately links their common ground and creates a bliss-filled connection, but of course, we're all guilty of feeling less inspired to work hard when things are good. That's really the only drawback of a trine: it brings an abundance of luck and auspiciousness, yes, but because of that we could be tricked into thinking that we have nothing to worry about. As long as we don't float off into space on a trine's cloud nine, we can celebrate the burst of positive energy and use it to our advantage, regardless of what cosmic chaos might come next.

OPPOSITION

An opposition occurs when planets are at a 180-degree angle from one another (or within an allowable orb of that angle), or, as the aspect's name implies, directly opposite from one another on the zodiac chart. Because of the opposing energies through which the involved planets are expressing themselves, this is considered a hard aspect. Under this aspect, planetary energies are butting heads in a rather dramatic showing. Their motivations and expressions are polar opposites, leading to obvious conflict, discord, and even explosive moods.

That said, the conflicts that arise from an opposition are very clear and out in the open. It's easy to see where things are misaligning, because one is simply opposite the other. This actually makes the conflict a little easier to navigate—it's based on polarity and duality, so if we can shift from a conflict setting to a balance setting, we can work with it. While finding balance between opposing forces can be difficult, it's also a little easier and less nebulous than some disagreements, and it can serve as the useful impetus for change. Sometimes it offers us a chance to look at something from an opposite side's perspective and find common ground in order to solve a problem. Oppositions are inherently about balance, and as you know, sometimes opposites even attract! Thus, there is much to work with under a planetary opposition, and while it likely requires patience, compromise, and a good amount of frustration, this aspect can bring intrigue, growth, and change, too.

A square aspect can serve as a bit of a roadblock on our journeys.

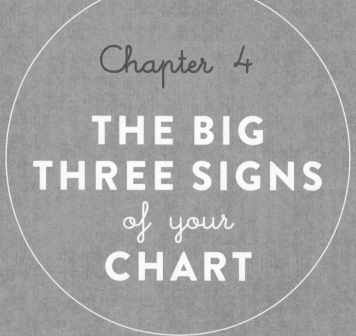

Chapter 4

THE BIG THREE SIGNS

of your

CHART

WE NEED NOT FEEL ASHAMED
OF FLIRTING WITH THE ZODIAC.
THE ZODIAC IS WELL WORTH
FLIRTING WITH.

—D. H. Lawrence

Now that you're familiar with the major planets in astrology, the twelve zodiac signs, *and* the basic ins and outs of a birth chart, you're gaining a more solid grip on some of the major energies that work together to influence us on a daily basis *and* blend to create your personal cosmic blueprint.

Now, let's get *personal*.

Most people's experience with personal astrology is via their horoscope, but here's the deal: If reading daily 'scopes is all you're doing with astrology, keep in mind that you're scratching the surface. This is fine, but there's a lot more to work with that will likely serve you in much deeper, more useful ways. Astro-skeptics often dismiss astrology based on horoscopes alone and how general they are, noting that there simply can't be only twelve different ways a day could play out for all of the billions of people on this planet. And of course, that's totally accurate. Horoscopes are super generalized! That doesn't mean they're not fun to read, or that they don't have actual value as a tool for your self-awareness, because they often do. But if you're looking to sink your hungry lil' teeth deeper into the astrology that affects you on a daily, weekly, monthly, or long-term basis, then looking into your birth chart and getting to know your big three signs is a good way to start.

As you know if you read the last chapter, your birth chart contains each and every one of the planets *and* all twelve of the signs, meaning that *all* of these energies are significant to each and every one of us. But let's zoom this lens in a little closer to home and make this a little bit more specific to *you* personally. There are three major signs that are considered more significant than the rest, and are arguably the most important foundational pieces of your chart and who you are. These are your **Sun sign**, **Moon sign**, and **rising sign**.

Yes, each of your planets expresses itself through one of the twelve zodiac signs, and each one is important, as discussed—Venus is how you love and value, Mars is how you fight and take action, Mercury is how you think and communicate, and so on. But the two luminaries, the Sun and the Moon, hold a *particularly* strong significance over who you are. As the singular star and moon on the list of major planets, they hold a stronger, *brighter* significance. This is even true simply from an astronomical standpoint: Think of the way the Sun is the only "planet" around which *our* planet orbits, and the Moon is the only "planet" that orbits *us*. The Sun is the father figure of the zodiac, and the Moon is the mother. Together, our **Sun sign** and our **Moon sign** are our astrological "parents," so to speak, and they are integral to who we are.

The **rising sign** (also called the *ascendant*) sails us into a new territory, as it's actually *not* a planet but a point in the sky and on your birth chart (we discussed these angles of the birth chart in depth in chapter 3, if you need a refresher). Your rising sign is perhaps the most significant angle in your chart and the most influential on your personality. Because this point traverses the entirety of the zodiac in a single day, you'll need your exact birth time in order to figure out what it is.

How to Find Your Signs

Virtually everyone knows their Sun sign already. It's the sign you'd name if someone asked what your sign is. And if you're already into astrology, you might also have become familiar with your rising sign and your Moon sign, too.

Unlike your Sun sign, for which all you generally need is a birthday to figure out, both your Moon and rising signs require an exact birth *date* (year included!) and usually a *time* in order to calculate accurately. This is because this planet and point don't move through the signs in a way that aligns with the calendar year, the way the Sun tends to. This means a birthday isn't enough—a full date and, in many cases, an exact *time* are needed.

Once you have that, you can set about finding your signs. One option is to use an online birth chart calculator or app to find out your Moon and rising signs. Many sites will generate a free birth chart and corresponding report if you enter your information (but remember to cross-reference things and do your research, as there's no guarantee that a random site's calculations are accurate). Alternatively, you could consult a professional astrologer about your birth chart, and they can consult an ephemeris or other reputable software to give you all your signs with accuracy (plus *many* more personalized insights, too).

Without further ado, let's get acquainted with a big, sparkly trifecta of zodiac signs that comprise the foundation of your chart: the makeup of the astrological *you*.

MEET your SUN SIGN

The Essence
of You

At this point, you know at least a little somethin' somethin' about your Sun sign. We've already discussed the significance of the Sun as a planet in and of itself, as well as the twelve different signs' energies through which it could be expressed in the zodiac. And of course, our Sun sign is the sign most of us refer to ourselves by and the one that many people strongly identify with. That said, it's still true that *yes*, you are *much* more than a Sun sign alone—just as the practice of astrology on the whole is about much more than Sun signs! But it's obviously a big one, so what *does* the Sun mean for you, and why is there so much emphasis placed on it?

The Sun shows us how we shine as a person. Our brightest, shiniest, and most powerful, notable, and memorable qualities can often be seen in our Sun sign's expression. If you go back to the section of the book that discusses the energy of each zodiac sign, you'll likely identify with a lot of the qualities associated with your Sun's sign. While those descriptions are about each sign's energy in *general*, they certainly apply heavily to Sun signs, as the Sun's spotlight offers each sign a lot of power and creative control over its expression as it travels through the sign's territory of the zodiac each year. In other words, you don't need to skew those qualities too much the way you might need to with other planets. The Sun is so bright that it simply highlights *all* of them.

The qualities of your Sun sign often shine through stronger and brighter than some other planets' signs do, because while you might act or feel or value or relate to things based on all different planetary factors, the Sun speaks to who you *are*. So yes, your Venus sign will certainly show up when you're courting a crush, just as your Mars sign will rear its head when you're competing for a new job, but the Sun is *always* there, because the Sun shows up when you're just being *you*. Your Sun sign is the center of your personal solar system, just as the actual Sun is the *literal* center of ours.

Let's look at astrology as self-serve frozen yogurt, because why not! The toppings are obviously a *big* part of the experience. There's usually a huge selection of different toppings that fill brightly lit plastic buckets, containing everything from chopped fruits and nuts to chocolate chips and candies, plus sauces and whipped cream and sprinkles galore, of course. So even though there may only be, oh, twelve different froyo flavors (ahem, *zodiac signs*), the possible combinations of toppings are virtually *endless*, making each one totally unique. We can think about Sun signs in this way, too. The whole froyo is your birth chart, and your Sun sign is the frozen yogurt flavor itself—it's the base of the dish, the foundation that's laid down before the rest of the toppings (aka the other planets and their signs in your chart) get sprinkled on top to jazz it up and make it unique. Some people may pile their toppings on so high that you can't even *see* what flavor of frozen yogurt lies underneath, while others might keep it simple and let the froyo itself take center stage. Sometimes we might have *so* many intensely flavored toppings that we can't really *taste* the froyo—but it's there, just like your Sun sign is there, and you'll get to it soon enough. Without the frozen yogurt base of the Sun, this dessert wouldn't even be froyo; it would just be a paper bowl full of toppings. So remember: No matter how powerful your other planetary influences may be, at the core of it all is *always* going to be your Sun sign.

Why the Obsession with Sun Signs in Mainstream Astrology?

Obviously, the Sun is *très important*, but how the heck did it become the be-all and end-all, superstar sign in pop culture astrology, and in many cases, the only sign that some people even *know* about? Let's not get it twisted: The Sun *is* a star, and has *always* been one of the zodiac's major players throughout the entirety of astrology's millennia-long history. But back in the early days of astrology, no one would have even *dreamed* of looking at *just* a Sun sign to determine anything about a person's personality or life or future.

Here's how the focus on Sun signs happened. When astrology began inching its way into the mainstream back in the first half of the twentieth century, newspapers and other publications were seeking a way to bring personalized astrology readings to a broader audience on a regular basis. Obviously, because everyone's birth chart looks different (even if two people were born on the same *day*), there was no way to generalize all of that information and deliver a typical reading to the masses.

So what did clever astrologers develop to remedy this issue? Sun sign horoscopes, which only require someone to use their birth date (not even birth year) to identify. That's because the Sun is the only planet that transits through the same signs at approximately the same time every single year, so it's the only sign that astrologers could use to share simple, generalized horoscopes by referencing birthdays and nothing more. No one would have to book a consultation with an astrologer or check a wildly large chart of dates and transits for their exact birth date, year, and time; they'd simply identify the Sun sign that corresponded with their birthday and be done with it. Simple and with mass appeal.

Using this new method, astrology writers could draw up a chart for each of the twelve Sun signs, using the Sun sign as the first house of the chart (rather than the ascendant, as we typically would) and then from there, look at how the *other* planets were interacting in said chart. That's not what someone's traditional birth chart looks like, as you know, because this was developed as a method of generalizing in a way that the average reader of a publication could easily comprehend. So, of course, there are more than twelve ways someone's day, week, or month is bound to go. And there are also obviously more than twelve basic personality types (remember the froyo analogy?). But pop astrology boils all your signs down to just one: the Sun sign.

ARE HOROSCOPES ACCURATE?

Now you know that the hyper-focus on Sun signs and their corresponding horoscopes are very much a modern-day practice that developed out of convenience and general entertainment value. Is it fun to read? Absolutely! Is it accurate? Oftentimes yes, despite being quite generalized, especially if you highly identify with your Sun sign, have a prominent Sun placement, or have other significant planets or points that share the same sign (especially your rising sign).

Once you dive into your actual birth chart (deets in Chapter 3), you'll be able to see even more clearly how *your* Sun sign manifests personally. You already know by reading the section on your Sun sign's energy how your Sun's power manifests, and that likely resonates with you and who you are inside. But there's even more. For example, the area of your life where you're likely to have the most vitality, star power, and strongest ability to shine would be in the *house* that the Sun resides in within your birth chart. You'll also consider the Sun's *aspects* in your birth chart, or the relationships it forms with the other planets that can affect the way it's expressed.

WHY DO I SEEM SO DIFFERENT FROM OTHER PEOPLE WHO SHARE MY SUN SIGN?

I'm sure you've met plenty of people with the same Sun sign as you who seem completely different in their personality, motives, and expression. There are several reasons for this. The first is that, obviously, there are more than twelve basic types of people, and we shouldn't use astrology to put people in boxes using vague categorizations, erasing individuality. We're all one-of-a-kind individuals made up of fully unique life experiences, backgrounds, upbringings, genetic predispositions, free will to make choices, you name it. That's a given—you're *you*, a full-fledged and autonomous human being, and a birth chart could never portray or predict every single thing about you!

The reason that Sun signs (which people also often refer to as their "star sign" or "zodiac sign") are so notorious today is actually because of the popularity of tabloid horoscopes.

Another reason people with the same Sun sign might seem nothing alike is because, as you've learned, everyone has a whole unique chart full of planets and signs *beyond* our Sun sign, all of which have varying levels of influence over the way our Sun sign qualities manifest. Astrologically speaking, *you* are composed of so much more than a Sun sign alone.

There are lots of reasons why not everyone born under the same Sun sign is going to see their energy expressed in the same way. But even within a single planet's journey through a single sign, there are different influences as to how the energy will express, which makes astrology even more personalized and intricate.

Decans: Making Your Sun Sign Even More Personal

If you've read the section about the zodiac signs, then you already know the general deal with your Sun sign's energy (and I'm guessing this probably wasn't your first-ever introduction to it if you've ever dabbled in astrology prior to reading this book), but did you know your Sun sign can be even *more* personal?

One of the ways you can further personalize your sun sign is by looking at decanates, or *decans* for short. Decans are subdivisions within each sign, and each sign has three different decans. Decans change the way a sign's energy is expressed. You could be born within any of the three decans depending on when the Sun voyaged through your sign's chunk of the zodiac. Remember how each sign has exactly 30 degrees through which a planet travels? The decans are based on that: the first, second, and third sets of 10 degrees within a sign represent the first, second, and third *decans* of the sign.

Decans are about to get a little complicated, but bear with me. Within each zodiac sign, each of the three decans is "co-ruled" by a different planet. The co-ruler of the first decan is always the same as the sign's traditional ruling planet. For the other two co-ruling planets, we look to

We have to take into account the *influences* of all the planets in our chart that represent important parts of us, not just our Sun.

the ruling planets of the other signs within the same element—the ruling planet of the other two decans will always correspond with the planets that rule those two other signs. So first decan Aries are purely ruled by Mars. Second decan Aries are also ruled by Mars of course, but they are influenced by the Sun as well (because that's Leo's ruling planet, and Leo is the next fire sign after Aries). Which means third decan Aries would be ruled by Mars but influenced (or co-ruled) by Jupiter, because that's Sagittarius's ruling planet (and Sagittarius is the next and final fellow fire sign).

HOW TO FIND THE DECAN OF YOUR SUN SIGN

Decans can be applied to the placement of *any* natal planet, but because Sun signs are used most widely, it's fun to find out how yours might differ from the rest of your Sun sign crew. If you want to find out which decan you were born in, you'll have to consult your trusty birth chart and look at the degree, between 0 and 29, at which your Sun is located. But if you don't have a birth chart handy, you can also guesstimate which decan you're born in by looking at the days your Sun sign's season began and ended, then calculating which third of the month you were born in—just divide up the number of days by three and count it out (approximate dates are included below). Just note that if your birthday falls near the approximate date of the first, second, and third decans, you'll really need to check your chart in order to know for sure, as these dates can vary slightly from year to year.

If you want to know more about your Sun sign in general, look up your sign's energy in Chapter 2—knowing, of course, that with only twelve signs, the descriptions for each are pretty broad! We know you're a unique snowflake, and understanding which decan you were born under can tell you more specific and personalized details about how your Sun sign's energy is expressed in you. Read on to find out about the unique way that your Sun sign's energy manifests based on the **decan** in which you were born.

What Kind of Aries Are You?

If you were born with an Aries Sun, you probably know what the deal is with your sign, but knowing which decan of Aries you were born under can tell you more specific and personalized details about how your Sun sign's energy is expressed.

Aries Decan 1: Purely Aries

Sun between 0° and 9°

Born between approximately March 20–March 29

Ruled solely by Mars

First decan Aries possess most of the stereotypical Aries qualities, but perhaps exaggerated to an even more energetic degree—you're like Aries on speed. Remember when I said Aries was the energy drink of the zodiac? Well, as a first decan Aries, you are basically double-fisting said energy drinks, and loving it. Brimming with self-confidence and tenacity, these go-getters can make something out of absolutely nothing. You're likely physically energetic with lots of stamina and possess a willful drive that few other decans of *any* sign could compete with. Speaking of competing, you're the most competitive breed of Aries, and you likely have absolutely *zero* ability to resist a challenge. With Mars as your sole ruler, your passion, courageousness, and power are unbeatable. You're quick to fire, but just as quick to show your love, and if anyone can keep up with your fiery spirit, they'll be lucky to have you on their team.

Sun between 10° and 19°

Born between approximately March 30–April 9

Influenced by the Sun

Second decan Aries are ever so slightly more regal and defined than your average Aries. With the influence of the proud and mighty Sun in your corner, your bold and aggressive Mars-ruled impulses are slightly tamed and smoothed out with the warm and glittering glow of the golden Sun. You've got all the passion of a typical Aries, but with a little added dose of style. With the Sun's influence, you may be more self-aware, devoting yourself to making your appearance a little extra glossy. Aries energy throws itself head and heart first into all endeavors, but as a second decan Aries, you have a little more concern for your reputation, as you are much more conscious about what other people think. This also means you're more prone to flattery than a typical Aries, who usually wouldn't be too concerned with the opinions others have of them. You're likely to channel all your cardinal energy into a creative pursuit and are especially good at getting passion projects off the ground.

Aries Decan 3: Aries with a Side of Sagittarius

Sun between 20° and 29°

Born between approximately April 10–April 19

Influenced by Jupiter

Aries are known for their hardheaded stubborn streak, but with an influence from expansive Jupiter, third decan Aries are more flexible than most. That said, you won't be pushed too far, as you love your freedom above all else! You're likely to have more of an interest in (and patience for) studying and engaging in intellectual conversations about philosophy and spiritually than your Aries siblings, and higher knowledge is one of the areas toward which you channel your excess of fiery energy. Aries are impulsive, but you're even a little *extra* spontaneous. You've got a big taste for adventure—it's especially hard for you to say no if someone offers you the chance to try something new or run off for a good time. The freedom to run as far as you'd like (with your endless supply of Arian energy!) and do as you please is one of your most important values.

What Kind of Taurus Are You?

If you were born with a Taurus Sun, you probably know what the deal is with your sign, but knowing which decan of Taurus you were born under can tell you more specific and personalized details about how your Sun sign's energy is expressed.

Taurus Decan 1: **Purely Taurus**	Sun between 0° and 9° Born between approximately April 20–April 30 Ruled solely by Venus

A first decan Taurus is the most *classic* Taurus, and will likely identify with most of Taurus's typical descriptions. You move at a slow but steady pace in all matters, and are incredibly reliable—your bosses, friends, colleagues, and lovers know this and appreciate this about you! Stability and commitment are important to you, and your jobs, relationships, and friendships are all likely to last a long time. As Venus is your sole Sun ruler, you're extra prone to being swept up in life's sensual pleasure, which means you probably work very hard in your career to ensure you can afford the comfortable and occasionally luxurious lifestyle that you love to lead. As a Venus baby, you're so deeply sensual that you might be a little extra prone to hedonism, too—but c'mon, you can't help the fact that you love delicious food, fancy drinks, comfortable clothing, expensive art, and great sex! Who doesn't, really? You don't feel bad indulging in such things, because you know you always put in the work that earns you the time for such relaxation.

Taurus Decan 2: Taurus with a Side of Virgo

Sun between 10° and 19°

Born between approximately May 1–May 10

Influenced by Mercury

A second decan Taurus tends to talk, walk, and move a little more quickly than your average Taurus. With influence from quick-witted and even quicker-footed Mercury, you likely make a little more haste in your endeavors, and you also likely have a little more energy! It's in the Taurus nature to enjoy bountiful relaxation time, and while regular sensually restoring recharge periods are still a high priority for you, you can pull off being more of a busybody than most. In fact, you probably get a little restless if you spend too much time lazing about. Virgo's altruistic influence on your Sun sign makes you a helpful person, more willing to share your time, hard work, and luxuries with others. You're also more social than the standard Taurus—Venus's beauty mixed with Mercury's knack for communication make you a sparkling conversationalist and host. Taurus is known to be stubborn, but you're a little more open to new ways of doing things than most, and can bring a little extra flexibility and resilience to your plans.

Taurus Decan 3: Taurus with a Side of Capricorn

Sun between 20° and 29°

Born between approximately May 11–May 20

Influenced by Saturn

All Taurus energy puts the *bull* in *bulldozer*, but a third decan Taurus? Your energy is practically unstoppable. With the strict guiding influence of Saturn, which bestows you with discipline and a tireless work ethic, there is an added layer of ambition and determination to everything you do. All Tauruses appreciate material wealth and security in all facets, and are willing to work for it, but your approach to everything from moneymaking to love is even more calculated and controlled, as you have a heavier scarcity mentality and are constantly fearful of losing what you've worked for. That said, this only makes you *more* tenacious and motivates you to bring your A-game 24/7 (which you pretty much *always* do). Only *then* do you allow yourself to indulge in the Venus-ruled pleasures that make all the work worth it. You exert much more self-control over the hedonistic Taurus habits than the rest of the bunch.

What Kind of Gemini Are You?

If you were born with a Gemini Sun, you probably know what the deal is with your sign, but knowing which decan of Gemini you were born under can tell you more specific and personalized details about how your Sun sign's energy is expressed.

Gemini Decan 1: Purely Gemini

Sun between 0° and 9°

Born between approximately May 21–May 31

Ruled solely by Mercury

First decan Geminis are pure, true, unadulterated, slightly chaotic Gemini energy. A fantastic conversationalist with a quick wit and an encyclopedic knowledge of a variety of subjects, you make your ruling planet Mercury proud with the speed, objectivity, and intelligence level at which you think. You deeply embody the mercurial nature of your sign, easily existing at two extreme ends of a spectrum simultaneously. You can be both the most understanding *and* the most judgmental person in the room at any given time, and it's sometimes hard for people to keep up with the constant rotation of topics, ideas, and opinions that roll off your tongue with endless charisma and energy.

Gemini Decan 2: Gemini with a Side of Libra

Sun between 10° and 19°

Born between approximately June 1–June 10

Influenced by Venus

Second decan Geminis have a softer and more gentle edge to their personalities than most. You're less likely to stir the pot and are more diplomatic and thoughtful in the way you express your many opinions, as you appreciate keeping the peace. This makes you more comfortable moving at a slower pace than most zippy Gems. While all Geminis are born with the gift of gab, you're the biggest flirt of them all. Mental stimulation is always your number one goal, but with sensual Venus as your co-ruler, you're more prone to fall for lusty, earthly pleasure. Libra's diplomatic influence on your demeanor makes you much less prone to drama and more inclined to try to keep the peace than the average pot-stirring Gem. You're slightly more reserved with your more controversial opinions and don't get much enjoyment out of arguments. You'd rather socialize all night about topics and fun facts that *everyone* around can get down with.

Gemini Decan 3: Gemini with a Side of Aquarius

Sun between 20° and 29°

Born between approximately June 11–June 20

Influenced by Uranus

You've got a slightly edgier, less-agreeable side to you than the average Gemini, as you're much less likely to change your mind on your opinions. Third decan Geminis know *exactly* where they stand on most issues and are more interested in social justice. While the average Gemini is hyper enough to entertain itself, you are more inclined to play as part of a group, as you understand the value of bringing power to the people. You're more likely than any other Gemini to use your smarts for building bigger ideas; you're still full of fascinating factoids, but you're much less interested in small talk and much more concerned with broader topics that are more applicable to people's lives. While being a little less emotional than the other decans, you also are more likely to invest yourself in the community.

What Kind of Cancer Are You?

If you were born with a Cancer Sun, you probably know what the deal is with your sign, but knowing which decan of Cancer you were born under can tell you more specific and personalized details about how your Sun sign's energy is expressed.

Cancer Decan 1: Purely Cancer	Sun between 0° and 9°
	Born between approximately June 21–July 1
	Ruled solely by the Moon

First decan Cancers are exactly the maternal, nurturing, sensitive, and grounding forces that we expect from the classic lunar-ruled sign. Regardless of your gender, you have an innate maternal instinct, and family—chosen or biological—is extremely important to you. You're the first to offer up a gentle touch, sympathetic ear, and soothing words. This kind of intimate and emotional human connection is where you come alive, and it makes you feel as grounded as the person with whom you're interacting. You've got a huge heart and will open it up to anyone who seems willing to be vulnerable with you. Your compassion knows no bounds, and learning boundaries when it comes to taking on others' pain is an important part of your journey. As a crab, through and through, you *do* have sharp claws, and you won't hesitate to use them. You'll be as crabby as a crab and as moody as the Moon phases if someone hurts your feelings or doesn't appear to reciprocate the care and love you so generously offer up to others.

Cancer Decan 2: Cancer with a Side of Scorpio

Sun between 10° and 19°

Born between approximately July 2–July 11

Influenced by Pluto

If you can imagine a Cancer who is even *more* protective over its feelings than a typical one, then you already know what to expect from a second decan Cancer. Thanks to transformational Pluto's influence, you feel each of your feelings with the earthshaking intensity of a Scorpio, but in order to keep your emotions from totally taking control, you feel compelled to put up a bit of a shield to protect your heart, making second decan Cancers appear a little more distant and closed off than the others. Because of your more reserved and guarded nature, it might feel as though, even if you have a lot of friends, no one really *knows* you outside of your closest inner circle. But that's okay, because those few in your inner circle understand the fierce loyalty and devotion you grant to people lucky enough to penetrate your protective shell. You'll do anything to protect your loved ones, and will even put your heart, which you work so hard to protect, on the line.

Cancer Decan 3: Cancer with a Side of Pisces

Sun between 20° and 29°

Born between approximately July 12–July 22

Influenced by Neptune

Dreamier, more sensitive, and more vulnerable than the rest, third decan Cancers wear their hearts on their sleeve in a way the other crabs wouldn't feel safe doing. Your Cancerian maternal instinct is elevated to an ability to actually *heal* others, as Neptune's influence on your decan helps you lean more into your spiritual side and seek out the wounded who need your selfless compassion. Like Pisces, you're deeply drawn to expressing your feelings through creativity, and it will especially manifest in the domestic realm: You're likely to keep a beautifully decorated home and be a master of the domestic arts. You know that your compassion is a gift, so you willingly choose to keep your guard down. In fact, you are considered to be one of the most highly sensitive people in the entire zodiac. Your empathy for others and deep understanding of emotions is boundless! But this also means you should be choosy about the people and energies you surround yourself with, as you're extra sensitive to negativity.

What Kind of Leo Are You?

If you were born with a Leo Sun, you probably know what the deal is with your sign, but knowing which decan of Leo you were born under can tell you more specific and personalized details about how your Sun sign's energy is expressed.

Leo Decan 1: Purely Leo	Sun between 0° and 9° Born between approximately July 23–August 1 Ruled solely by the Sun

First decan Leos are the most Leo of all Leos. These are the superstars of the zodiac, who are *absolutely* built for the pressure and heat of the limelight. You're blessed with the work ethic, creativity, ambition, confidence, *and* charisma that it takes to make it in show business—or any other business or endeavor you put your mind to, for that matter. It's helpful to remember that your humble brag probably doesn't sound too humble once it hits another person's ears, and you *do* have a tendency to get a little bit self-absorbed and narcissistic. But if that's the only consequence of having the confidence, warmth, and positivity that you possess, then no biggie—it's worth it. Because once you learn to shift your focus outward while still maintaining your iconic personal brand of self-expression, there's no limit to what you can achieve.

Leo Decan 2: Leo with a Side of Sagittarius

Sun between 10° and 19°

Born between approximately August 2–August 12

Influenced by Jupiter

More than any other brand of Leo, you're able to confidently assert your intelligence and wit, as you tend to get a little more philosophical in the way you think about things and are more articulate than your fellow lions. You love to learn, travel, and expand your horizons, so while some Leos may be satisfied being the big fish in a small pond, that couldn't be further from who you are. You thrive on exploration and growth, and you're constantly looking for new ways to express who you are, often in the most theatrical, wild, and mystifying ways. Of course, *all* Leos tend to think of themselves as the center of the universe, and that's true for you, too, so beware of becoming *too* opinionated and harsh in asserting your thoughts (or condemning those of others'). But thankfully, your jovial positivity and love for spontaneity make you easy to forgive.

Leo Decan 3: Leo with a Side of Aries

Sun between 20° and 29°

Born between approximately August 13–August 22

Influenced by Mars

All Leos take pride in their work and their image, but none are as goal-oriented, powerful, and driven as a third decan Leo. With the influence of action-packed warrior planet Mars on your personality, you're the most ambitious of the bunch, often setting many goals for yourself at once and putting your entire heart and passion into making them a reality. Because for you, goals aren't just hopes and dreams, or ways to obtain riches and success. Your goals are a reflection of who you *are* and what your legacy will be. Third decan Leos not only need to be the star of the show, but also the leader of the pack. You're naturally suited for a leadership role, have a clear vision of what you want, and know how you can organize others to help you make it happen. Because of this, you expect absolute devotion from the people in your life, and you're willing to reciprocate with the same!

What Kind of Virgo Are You?

If you were born with a Virgo Sun, you probably know what the deal is with your sign, but knowing which decan of Virgo you were born under can tell you more specific and personalized details about how your Sun sign's energy is expressed.

Virgo Decan 1: Purely Virgo	Sun between 0° and 9° Born between approximately August 23–September 2 Ruled solely by Mercury

Typical of the Virgoan nature, through and through, first decan Virgos are meticulous, thorough, committed, and dedicated to being helpful—imagine all the standard Virgo traits exemplified, and that's you! Your attention to detail is unparalleled, and your practical, down-to-earth nature is generally received as a gift to anyone who knows you. Due to the heavy Mercury influence on your nature, you're an especially gifted editor—not just of words, but of spaces and energy, too. You're extra sharp, organized, perceptive, and observant. You're also the most intellectual of the maiden's three faces, and can easily communicate your thoughts, observations, and even criticisms with well-received words. You seek improvement just as zealously as you seek to help improve the world around you: Your patience, meticulousness, and care make you an excellent teacher, while your organization skills, intelligence, and attentiveness make you a top-notch student, as well.

Virgo Decan 2: Virgo with a Side of Capricorn

Sun between 10° and 19°

Born between approximately September 3–September 12

Influenced by Saturn

The reputation of a Virgo for being a perfectionist is taken to new heights by the high-achieving second decan Virgo. You're perhaps the most pragmatic and hardworking of the bunch, and it's impossible for you to leave a task behind until you've successfully mastered it and produced a result that you're satisfied with (and that's no easy task, as you're a hard sell, even to yourself!). You are bestowed with the gift of knowing that your hard work will pay off, because it always does! Learning to be less critical of yourself can help you loosen up and have more fun with your projects, as your skill level and willingness to work for improvements make you capable of virtually *anything*. You can be a bit of a lone wolf, but once close with someone, you bring the classic Virgo warmth, care, and earthy depth.

Virgo Decan 3: Virgo with a Side of Taurus

Sun between 20° and 29°

Born between approximately September 13–September 22

Influenced by Venus

Earth goddess alert! Third decan Virgos lean into their goddess-y, earth maiden natures more than either of the former decans. Your earthly senses are strong and you rely on them heavily, and your observant, detail-oriented nature manifests in you being quite sensitive to the spaces, visuals, and energies around you. Venus's influence also gives your decan a more creative eye than the others: You're likely to apply your incredible attention to detail to artistic endeavors, which gives you a strong aesthetic sense. This means your home is likely to be clean, organized, *and* thoughtfully decorated. If we look hard enough at nature, we can see the art and beauty of it—the sacred geometry, the perfect balance, the spectrum of colors and shapes and textures. You have the beautiful natural ability to see this, which to you makes the natural world the most beautiful artwork of all.

What Kind of Libra Are You?

If you were born with a Libra Sun, you probably know what the deal is with your sign, but knowing which decan of Libra you were born under can tell you more specific and personalized details about how your Sun sign's energy is expressed.

Libra Decan 1: Purely Libra	Sun between 0° and 9° Born between approximately September 23–October 2 Ruled solely by Venus

The most prince and princess-y Libras of the bunch are the first decans. With Venus as your sole Sun sign influence, you're as charming, popular, and sugary-sweet as they come. Bringing peace and balance to any situation you encounter is truly your sole mission; you crumble under the discord of conflict and aggression and use your diplomacy skills to maintain harmony in all of your relationships. You care deeply about being loved and will do just about anything to ensure it. This makes you the most charming and entertaining lover, and the most fun-loving and understanding friend, but it can leave you feeling drained, trapped behind a need to be adored, and unable to express your negative feelings. Even when you're flaky, indecisive, or have fudged the truth, it's hard not to forgive you, as your impeccable sweetness and diplomatic style of communication make anyone who speaks to you—even a passing stranger—feel like the object of your utmost affection.

Libra Decan 2: Libra with a Side of Aquarius

Sun between 10° and 19°

Born between approximately October 3–October 12

Influenced by Uranus

Second decan Libras are some of the most powerful Libran forces—and certainly not a group to be underestimated! You've got the face of a poker player combined with the intellectual ability of a lawyer. While all Libras may enjoy the perks of being charming, stylish, and diplomatic, it's you who knows best how to *use* those talents to get what you want, occasionally downplaying your intellectual air sign nature while playing up your innocent and people-pleasing Venusian sweetness in order to gain the upper hand. That said, you're actually the most serious, stoic, and thoughtful of the Libran family. And while you can easily play the role of everyone's best friend, it can be challenging to open up to others, as your need for balance can morph into a desire to maintain control. With influence from community-oriented Aquarius, you're also the biggest social butterfly of the scales, and you likely fill your calendar with social events with *many* different people and care deeply about a variety of causes.

Libra Decan 3: Libra with a Side of Gemini

Sun between 20° and 29°

Born between approximately October 13–October 22

Influenced by Mercury

The third decan Libra is the more *mercurial* of the bunch, thanks to the sprinkling of Mercury and Gemini in your personality. While peace and balance are still a matter of great importance to you, so is justice—and you're more willing than any of your fellow scales to rock the boat a little bit in order to stand up for what's right (although, of course, you're likely to deliver such opinions with so much grace and diplomacy that no one will be sure whether or not you're *actually* disagreeing with them!). You tend to wear your intelligence on your gorgeous, velvety sleeve, combining your Venusian sex appeal and sweetness with witty and quick Mercurial communication skills. And while all Libras are gifted conversationalists, few can keep up with the impeccable wit, charm, and style with which you conduct each and every interaction. Unfortunately, this tireless perfection-driven performance can lead you to periods of withdrawal.

What Kind of Scorpio Are You?

If you were born with a Scorpio Sun, you probably know what the deal is with your sign, but knowing which decan of Scorpio you were born under can tell you more specific and personalized details about how your Sun sign's energy is expressed.

Scorpio Decan 1: Purely Scorpio	Sun between 0° and 9° Born between approximately October 23–November 1 Ruled solely by Pluto

First decan Scorpios embody the typical Scorp reputation of being the zodiac's dark horse. Your stinger is a weapon, but *you* choose whether you want to be a weapon of destruction or protection. Your incredibly controlled (and yes, sometimes calculated) ability to remain cool and calm on the outside is all the more impressive when you realize that underneath it lies the depth and intensity of a black hole. This also gives you an insane ability to get things done, as you conquer your goals quietly without demanding any attention along the way; in fact, you'd rather fly under the radar, as you can be a little paranoid about people noticing that you're competition and subsequently trying to tear you down. You feel things in the most extreme nature: You might rage hard, yes, but you also love even harder. Your ruling planet Pluto transforms things on an extreme and foundation-shaking level, so it's no surprise that you experience the world with a similar emotional intensity.

Scorpio Decan 2: Scorpio with a Side of Pisces

Sun between 10° and 19°

Born between approximately November 2–November 11

Influenced by Neptune

Extra mysterious, magnetic, and refined, second decan Scorpios are sprinkled with an extra touch of mysticism and sensitivity thanks to the dreamy influence of planet Neptune. This manifests as your being almost *psychically* perceptive of even the tiniest shifts in energy, which enhances your built-in ability to strategize and see things that are beyond the surface, things that remain invisible and imperceptible to most people. But of course, in the typical Scorpio fashion of extremeness, this can either be used to heal and soothe people, or it can be used to judge and attack others. The elusive Neptunian vibes combined with your intense Plutonian energy make you a master of illusions—no one will find a crack in your facade, nor can they pull a fast one on you, as your brain is a Rolodex of receipts that can serve as ammunition if necessary.

Scorpio Decan 3: Scorpio with a Side of Cancer

Sun between 20° and 29°

Born between approximately November 12–November 21

Influenced by the Moon

The most emotionally sensitive Scorpios fall right here in the third decan. Given the influence of the night's luminary—the Moon—you prefer to do your work in the shadows, playing up the classic Scorpio obsession with privacy. You're not necessarily paranoid about stepping into the light, though; it's simply that you feel freer to roam and explore the depths of your rich emotional world under the starry veil of darkness. There's a heavy theme of sacrifice attached to your decan: Like the maternal Cancer, you have an instinct to nurture and are willing to sacrifice bits of yourself in order to protect the people, places, and feelings that are meaningful to you. That said, you're still a strategic Scorpio and are also willing to sacrifice the well-being of another if it brings about what you see as a greater benefit to all.

What Kind of Sagittarius Are You?

If you were born with a Sagittarius Sun, you probably know what the deal is with your sign, but knowing which decan of Sagittarius you were born under can tell you more specific and personalized details about how your Sun sign's energy is expressed.

Sagittarius Decan 1: Purely Sagittarius	Sun between 0° and 9° Born between approximately November 22–December 1 Ruled solely by Jupiter

Classically adventurous, knowledge-hungry, and optimistic, first decan Sagittarians embody the typical Sag-like traits. With Jupiter as your one and only Sun sign ruler, all of your Sag qualities are enhanced and magnified by the giant planet. You're truly the archer, with a passion for learning, experiencing, and philosophizing, always looking to transcend beyond any boundary you may face. You seek growth and expansion in everything you do: You want every conversation, every revelation, and every adventure to be bigger and more mind-expanding than the last! This puts a fire under you, and you're likely to constantly be on the move, impossible to hold down when it comes to your pursuit of knowledge and fun alike. This also, however, makes you easily restless and quickly bored, as you require constant stimulation and excitement.

Sagittarius Decan 2: Sagittarius with a Side of Aries

Sun between 10° and 19°

Born between approximately December 2–December 11

Influenced by Mars

The second decan Sagittarius is perhaps the most uncontained of the bunch! Your classic Sagittarian spontaneous and excitement-loving nature is enhanced by the bold and action-packed presence of Mars in this decan, making you extra headstrong, impulsive, and ready to drop everything at a moment's notice to take on your next unplanned adventure (midnight flight to Paris, anyone?). Like fellow fire sign Aries, your leadership qualities take the spotlight, and you can become a sort of warrior when it comes to propelling your ideals, hunger for knowledge, and growth of humanity. That said, your blunt and straightforward Sagittarian communication style is sometimes taken to new levels of combative intensity thanks to warrior planet Mars's influence, and what feels like simple honesty to you might come off as a scathing takedown to the recipient of such a tirade.

Sagittarius Decan 3: Sagittarius with a Side of Leo

Sun between 20° and 29°

Born between approximately December 12–December 21

Influenced by the Sun

You know how we discussed Sagittarians being good at a party? Well, no archer can attract a crowd, command a room, and own a spotlight quite like a third decan Sag can. You're a born performer with an endlessly fascinating and entertaining personality, and your charisma and confidence are unparalleled. These sparkly qualities give you the ability to connect with an even wider range of people and experiences—you make friends everywhere you go. Your natural sense of optimism is enhanced even further by the influence of the always bright 'n' shiny Sun, making you a joyful and gregarious presence. However, your booming confidence and boundless positivity combined with your classic Sagittarian spontaneity and taste for adventure can make you quite the risk taker and feed into your occasionally reckless nature, so be careful not to let your confidence make you short-sighted.

What Kind of Capricorn Are You?

If you were born with a Capricorn Sun, you probably know what the deal is with your sign, but knowing which decan of Capricorn you were born under can tell you more specific and personalized details about how your Sun sign's energy is expressed.

Capricorn Decan 1: Purely Capricorn	Sun between 0° and 9° Born between approximately December 22–December 31 Ruled solely by Saturn

The first decan Capricorn might very well be *the* capstone Capricorn. When you work, you work *hard*—and there are absolutely *no* exceptions for you, are there? You are proud and honorable, determined and focused, tireless in your efforts like a goat working its way up a mountain. For better or worse, you have an insane amount of self-discipline—it's as if there's a constant threat of the whip lurking just behind you, motivating you to work with an amount of energy and focus that most people couldn't muster up for even the most *passionate* of their passion projects. You're a true crusader in all that you do, and your presence will always be noticed and felt by everyone around you, whether or not you're the silent and serious type or a more gregarious Cap. Even if you enjoy lightheartedness and fun, there's always a serious, goal-focused tone: You never take your eye off of what you see as the prize!

Capricorn Decan 2: Capricorn with a Side of Taurus

Sun between 10° and 19°

Born between approximately January 1–January 9

Influenced by Venus

Notably less serious and more relaxed than your average Capricorn, second decan Caps allow themselves room to enjoy the finer things in life—the finer things, of course, that they've rightfully earned. Venus's luxury-loving influence highlights your fantastic ability with money; you were born for material wealth, and like all Caps, financial stability is a necessity for you. Balancing a checkbook becomes an extreme sport under your watchful eye, and counting up your pennies (or, more likely, your stocks) might be one of your favorite hobbies, as having money to afford the beautiful things you love and that bring you comfort actually matters more to you than the constant success that other Caps crave. Everything you do becomes an art form: Your work is your artistry, and you treat every responsibility with the care and pride of an artist in front of a canvas. Your high taste level and work ethic combined can make you arrogant, so call on your earthy nature to keep you grounded!

Capricorn Decan 3: Capricorn with a Side of Virgo

Sun between 20° and 29°

Born between approximately January 10–January 19

Influenced by Mercury

All Capricorns are wunderkinds in a sense, with their infallible goal-conquering nature, but being the best comes with an almost *disturbing* amount of ease for the third decan Capricorn. Thanks to Mercury's fast-footed and quick-thinking influence, you're bestowed with a swiftness and sharpness that's unusual for your notoriously slow-but-steady and yes, sometimes old-school sign. This levels up your natural Cap wisdom by also adding sheer intellectualism, which makes you quite shrewd and competent when it comes to acquiring material wealth and success. Virgo's influence also highlights your relentless and obsessive effort to be your best at all times. Like all Capricorns, you refuse to quit before you reach your goal, but you'll also refuse to reach your goal unless you're reaching it with the amount of meticulous effort and perfection that you constantly expect of yourself. Few can deliver, but you? Always.

What Kind of Aquarius Are You?

If you were born with an Aquarius Sun, you probably know what the deal is with your sign, but knowing which decan of Aquarius you were born under can tell you more specific and personalized details about how your Sun sign's energy is expressed.

Aquarius Decan 1: Purely Aquarius	Sun between 0° and 9° Born between approximately January 20–January 29 Ruled solely by Uranus

First decan Aquarians are every bit the originality-focused, avant-garde, forward-thinking, practically alien beings that we expect an Aquarius to be (and love them for!). Your progressive, quirky, out-there nature shows through with effortless zeal, and any attempts to tone down your individuality or uniqueness are truly fruitless! With such a heavy-handed influence from zany, inspiration-giving, revolution-starting Uranus, you're a powerhouse when it comes to generating innovative and out-of-the-box ideas and creating visionary utopian ideals for the future. You have the uncanny ability to relate to almost *anyone*, no matter how different their life and experiences have looked; that's part of what makes you such a natural-born humanitarian! Yet at the same time, you may sometimes feel the need to isolate yourself completely due to the fact that you don't seem to relate to *anyone*. Such is the paradoxical nature of the first decan Aquarius.

Aquarius Decan 2: Aquarius with a Side of Gemini

Sun between 10° and 19°

Born between approximately January 30–February 9

Influenced by Mercury

Sharp as a tack and quick as a bolt of lightning: this is the second decan Aquarius. Your behaviors and ways of thinking might come off as less unpredictable and wily than the average Aquarius, as you lean heavily into logic and have a methodical, organized, and intellectual way of thinking; in other words, you've got your system down. That said, you are *forever* young at heart, full of a childlike energy and excitement. Thanks to Gemini's incredible communication skills (and need to say *everything* that crosses their mind), this sign's influence allows you to easily communicate your avant-garde thoughts and ideas to the world. This is wonderful, as it allows you to connect with people and see eye to eye (which can be a struggle for our out-there, one-of-a-kind Aquas), but it also slightly lessens your mystique, so instead of seeming like a bizarre alien being, you're more likely to be seen as a really fascinating human. Still a good thing. That said, you easily maintain your classically Aquarian free-thinking and unconventional nature.

Aquarius Decan 3: Aquarius with a Side of Libra

Sun between 20° and 29°

Born between approximately February 10–February 18

Influenced by Venus

The most socially charming and *people*-people of the bunch, third decan Aquarians have the warmest and most social personalities of all. Because you're more willing to show (and feel!) emotions than your fellow Aquas, this actually makes you extra mysterious, as it allows people to feel a little bit closer to you than if you were completely closed off. With loving Venus in your corner, you can be quite a flirt. You're like a beautiful alien, and the things that make you different and unique are *exactly* the things people are drawn to you for. Sweet and sugary Venus also highlights your natural idealism: You have a firm belief that the future should be *beautiful*, and your desire to ensure this drives almost everything you do. You could spend all day fantasizing over the magical utopia you seek to build for future generations, but you can also get lost in your head, making you come off as loopy and perhaps even a little ditzy.

What Kind of Pisces Are You?

If you were born with a Pisces Sun, you probably know what the deal is with your sign, but knowing which decan of Pisces you were born under can tell you more specific and personalized details about how your Sun sign's energy is expressed.

Pisces Decan 1: Purely Pisces	Sun between 0° and 9° Born between approximately February 19–February 28 Ruled solely by Neptune

First decan Pisces are sweet and gentle little fish indeed. You're dreamy and creative, constantly drawing inspiration from the universe within which you feel so deeply connected. You're bestowed with an incredible gift to turn your deep feelings into art (or at least express yourself via creative means *somehow*). Generally quite passive, you tend to have a sweet if not slightly loopy demeanor and the only thing that can get you *really* riled up is hate and cruelty—there's no place for such low-vibrational and unpleasant qualities in your corner of the sea. Part of why these things are so intolerable is because of your deep, unshakable empathy that allows you to almost psychically sense the thoughts, feelings, and insecurities of others. This is what makes you so beautifully compassionate, but can also be a source of great pain, as you have a tendency to take on other people's problems and feel the sting of their sorrow as if it's your own.

Pisces Decan 2: Pisces with a Side of Cancer	Sun between 10° and 19°
	Born between approximately March 1–March 9
	Influenced by the Moon

While all Pisces wear their hearts on their sleeves, second decan Pisces may be the most emotionally vulnerable of them all. Regardless of your gender, you've got a classic feminine mystique about you. The moody Moon, queen of the darkness, influences you by making you slippery and shadowy. You're rather ethereal in nature and it can be difficult for anyone to see your complexities by looking straight on. Like the fish you are, you absorb your environment straight through your skin with an incredible show of empathy. This is a gift, yes, but if you don't take care to stay aware of your surroundings and protect yourself against toxic and abusive people, you could be seen as a target and easily taken advantage of. That said, the transparency with which you operate is what also makes you one of the most sparkling, beautiful, and mystical souls. You were built for a world much kinder and gentler than ours, but the fact that you refuse to let it harden you or make you callous is truly an act of resistance.

Pisces Decan 3: Pisces with a Side of Scorpio	Sun between 20° and 29°
	Born between approximately March 10–March 19
	Influenced by Pluto

The third decan Pisces have an edge that their fellow fishes simply don't possess. You have a fierceness and tenacity that can pull you out of your classic Piscean fantasy world and actually help connect you to the tangible space within which your corporeal body operates. You certainly prefer your dreamlands, but the real world can be fun too, huh? Unlike the other decans, you're even known to have a bit of a competitive streak, although your deep compassion for others keeps you from getting carried away with the more aggressive aspects of such a quality. Your driven nature combined with your natural idealistic and whimsical imagination can sometimes make you an impulsive person: You love to experiment, take risks, and reach levels of intensity that make you *feel* things, especially *new* feelings. That said, you're sometimes unable to see the danger that could lie ahead in your endeavors, so while this can make you prone to trouble, it also allows you to reach a little further in the material world than some Pisces care to put their energy toward.

MEET *your* MOON SIGN

You at
Your Realest

While your showy Sun sign prefers to be in the driver's seat of your personality car (as well as in the spotlight of pop culture's view of astrology), your Moon sign is always in the vehicle, too, occasionally taking the wheel when the Sun goes down, which is when the vulnerable shadow sides come out and reveal things you wouldn't reveal in the sunny light of day. **In many ways, your Moon sign is *just* as pertinent to the cosmic puzzle of who you are as your Sun sign is.** Because while the Sun may be the great father of the zodiac, representing the divine masculine energy in all of us, the Moon is our astrological mother. If you've read the section on the planets, then you already know the deal with the Moon and what it represents in astrology in general: She's nurturing, emotional, sensitive, and intuitive. She appreciates safety, family, comfort. She's focused on gently creating a home within each of us where we can be vulnerable, feel our feelings, trust our intuition, care for ourselves, and express ourselves emotionally. But depending on where the Moon falls in your chart (and what sign its energy is expressed through), you likely express and seek these qualities in very unique ways.

Only those closest to you have the pleasure of seeing you step into the soft, ethereal glow of your Moon sign on the regular. Just as the Moon itself generally shows its face only at night, your Moon sign is also more careful and cautious about who it expresses itself around. It appreciates having the security blanket that the night's darkness provides.

Because of the Moon's maternal and nurturing nature, your Moon sign can also be indicative of your mother or another motherly figure in your life, and it speaks to your *own* ways of being nurturing and maternal to others. Of course, the Moon is also extraordinarily important in romantic relationships, within which we usually feel very vulnerable and emotional, and through which we seek (and provide) comfort, nurturing, and emotional safety.

Whenever we're not under the intensely bright and public spotlight of the Sun, we can comfortably slip into our pajamas and embrace our more gentle, sensitive, and vulnerable lunar qualities. Our Moon sign shows us how we express emotion, how we nurture and want to be nurtured. In the quiet of the Moon's night, we can hear our intuition through whichever of the zodiac signs' lenses our nighttime luminary happens to shine through.

Just as we occasionally see the Moon's face floating in the sky in the middle of the daytime, the people outside of your inner circle may catch flashes of your Moon sign in your everyday life, too. Your Moon sign

When you're alone and no one's watching and you can really, truly be yourself—no pretenses, no masks to put on, no performances to upkeep—*that's* when your Moon sign comes out. Similarly, your Moon sign comes out when you're with people you feel safe with and are most comfortable around—the people you're not afraid to be vulnerable with.

shows up to the party if you're feeling emotional, *or* when you want to self-soothe to help regulate your emotions. It shows up if you're having a rough day and just want to be babied, *or* when you're showing a little TLC to someone *else* who is having a rough day and needs some babying. When your ego starts to break down (the ego that is represented in astrology by the Sun, of course), your Moon sign begins to rise. Your Moon sign is the raw, emotional, uncensored version of you.

The Moon may not run the world like the Sun does, but it *does* control the tides. In other words, the Moon rules the undercurrents of our Sun sign's brighter personality. Like the other planets, it gives nuance, but in the case of the Moon, it's a part of ourselves that we interact with internally every day. For example, an Aries Sun person with a Pisces Moon may be gentler and more sensitive than your average headstrong, foolhardy Aries. Or a typically reserved and down-to-earth Virgo Sun might be extra dramatic and performative in their emotions if they have a Leo Moon.

In order to calculate your Moon sign, you'll need your exact birth *date* (the day *and* the year), and in some cases, you'll need your exact birth *time*, too. To refresh your memory, the Moon is the fastest moving of the major planets and transits into a new sign about every two and a half days. This means someone born on March 11 *this* year will likely have a different Moon sign than a person who was born on March 11 *last* year. There are lots of free charts available online that will show you the transits of the Moon over the past decades, so you can look up your exact birth date to track its location. But if you are one of the approximate one-third of people who were born on a day during which the Moon switches signs, you'll need your exact birth time so you can identify exactly which of the two signs the Moon was actually in when you were born.

Moon in Aries

Aries is a self-starting cardinal fire sign, so they rush toward their emotions on high-speed, which means that, yes, they sometimes crash and burn. But such is the exciting roller coaster of feeling with an Aries Moon! When this Moon feels something, they *really* feel it. They'll wear every last shred of their heart on their sleeve. Fair warning: These impulsive types aren't very careful with their emotions, and they subsequently may not be the most careful with yours, either. But this isn't because they don't care; it's simply that Aries Moons can be emotionally reckless, jumping straight into situations that could easily shatter their own hearts or someone else's. Fire signs are all passion and not necessarily *emotion*, so while Aries Moons are zealous and excitable in their happy feelings, it may be hard for them to express their darker, more difficult, or more nuanced emotional experiences.

How to Show an Aries Moon You Care: Aries Moons can be a little bit babyish in the way they process their feelings, so when it comes to a nurturing response, fight their fire with fire and up the babying factor here. Let them throw a little fit (for a few minutes, anyway) to show them you can handle it, and go out of your way to coddle and cradle. They have very little patience, but ironically *extra* patience is what these Moons require. Indulging in their requests, however pouty, will make them feel super loved.

Moon in Taurus

As fixed earth signs, Taurus Moons are reliable, slow moving, and perhaps even a bit cautious with their feelings. The general steadiness of this sign gives stability to their emotions, and that peaceful stability is part of why the usually moody Moon is so happy here (it's the sign of her exaltation)! They're naturally grounded *and* gentle, a lovely combination that allows them to help others sort through their emotions in a practical, drama-free way. Taurus Moons deeply appreciate safe and comfortable spaces (in the form of their homes, families, friendships, or romantic relationships), and once they get into a groove of a comfort zone, they won't be quick to find reason to leave. In fact, it can be hard to make a stubborn Taurus Moon do anything outside of their usual routine. Earth signs tend to focus more on their physical senses than their intuitive ones, so Taurus Moons feel their feelings and intuitions in their bodies, like a sixth sense.

How to Show a Taurus Moon You Care: Comfort and luxury is the love language for a Taurus Moon. They relate to both the outside world *and* their inner selves through their senses, so show them you care by taking them out to get some delicious comfort food, pouring them a glass or two (or five) of fine wine, or offering them a nice full-body massage. Showing them kind and loving physical touch and sensory pleasure makes them feel super nurtured.

Moon in Gemini

Gemini Moons are mutable air signs, and they spend a lot of time verbally making sense of their constantly changing emotions. Given the Mercurial nature of Gemini energy, Gemini Moons can be a little extreme in the polarities of their feelings. Get a Gemini Moon comfortable enough with you, and you'll see that they can be hot one second, cold the next, and often experience feeling two conflicting ways at once. That said, this also means they can snap out of a dark mood with relative ease and maintain a good level of positivity, and they can be quite uplifting emotionally to others. Gemini Moons appreciate talking through their emotions and are quite adept at expressing themselves verbally, although they might have a tendency to go a little TMI on the details. Similarly, their curious nature can sometimes lead them into crossing some privacy boundaries with the people they're close to, as they're not always easily able to tell the difference between prying and inquiring.

How to Show a Gemini Moon You Care: Be a good listener (this sign *loves* to talk) and allow them to talk through their feelings, fears, and emotions with you, then offer honest and thoughtful feedback in return. Ask questions that can help them process their thoughts and show that you're paying attention. This is the sign of communication, so having a safe space where they can freely break the big, scary feelings down into *words* feels warming and comforting to them.

Moon in Cancer

As the premiere and cardinal water sign, Cancer Moons are deeply in touch with their emotions and highly sensitive in *every* way. Any attempt to suppress their many emotions will leave them feeling super moody and out of touch with themselves, which can subsequently lead them to withdraw into their crabby shells and lick their emotional wounds all alone. They have a *ton* of emotion, but truly do need the safety and protection of the night's sky—aka a *really* comfortable place or person—in order to come *out* of that security blanket of a shell. Cancer Moon people are also highly sensitive and perceptive. They're natural-born nurturers, and can spot a wounded bird or a tearful eye from a mile away. And when they do, they'll rush to the rescue with their emotional first-aid kit. The Moon is in its domicile in Cancer, so this is often a dominant placement for people, meaning that no matter what the person's Sun sign, the Cancer Moon's emotionally centered energy will shine through.

How to Show a Cancer Moon You Care: As the most domestic of the Moon signs, Cancer Moons would appreciate scheduling a low-key night at home to talk and cuddle under warm blankets, as they enjoy retreating into a safe and cozy space for emotional healing. Cooking a homemade meal for them will *more* than show the love. Better still, why not let them nurture *you*? This maternal sign feels most confident and appreciated when taking care of others, so accept their offer to pamper you and coddle *your* feelings in return, even if it makes you blush.

Moon in Leo

This fixed fire sign is full of passion and isn't afraid to let its emotions take center stage—and center stage they will take, because this Moon placement has a flair for the *dramatic*. Let's just say it: Leo Moons *love* drama. Even if their Sun sign hates it and their Mercury sign wants to kill them for it, they can't help it: Moon in Leo people are natural-born performers when it comes to their emotions. They might fly off the handle and punch a wall when angry, sob their eyes out when sad, or do a happy dance when they're elated. If they love someone, expect them to launch into a gushing soliloquy about their feelings. When they feel something, they really do need to express it, so art is a wonderful emotional outlet for this placement. Writing stories, monologues, or music about their deepest feelings can lead to some really honest and beautiful work.

How to Show a Leo Moon You Care: A Leo Moon's emotions need a spotlight *and* an audience, so make them feel emotionally *seen*: When they're in the feels, maintain eye contact, don't interrupt them, and let them know they've got your attention. Practice conversational skills that acknowledge that you're truly *hearing* them (like repeating what they say for clarity), and be an active audience for their emotional form of storytelling. Knowing they can safely show you their dramatic emotional side makes them feel safe.

Moon in Virgo

As mutable earth signs, Virgos are grounded in their emotional energy, and maybe a little willing to suppress it altogether. Their relaxed demeanor around emotionally fraught situations makes them stable and reliable, but also hints at what a struggle it can be for them to get lost in a feeling, or even acknowledge that a feeling is there at all. That's because Virgo Moon people really want to *rationalize* their emotions, but they must remember that feelings aren't necessarily problems to be solved. They love order and organization, which, of course, is a virtually impossible ask when navigating the free-flowing and often messy waters of emotions and the not-always-logical realm of their own intuition. That said, Virgo Moons are naturally caring and nurturing. They prioritize health and purity, so if they feel an emotion building up beyond their ability to suppress it, they will seek a healthy outlet. They're natural-born fixers, so expect for them to immediately start writing up a list of ways you can solve your problems if you turn to them for emotional advice.

How to Show a Virgo Moon You Care: Always pay attention to the details, and do them a practical favor if they're stressed, overwhelmed, or feeling down—think washing their car while they're out of town, offering to jot down a shopping list and hit the grocery store for them during a busy week, or even just texting them a gentle reminder about something they mentioned needing to get done. Knowing that they can count on you to be sensible and on top of stuff is the most comforting gift you can offer.

Moon in Libra

These cardinal air Moons are all about balance and seek harmony within their inner selves. They're very socially conscious about maintaining equality in relationships, so you'll rarely catch them emotionally dumping or bringing others down with moodiness, and they're always willing to listen to *you* in return for your time. But this can also lead to them constantly "keeping it light" with their feelings in order to not bring about any discord or rock the boat. Libra Moons are very social and love to feel popular, but also require a balance of deep, quality heart-to-heart time in addition to their wild outings. They're not above booking themselves silly with social engagements in order to ignore the emotions lurking just beneath their surface, so be sure to plan quality time with a Libra Moon, too, where you can dive into deep conversations and really connect.

How to Show a Libra Moon You Care: Libra Moons want to be your sought-after party friend, yes, but they'll feel *extra* special if they know you're also the friend they can turn to in a heartbreak. They have trouble saying when they're struggling, so text them first and ask how they are repeatedly if you have an inkling that they're down. Or just forget all this and let them give you a makeover—these Venus-ruled Moons equate beautifying something with making it better, so indulge their need to aesthetically enhance.

Moon in Scorpio

Scorpio is a fixed water sign, and the Moon here can make someone extremely intense, deep, and committed in their feelings. While the other water Moons (Cancer, Pisces) tend to wear their hearts on their sleeves, Scorpio Moons are better at hiding their highly emotional (and sometimes emotionally *volatile*) nature—that is, until they get moody or feel betrayed or hurt and start lashing out vindictively. However, Scorpio Moons have perhaps the deepest capacity for taking on the emotional burdens of others. They'll go to hell and back with the people they care about, and no amount of intensity or raw feeling could scare them away. Having them in your corner when times get tough feels like having an emotional warrior by your side. Similarly, they throw themselves wholeheartedly into each of their own feelings, no matter how dark, which can be overwhelming, so having healthy creative outlets and a trusted inner circle to help them dissect their moods is helpful.

How to Show a Scorpio Moon You Care: Building trust is a *must*. Sticking around for the long haul with a Scorpio Moon and proving to them time and time again that their secrets, insecurities, and darkest thoughts are safe with you is requisite if you want to make them feel cared for, as they deeply value privacy and loyalty, and get paranoid they'll be betrayed if they show their vulnerability. They're also the sign of transformation, so offer up your unconditional acceptance as they evolve into new feelings and continually reinvent their paradigms.

Moon in Sagittarius

As the mutable fire sign of the bunch, Sagittarius Moons are the zodiac's emotional free spirits. They treat all emotional and spiritual experiences as opportunities to learn and expand their awareness, and they're whimsical and go-with-the-flow with their feelings; they're not big "dwellers" and would rather greet their emotions and then wave goodbye when it's time to move on. Sag Moons tend to have a wild and adventurous streak, even if their Sun sign makes them *usually* more reserved, so they're willing to be spontaneous and take risks, and they don't fear the consequences of pain and heartbreak the way some lunar signs may, thanks to their boundless optimism. Always honest to the point of being blunt, Sag Moons don't want to hide what's on their mind or in their heart. They enjoy keeping their spirits light. They'll toss their baggage out wherever they can to lessen the load, so don't take it personally if they tell you their troubles and then jet off to the next exciting thing!

How to Show a Sagittarius Moon You Care: Space and freedom are absolute *musts* for these fire Moons, so never smother them, demand things of them, or back them into a corner if they're feeling down. They're natural-born emotional explorers, so letting them navigate their feelings without too much interference (but sticking nearby for when they *do* need support!) makes them feel safe but not suffocated. Always reciprocate their honesty and straightforwardness with more of the same, as they prefer everything to be out in the open.

Moon in Capricorn

Capricorn is the cardinal earth sign, so these Moons have a pragmatic and goal-oriented approach to the world of emotions. They tend to deal with feelings (their own and others') in a very matter-of-fact and reserved way: They accept that feelings exist, but that doesn't mean they're going to indulge them or make them obvious. Expect them to be *this close* to making an Excel spreadsheet that helps them track and better control their feelings at all times. But despite their serious and sometimes taciturn nature, they *do* feel a lot inside; they just direly don't want their feelings to be a distraction from their material goals (or anyone else's), and they feel obligated to make sense of and justify emotions. Because of their logical nature, they can also struggle to give much credence to their intuition, so it's important for them to take conscious time to give their vulnerable side some fresh air, open up to the people they trust, and shush their inner critic.

How to Show a Capricorn Moon You Care: Offer up an objective, nonjudgmental ear—oh, and your complete and total loyalty. Because Capricorn Moons are some of the most responsible people around, they need to know you're reliable and committed to being there for them; they'd never mess with someone's feelings, and they expect the same from their few confidants. Indulge them when they inevitably crack a self-deprecating joke or two—comic relief, especially at their own typically serious expense, is one of their favorite ways to let off steam and process their feelings! Oh, and they love money, so make sure your gifts are only the highest quality and *nothing* cheap.

Moon in Aquarius

The fixed air sign of Aquarius has a reputation for being a little detached from the world of feelings, so this lunar placement can breed a slightly emotionally unaware type, but that doesn't detract from how thoughtful and caring they are. It's not that Aquarius Moons don't have emotions—they do, of course, as we're all human! It's simply that they are extraordinarily forward-thinking, global people by nature, so the idea of getting swept up in a whirlpool of *personal feelings* (their own or someone else's) sounds rather unpleasant to them, and sort of like a waste of time. That said, this detachment gives them the gift of being able to view emotions from a very objective place, making them thoughtful advice givers who care deeply about the suffering of people on the whole. Because Aquarius Moons struggle to identify their feelings, they might sometimes come bubbling out of them in a self-righteous way, as if they're be-all and end-all facts instead of simply fleeting emotions. It's important that they find ways to access the vulnerable side of their heart.

How to Show an Aquarius Moon You Care: These Moons require space to explore their foreign feelings privately, so avoid prying or trying to force anything out of them. For as naturally social and friendship-oriented as they are, it's often easier for them to do this sort of processing alone. Knowing that you see them for the unique individuals they are—emotions and all—is all they need from you to feel safe and nurtured. Oh, and if they do open up to you, there's one rule: no blanket statements. They hate stereotypes or being clumped in with any one crowd or way of thinking!

Moon in Pisces

Pisces Moons are mutable water signs, meaning they're extremely in tune with their emotions and their intuition. This dreamy Moon placement makes people deeply empathetic and almost emotionally psychic, although it also gives them a tendency to get lost in a fantasy world and occasionally detach from reality during times of emotional crisis. Pisces Moons can't help that they're so easily swept away by whirlpools of emotion. They love to indulge their feelings: If they're sad, they'll probably watch a sad movie to feel even *more* sad. They're also naturally spiritual beings possessing a very clear connection to their intuition, often favoring it over facts. Pisces Moons tend to naturally gravitate toward expressing their emotions (or connecting with others' emotions) through creativity—think writing poetry, listening to or playing music, drawing and painting, and anything else that can give a symbolic form to a feeling.

How to Show a Pisces Moon You Care: Make your relationship with them a safe space that allows them total freedom in their creative expression *and* full emotional vulnerability—that means no emotional conversation is off the table, and no sad song is too depressing to be skipped on the playlist. Text them a link to any song that makes you cry, any poem that strikes an emotional chord, or any old photos that make you nostalgic; they'll appreciate the symbolic exchange of experiences and the fostering of emotional interconnectedness.

MEET
your
RISING
SIGN

You at
a Glance

Your rising sign is also known as your ascendant, and you might see it stylized as "AC" or "ASC" if you look up your birth chart. Just as the rising Sun is the first impression of light upon the day, your rising sign represents the first impression of *you* upon the world. Your rising sign is likely the first astrological influence that others will see in you at first glance. It's not necessarily who you are at your *core* (that would be your Sun sign), but it's more about who you are on the outside. It governs your impulse reactions, general disposition, and manner of presenting yourself. It's sort of a surface-level indicator of your personality.

Let's review what the rising sign even *is*, because it's not a planet. The rising sign is determined based on the point in the zodiac that the eastern horizon line is on at the time of your birth. This sign is integral to the layout of your birth chart, because it indicates the placement of the first house cusp (and therefore dictates the layout of all twelve subsequent houses on the zodiac wheel, too). The journey of the rising sign through the zodiac each day is a swift one, as it moves much faster than any of the major planets do—it switches signs approximately every two hours (which means that it makes a full rotation through the twelve signs of the zodiac approximately every twenty-four hours).

This means that while you might be able to figure out which sign each planet was in on your birthday *without* an exact birth time by consulting an ephemeris or an online chart calculator (assuming a planet didn't happen to switch signs on the day you were born, of course), the same can't be said for your rising sign. It's virtually impossible to know for sure what your rising sign is if you don't have a birth time—and if you don't know that, then you won't know which *house* your planets live in (since the cusp of your first house is dictated by the exact degree of your rising sign, and the rest of the houses follow suit). That said, checking your birth certificate or texting your parents is now a high-priority task if you want to figure that out!

Rising signs are obviously important when it comes to the layout of our birth charts, but they can also tell us a lot about our personalities, which is why they are considered one of the "big three" signs that make up the foundation of our astrological selves. Your rising sign is kind of your *brand*. It's the part of you that shows up when someone meets you for the first time or has a quick interaction with you. It also shows up strongly when you're in a social setting, especially when you're aware of the fact that you're making a social impression on people. Whichever sign our ascendant is in greatly influences our mannerisms, our demeanor, our immediate reactions to things, and even our physical appearance (yes, our rising sign rules over and even dictates our looks!). Thus, this sign has a major influence over the first impression that we make on others and our overall personality presentation. Obviously, we have a whole solar system full of planetary influences that contribute to who we are astrologically, but the rising sign is the face that we show someone upon first introductions, so it's a major one!

> Many people feel that it's your rising sign, not your Sun sign, that shows up most obviously when you meet someone. So don't be surprised if someone mistakes you for your rising sign, or vice versa!

Since I clearly love talking about frozen treats, you can think of the rising sign as the cherry on top of your zodiac sundae. The Sun is the ice cream flavor and the base of the dish, the Moon is the warm chocolate sauce that gets poured over everything like a cozy and comforting blanket, but your rising sign is that final touch that gives the first impression. It's your unique surface-level flair that catches people's eyes and makes you *you*.

One of the best ways to get to know the rising signs is to "meet them" at a party, because that's a great example of a place where our rising sign might take the front seat. So that said, welcome to your personal rising sign mixer.

ARIES RISING: Chill? Never heard of it. No matter what your Sun sign, having an Aries ascendant will give you an impulsive and wild firecracker of an edge. These are very energetic personalities who possess a bold and impossible-to-miss presence. Your hot-blooded energy can be divisive at times, as you can be very direct when it comes to expressing your emotions. Outbursts of passion, opinions, and even rage aren't uncommon for you, but your forward-charging attitude ensures that the storm can pass as quickly as it came on. Aries risings tend to be very physical and energetic people, so you like to wear things that you can move around in (whether it be on a dance floor or in a fistfight) *and* that show off your fire-sign confidence. Because Aries is the natural ruler of the first house, this is a very natural-feeling placement, and people will instinctively turn to you for your leadership qualities.

The Horoscope You Should Be Reading

Did you know that reading your horoscope for your rising sign may actually prove to be more accurate than reading it for your Sun sign? Most horoscopes are written under the assumption that the Sun sign is also the sign of the first house, but unless your Sun sign and rising sign are the same, that's not necessarily the most accurate reading (although it still holds some significance, given the power of the Sun in everyone's chart!).

That said, because it's actually your *rising* sign that dictates the way your birth chart's twelve houses align with the twelve signs of the zodiac, you're more likely to identify with the horoscope for your rising sign. I recommend reading *both* from now on and seeing which one resonates more deeply with you!

TAURUS RISING: Regardless of your Sun sign, having a Taurus ascendant brings a majorly grounding and stable energy to your presence. Talking to you at a party feels like the social equivalent of snagging the cozy corner of the couch—your clear sense of loyalty can put people at ease. You come off as super down-to-earth and aware of your physical senses. You love your comforts more than anything, so expect for there to be a part of you that's resistant to change and less inclined to leave your comfort zone. You really do appreciate security, to the point of being stubborn. Taurus risings are naturally sensual and luxurious, so your style is classic and you might occasionally enjoy showing off an expensive outfit, high-end haircut, or designer shoes every once in a while.

GEMINI RISING: Social, curious, and quick-thinking, a Gemini rising is a fun and buoyant personality type. You come off as inquisitive, social, and perhaps a little bit difficult to peg or put in a box. Your mind runs at a million miles a minute, which makes you hard to read. Gemini's influence is a flighty and slippery one! But you like it like that. While you're masterful at small talk and can chitchat for hours, you're secretly choosy about who you let get *actually* close to you. That said, you're great socially, and are definitely a chameleon when it comes to your ability to connect with all different groups of people. You're the person at the party who will have somehow chatted with everyone there by the end of the night. You probably enjoy experimenting with fashion and give a good amount of thought to choosing looks that express what you want to portray at any given event.

CANCER RISING: There's something about Cancer rising people that simply feels like home, so meeting one may feel like meeting someone you've already known. As a Cancer rising, you're a natural-born nurturer, so whether or not you *like* someone, you tend to find it in you to offer a thoughtful and sympathetic ear anyway. This can make you a magnet for people who want to dump their life story on you, which you handle with much grace and patience, but you're also cautious with who you share energy with given your need to protect your gentle soul. You appreciate feeling comfortable and secure, so being around chaotic personality types is not your style. You probably have a feminine and somewhat modest sense of style, and you're probably quick to change into a comfy pair of sweats immediately upon arriving home from the function.

LEO RISING: Regardless of how laid-back or reserved your Sun sign is, your Leo rising will always give you a flashy streak and a flair for drama. You feel comfortable being the center of attention (which happens easily and regularly, as you naturally attract lots of it), and you tend to be gregarious, highly charismatic, and warm in your personality. Upon meeting you, your unshakable sense of confidence really stands out to people: You usually appear quite sure of yourself, even if you're feeling insecure deep down. Although sometimes you're a little *overly* enthusiastic in your endeavors, maybe aiming a little too high, your magnetic warmth makes you easily forgivable. It's hard to take your eyes off a Leo rising in their element! You enjoy looking good and are not afraid to flaunt a flashy, eye-catching, or even revealing outfit—a few sequins or sparkles never hurt anyone, right?

VIRGO RISING: Let's be honest: If you're a Virgo rising, it always looks like you've got your act together, even when you definitely *don't*. Therein lies the power of your ascendant. You've got a practical and down-to-earth quality about you that makes you seem reliable, like people can trust that you'll come through in the ways that you say you will. This placement can make you come off as a bit reserved and shy, so it takes a minute for people to get to know you. You love a classic, simple fashion moment, and while you're not vain, you also like to look put together, so efforts are made in that department. Oh, and side note, you're definitely that person who has everything anyone could ever need in their purse, be it tampons, hair ties, pain medicine, lip balm, or maybe even a glue stick (hey, you never know!).

LIBRA RISING: Libra risings are some of the sweetest people around! It's always fun to meet a Libra rising, as their natural diplomacy and charm make even the most rushed bit of small talk somehow *not* awkward. No matter your Sun sign, you are bound to be friendly, personable, charming, and social, and you are a lovely addition to any party or social gathering, as you're a human antidote to awkwardness. Libra risings tend to take pride in their appearance and are masterful at achieving a natural look (even if you did spend two hours and $100 worth of makeup on it). They're almost always as pleasant to look at as they are to chat with, and tend to take care of their appearance, keeping themselves looking clean and natural.

SCORPIO RISING: These enigmatic people possess a cool, calm, collected, and maybe even *dark* air of mystery about them. A Scorpio rising has a very powerful presence, and people tend to want to listen to them when they speak (although they are thoughtful about what they choose to share). They have an intensity about them that can intimidate some people, but usually it draws people in. They also tend to give off a bit of an erotic and sexual vibe, even when they dress conservatively; their raw energy can feel a bit primal. Expect for the Scorpio rising person to have gone through a goth or emo phase at some point in their lives, as they like to express themselves in a slightly moody, edgy fashion—black clothing is a must. They're also known for their intense, dark, and mysterious eyes.

SAGITTARIUS RISING: Regardless of your Sun sign, a Sagittarius ascendant gives you an adventurous, spontaneous, and free-spirited nature. You're gifted at making new friends and meeting new people, as you're genuinely curious about others and extremely open-minded—plus, you'll say yes to any adventure, which leads you to many different types of social gatherings! You're naturally optimistic and pretty good at putting on a happy face, even if your mood is sour. And you won't stay down for long, as you have an internal drive to keep moving forward and take in all the world has to offer. Your sense of style is likely spontaneous and eclectic; for instance, you'll throw on a friend's hat or scarf while you're out together and suddenly, it morphs into an integral part of your night's outfit and somehow looks like you planned it. You also appreciate multicultural patterns and styles.

CAPRICORN RISING: As a Capricorn rising, you've got a serious and authoritative flavor to your personality that tells the world you're not to be messed with, and it can be both intimidating to others and quite attractive. Socially, you're super sharp, and you come off as intelligent and very much aware of what you're doing. People feel like you're in charge! Your Capricorn ascendant is truly a secret power, because no matter how sloppy life gets, you can whip yourself into shape *real* fast and start getting things done with mind-boggling efficiency, and everyone around you can see this, too. Style-wise, you prefer to keep things simple and classic, and don't feel a heavy need to prove yourself through your appearance. Clothing is mostly functional for you, although you can appreciate a well-made and well-styled look.

AQUARIUS RISING: This fun and quirky placement makes you social, interested, and very one of a kind—albeit a little harder to read, as you have an almost futuristic and otherworldly quality about you. You're definitely not typical, and that's exactly how you like it. You are quite opinionated and aren't afraid to express your views—however out there—to anyone who crosses your path. You're a naturally progressive and forward-thinking person, regardless of your age, which makes it easy for you to get along with and have interesting conversations with people of all generations and walks of life. You're a visionary by nature, so it only makes sense that your personal style would reflect this. You enjoy looking unique and can even be a bit of a trendsetter, so you're not afraid to try something new fashion-wise and take a risk with a funky or unusual look.

PISCES RISING: Dreamy, creative, and totally emotionally open, Pisces rising people wear their hearts on their sleeve. Your sweet demeanor makes you naturally compassionate and easy to get along with, and as long as someone is able to let go of their inhibitions and get mystical and emotional with you, you could chat with them (or sit with them in silence) all night. You don't need much attention as long as you have affection from the people you care about. Pisces risings have a veil of gentleness and raw emotion about them; this placement can soften any hard edges that a Sun in a brazen fire sign, rigid earth sign, or impersonal air sign might give you. You're naturally creative, so your style often reflects that: Your unique perspective and appreciation for the arts will show through in the way you present yourself.

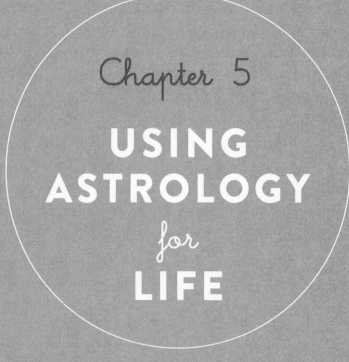

Chapter 5

USING ASTROLOGY *for* LIFE

ASTROLOGY IS JUST A FINGER
POINTING AT REALITY.

—Steven Forrest

If you've made it this far, congrats: You've hopefully gained a basic working knowledge of all of astrology's moving parts, and you've likely begun to understand more about your personal astrology, too. (And don't worry—if you skipped straight to this section, you can always go back and look things up as needed.)

Throughout the book, you've likely already learned many different ways to connect with the surrounding cosmos on a day-to-day basis, not only through the mystifying oracle that is your natal chart, but also by learning how to align yourself with the energy of each Sun season, show someone your love based on their Moon sign, and much more. With this chapter, we'll take the different energies you've developed relationships with—the planets and the signs—and help you figure out how to apply these concepts to your everyday life. We'll be pulling together your newfound knowledge of the planets and signs, as well as having you peek at your birth chart or check out some aspects in order to align with the current cosmic energies on a more personal level, too. Your new skills are definitely going to be put into practice now.

Astrology truly can be a part of your everyday life in *so* many ways beyond just reading your daily horoscope. Working with astrology in this way is beneficial to you in the sense that your plans will be more cosmically timed, and it will also make you feel a whole lot more connected to the surrounding universe. Plus, it's just more fun. Think of it as conspiring with the cosmos.

Transit vs. Natal Planets

Before we get started, let's chat about **transit planets** vs. **natal planets** which become more important to understand in this chapter.

We'll start with transit. A transit essentially indicates planets making moves—it could indicate when a planet either moves into a new sign or forms a relationship (or an aspect) to another point or planet. When we talk about which sign a planet is currently in, or an aspect that's taking place between two or more planets today, we're referring to planetary **transits**. The word *transit* implies exactly what you'd think—it refers to the planets *in motion*, interacting with each other and moving through the zodiac in real time. These transits affect the general population on a larger scale because they happen in real time.

When we're referring to a **natal** planet or aspect, however, that refers to the placement of planets in someone's birth chart. At the time of the person's birth, these were transits that affected everyone. But now, they're frozen in time as someone's natal planets and aspects, holding a lasting (but very personal) significance to the person whose chart they appear in. So, for example, while Venus may be in transit in Taurus today, my *natal* Venus is in Virgo. See the difference? Transit Venus is what's happening now, and natal Venus is Venus's placement in my birth chart. Another example: We all experienced a transit Saturn/Pluto conjunction in January 2020, and the energy affected us collectively. But that's much different than having a *natal* Saturn/Pluto conjunction in your birth chart, which would define you more personally.

Looking at the effect of planets in transit is a really fun way to feel more connected and aligned with the current happenings of our little corner of the universe. You already have a good idea of what each planet represents and how each zodiac sign can color their energy as they *transit* through them; now you can start applying these transits to your life in different ways and figuring out auspicious times to do certain things or play up certain qualities. At the very least, it can help you understand more about how astrology affects *you*, and that kind of self-reflection and awareness is a huge deal. Don't you feel even more connected to the cosmos already?

Much of the advice below focuses on **planetary transits** and how the energy affects us as a collective. While each transit affects everyone a little differently, based on their birth chart and the placements of their major planets, the overarching energy of the transit can be accessed by all and used to your advantage. For example, certain transits (like Mars transiting through Aries) might be generally auspicious for our goals and bode well for people starting new projects, while other transits (like Mercury retrogrades, for example) are a better time for everyone to slow down and hold off on starting anything new.

Our natal planets and aspects are unique to us and affect us throughout our lives; these help shape our personalities, preferences, and more. Transits, on the other hand, affect all of us collectively; these affect the overall landscape or "energy" of the moment, if you will.

Planets at Play

Transit planets can also *interact* with natal planets. For example, if you want to look at your personal astrology, you can look at the planets in transit (i.e., what the planets are doing right now as they move through the zodiac) and compare that to your birth chart, which depicts your natal planets. For example, maybe you'll notice that transiting Venus is forming a trine with your natal Sun tomorrow, bringing lots of creativity, social activity, and good luck in love— how exciting!

Transits and Deeper Truths

If you want to get more advanced, you can also dive deeper into your birth chart and take a look at the ways the transiting planets are activating the planets and houses in your own chart. For example, take a look at which houses in your birth chart are being hit with transiting planets (as this can activate energy in that house's area of your life), or examine some of the aspects that the transiting planets are forming with your natal planets (as this can stir up drama *or* offer you lucky opportunities). This takes a bit more research and expertise (and is an area in which a reading with a professional astrologer could be *very* helpful), but if you want to dig deeper into this mystical art, it's a good practice!

Lastly, if you *really* want to start learning about the ways astrology affects you, keep an astrological journal! Track the transits of the major planets (especially the fast-moving ones), and make notes about how you feel and different things that you're facing in your life under any given transit. The Moon changes signs every few days, so your entries about those transits will be more frequent and will probably deal with day-to-day things, like your mood and feelings. You can also make "recap" entries at the end of the longer-lasting transits that allow you to zoom out and focus on the overall themes and habits you notice yourself working with. When embarking on this practice, try not to be overly influenced by what astrologers tell you you'll feel—simply pay attention to what actually and naturally comes up for you. The more you do this, the more you'll be able to see how planetary energies affect you personally.

All in all, working with astrology on a day-to-day basis to keep track of the planets in transit can help you better pick up on the ways that you feel astrology's influence in your life, which will ultimately help you stay more in touch with yourself as a cosmic being.

HOW TO WORK WITH RETROGRADES

All of the major planets in astrology (except for the luminaries, aka the Sun and Moon) experience regular planetary retrograde periods, simply called retrogrades (and sometimes stylized as **Rx**). What this refers to is the occasional "backward" movement of the planet through the zodiac. Of course, ginormous planets don't just up and start moving in the opposite direction in the sky all of a sudden. It's just that every so often, a planet *appears* to temporarily go backward on its orbit—I say *appears* because, as you know (thanks to both astrology *and* elementary school science), planets only orbit in one direction as they circle the Sun. But thanks to a little optical illusion that affects our point of view here on Earth, every so often it looks like a planet starts moving backward—reversing on its course before resuming its usual forward motion again.

How Retrogrades Affect Us

Astrologically, retrograde periods have a deep significance. During a planet's retrograde, we feel a shift in the energy when it comes to everything that's ruled by the retrograding planet. We'll notice that things aren't flowing forward in those departments and may feel like they're at a standstill altogether. We're more likely to experience roadblocks and other issues that keep us from moving ahead in these areas of our life, and we might find that things tend to go wrong and mishaps are more common when we *do* try to carry on as usual. This frustrating retrograde energy really affects us—and in order to align ourselves with it, we have to be willing to take a few steps back, too.

Retrogrades often cause things from our past to circle back to us for review, so don't be surprised if you're suddenly lost in a stroll down memory lane or dealing with issues that you'd previously thought were long resolved. This energy could come in the form of revisiting past projects you started but never finished, finding secrets come up to the surface or discovering new information about old issues, being forced to dress old wounds that never fully healed or got resolved, or spending a lot of time in your memories and reminiscing about the past. Oh, and don't forget about past relationships—you might find that you're called to reach out to old friends or colleagues, or you run into people from your past. And many retrogrades are *notorious* for bringing ex-lovers back into the picture, for better or worse.

Retrograde Energy

Retrograde energy doesn't have to be a bad thing. Life goes by fast and we're always on a mission to push forward, especially in our always-on-the-move society, but consciously slowing down and working with a planet's retrograde energy can make a massive difference in the way the retrograde flows in our life. Charging forward on a project or an endeavor will feel like swimming upstream, and under a retrograde's energy that's exactly what it is. Charging forward is the *opposite* of what a retrograde encourages, but when we ignore its influence and attempt to charge forward *anyway*, that's when we're more likely to hit the roadblocks, mishaps, and drama that retrogrades are known for.

In addition to slowing ourselves down (particularly in the areas of our lives ruled by the retrograding planet), there are other general rules of the retrograde that we want to follow. First, we want to avoid making any major moves during a retrograde, particularly in any area of our lives that is ruled by the retrograding planet. Large changes, big decisions, either beginning or finalizing something important—all these things should be avoided during retrograde periods if possible, or approached with caution if they absolutely must happen.

Second, as mentioned, our pasts come back to us for review in a big way during retrograde periods, so we're likely to find that our energy keeps getting dragged back to past issues rather than being focused toward the future. That's okay! This is the cosmos's way of letting us know that there's some unfinished business that

Communications (and even reunions) with our exes are very common during all types of retrogrades, so look out for those random texts or long-overdue apology letters.

254

requires our examination before moving forward. If we don't understand our past, we're doomed to repeat our mistakes, right? Retrograde energy knows this, so it does everything it can to help us slow things down and review where we're at. It's a pause on the journey that allows you to stop the car, check your map, charge your phone, stretch, and take a little nap and then move forward. If we abide by the energy of the retrograde, it can actually *save* us from driving hours and hours in the wrong direction. All it asks is that we pause, then rewind, then review, then reassess.

You may notice lots of *"re"* words going on here as I describe retrograde energy. In fact, many astrologers note that the easiest way to understand the energy of a retrograde is to look at the prefix of the word itself: **re**. By definition, this prefix typically denotes one of two (or both) things: the repetition of something (a definition that uses the prefix itself in its construction) and backward movement. Whether we like it or not, retrogrades rewind things. They trudge things up out of our pasts and ask us to review, reassess, revise, and reconsider. Re, re, re.

Speaking of *re* words, let's talk about *reputations*, specifically those of planetary retrogrades. Retrogrades get a bad rep not because they're terrible, awful transits, but rather because they can cause problems in our lives if we choose to ignore the astrological flow and try to work *against* the energy of the retrograde. If instead of heeding the cosmic advice we try to carry on with life as usual, we better do so with caution—because the planet's energy is *not* going to be flowing as it usually does, and we're certainly going to experience some setbacks and road blockades. Every planet's retrograde functions a little bit differently, because each planet rules different parts of our lives, but these are good general rules to keep in mind.

> If you know you have a major decision to make, a contract to sign, or a big life change coming up, take the upcoming retrograde's effects into account and do what you can to manage the details beforehand (or postpone things until after).

Phases of a Retrograde Cycle

There are actually three phases to a planet's retrograde: **the pre-shadow retrograde period, the retrograde itself, and the post-shadow retrograde period**. All of these phases take place over the exact same degrees of a zodiac sign (or multiple zodiac signs). The two shadow phases take place when the planet is moving *forward* in those degrees (immediately before and after the retrograde itself), and the actual retrograde phase takes place as the planet is moving *backward* over those degrees. So all in all, during each retrograde, there is a chunk of the zodiac that is transited by the retrograding planet three consecutive times during these phases.

Here's how it works: A planet moves forward through the degrees of each zodiac sign as usual. The pre-shadow phase begins once a planet enters the **last degree that it will revisit during its retrograde**. Once it begins moving backward, the actual retrograde begins. And then, once the planet stations direct (which means it starts moving forward again, as it usually does), it enters the post-shadow phase until it **passes the degree at which the retrograde phase began**. The degrees that the retrograde passes over within a sign (or multiple signs) while moving *backward* are the same degrees that indicate a planet's pre- and post-shadow periods, which happen while the planet is moving forward.

The pre-retrograde shadow is all about *preparation*. It's a time to wrap anything up that could pose an issue during the retrograde and make sure your affairs are more or less in order. Nobody's perfect, but we can try! Start applying your precautionary retrograde practices here, because many people start feeling the effects of the retrograde building during the pre-retrograde shadow period.

The post-retrograde shadow is all about integration. It's a time to slowly ease back into the planet's direct flow and readjust to your normal life—with a whole slew of retrograde lessons in tow. Some of the retrograde's energy may still seem to affect you, but that's just a message to take it slow. There's no need to try to rush back into your usual swing of things. Pump the brakes and allow yourself a little time to let the lessons sink in before you charge forward.

Using Retrograde Energy to Your Advantage

No matter which planet is retrograde, it's always a good idea to jot down your thoughts, feelings, and experiences during its journey. The lessons learned during a retrograde are always useful for the future—after all, the whole point of a retrograde astrologically is to help us slow down and review the things going on in our lives, heads, and hearts! Keeping track of the lessons you've learned during a retrograde, then integrating them into your life during the post-retrograde shadow period, is a great way to make sure you get the most out of the transit.

Obviously, life goes on during a retrograde whether we want it to or not. We're not always going to be able to avoid the "unadvisable" behaviors during any particular retrograde, but that's okay. Simply being aware, taking precautions, and doing what we can to *embrace* the retrograde energy will help us feel more in control and interconnected, and maybe make these transits less unpleasant. Here's how to work with each of the major personal planets' retrograde periods (and what to beware of).

Working with Mercury Retrograde

We'll start with the most well-known (and certainly most infamous) of all the planetary retrogrades: Mercury retrograde. Some people may not even be aware that any other planet even has a retrograde—*that's* how notorious and highly discussed (and maligned) Mercury's retrogrades are!

Mercury retrograde periods typically happen three (but sometimes four) times per year, and they last for about three weeks each, on average. Mercury retrogrades are somewhat frequently compared to the other major planets, and this planet also rules over *many* different things that affect most people's daily lives in a major way, which is probably why its retrograde periods are so damn notorious. Mercury rules thinking, timing, communication, and all things logistical in nature—so like, everything we typically have no choice but to deal with when it comes to work or getting things done. The logistical matters of our day-to-day life heavily depend on Mercury stuff—communicating with people, making plans, scheduling things, getting from place to place, and formulating our thoughts and opinions *all* fall under Mercury's umbrella.

Thus, when the planet goes retrograde, all these parts of our life seem to start malfunctioning. Anything related to thinking, intellect, and logistical matters are made messier—we may find it harder to mentally process or make sense of things and could find ourselves getting mixed up on dates, numbers, and details. Mercury also rules over communication and the sharing of information (which includes the many information-sharing tools of technology), meaning that we start to struggle to express ourselves clearly. Conversations may not go the way we want (and misunderstandings may run amok), and we're more likely to overlook email typos, send a text to the wrong chat, or totally misread something ourselves. On the tech side, it affects our devices: Apps crashing, phones freezing, and laptops dying are just a few messes typical to Mercury retrograde. Additionally, Mercury rules over timing, scheduling, and transportation, so expect to hit a lot of unexpected traffic, miss a deadline or two, or accidentally show up at the wrong place for a date. People often find themselves seeking communication with past friends, lovers, and colleagues during a retrograde, so don't be shocked when you get a random message or text from someone you haven't spoken to in years.

Mercury retrograde can be productive and chill—I promise. Here's what to *focus* on during Mercury retrograde.

Slow down your schedule and lighten your load.

I know, it's hard to think about clearing your calendar for three weeks, but this is exactly what the retrograde is asking you to do. Now is not the time to burn the candle at both ends. As the planet of timing, Mercury's retrograde asks us to examine how we've been spending our time, but if our schedules are so jam-packed that we don't have a free moment to ourselves to reflect, then how can we truly follow this cosmic prompt? See if you're able to pare things down in your schedule to just the essentials in order to free up some time. Logistical things are a mess under Mercury retrograde, so give yourself permission to chill: Don't take on extra projects unless you have to, and be a little choosier about your social engagements. Obviously, we don't have the luxury of taking three weeks off of work and pausing our social lives—it's just an impossible task. But it is helpful if you can lighten your load a little bit to allow yourself more time and space to explore and reassess your current workload, trajectory, and headspace.

Revisit old work projects and ideas.

If we allow the retrograde energy to lead us, we'll often find ourselves suddenly focused on projects or goals from the past that we may have lost steam on, or even fully lost track of. Starting a brand-new project or embarking on a brand-new path—especially as it may pertain to work, communication, writing, number-crunching, or any logistical matter—is highly *inadvisable* under a retrograde. But revisiting older projects and past ideas is actually *supported* by this energy. In fact, these things might even fall into your lap naturally, and if they do, embrace them! The retrograde can offer you a shifted perspective that can breathe new life into an old idea.

Practice being a better communicator *and* listener.

It's time to be more attentive to the way you express thoughts and information to others. Use Mercury retrograde as a really good challenge to yourself to be truly precise and clear with your words. Practice mindfulness and think before you speak, because under this transit, it's really easy for things to come out wrong or be misinterpreted. The clearer you are about what you're communicating—whether it's what time to meet someone or how you feel about an outfit—the better. The perks? This is a skill that can benefit you long beyond the retrograde, and practice makes perfect. This is also a time to practice patience and understanding when interpreting what others have to say. Try not to take things personally if plans get messed up or someone says something that makes you feel sensitive. *Everyone* will be struggling to express themselves clearly under this transit, so remember that you, too, will be prone to misunderstanding someone's point or getting confused about details. Open yourself to being a better listener and being more flexible in the way you interpret things.

Of course, we want to make the most of Mercury retrograde, but let's also acknowledge its power to deviate us from our norms. Here are some quick notes of *caution* when it comes to navigating a Mercury retrograde period.

Read and reread anything that's even vaguely important.

Under a retrograde, we're way more likely to misunderstand others (and unintentionally set others up to mis-understand *us*), so make quadruple-checking *everything* your personal retrograde rule. Be super careful when it comes to tech communication, like texting, emails, and social media. For example, watch what you say via text, because you never know who could see it (or if your tone could be misinterpreted). Triple-check that you're tex-ting the right person (because we're more likely to get mixed up and reply to the wrong thread under this transit). And reread emails and work files before you send or submit them, as you may realize that you're being unclear, forgetting to include information or attachments, or overlooking a crap-ton of typos that you didn't see initially.

Avoid major decisions, big moves, or finalizing agreements, if possible.

Because Mercury rules information and communication, its retrograde periods can lose things in translation. If wires get crossed on something simple, it's not a big deal (just an annoyance at worst), but when it comes to anything binding and important—like signing contracts, making major purchases (especially on Mercurial things, like tech items), or accepting any big offers—the misunderstandings could have lasting consequences, and *that's* where you want to be extra careful. Often, we find out *after* a retrograde that we didn't fully under-stand the situation we got into—perhaps we weren't actually clear on the terms of our contract, or the item we purchased turned out to be not the best fit for what we needed. That's why it's best to avoid moving on anything with lasting consequences during a retrograde. But of course, if you must move forward on some-thing, counteract it by going overboard with your attention to detail. Read every bit of fine print, triple-check the details of any agreement, clarify anything you're unsure about, and keep a paper trail for *everything*.

Leave room in your schedule or travel itinerary for timing issues.

During a retrograde, we're much more likely to hit timing snags, like hitting unexpected traffic, sleeping through an alarm, or missing a calendar app notification. That said, operate with the notion that time is *not* on your side. Don't schedule things back to back, leave early when you need to get somewhere, and beware of rushing, as you're more likely to forget something or miss details.

And Mercury can mess with more than our day-to-day transportation. More classic Mercury retrograde advice? Avoid traveling and taking trips. If you do have a trip booked, be sure to quadruple-check your itinerary (flights, times, locations, addresses, *everything*), be ultra-prepared (full tank of gas, hard copies of your itinerary, and a fully charged phone at all times), and leave to get anywhere with tons of time to spare, as Mercury rules timing and its retrograde periods tend to cause all sorts of unexpected delays.

Don't be overly reliant on technology.

Mercury rules tech, so back up your phone and your irreplaceable files, change your passwords, and be really careful with your devices. Mercury rules over information as well as technology, so our gadgets (think phones, laptops, smart devices, and even cars) are fully under fire during Mercury retrograde. Tech glitches are common here, but so are potentially disastrous freak mishaps—like accidentally deleting something you really needed, losing your thumb drive, having one of your online accounts hacked, or breaking your phone only to realize you hadn't backed it up. The cloud is your friend, people, as are your external hard drives. Use them, and do it *before* the retrograde hits to avoid issues.

Working with Venus Retrograde

Planet Venus takes a retrograde approximately once every year and half, and it does so for approximately 40 days. Venus is the planet that rules love, luxury, and beauty—this planet is in charge of what we *value*. Venus rules all things love and romance, including crushes, flirting, sexual and sensual pleasure, and relationships. Additionally, Venus rules over another kind of love: self-love. Our self-esteem and self-worth could be seen as Venus territory, as well, and so does the way we show affection to friends and family. Lastly, Venus is also in charge of the other things that are inherently valuable or pleasurable; things like beauty, aesthetics, art, money, and luxury fall under its jurisdiction, too. Venus is a highly creative and visually oriented planet.

During a Venus retrograde, we're forced to grapple with and sort through issues pertaining to what we value and what brings us pleasure, which could mean getting through some tough times in love and money. It becomes difficult to move forward functionally in our romantic relationships, as we may find that new issues (or often old, unresolved issues) are coming up really strong and relationships are falling short of expectations. We're forced to answer for things in both our love lives *and* financial lives under this transit, so we're often reassessing and reformulating our idea of what we find valuable. Venus also rules over art, aesthetics, and beauty, so we'll find that we don't have a clear vision of what we're attracted to—this is true for both sartorial and creative sensibilities.

Venus retrograde can actually help us work toward a better place when it comes to love and money, and we can come out the other side with a clear vision of what we want to attract romantically, financially, and artistically. Here's what to *focus* on during Venus retrograde.

Be willing to work through your relationship issues with honesty.

No more glossing over the less-than-beautiful things going on under the surface of your relationship—Venus retrograde is here to drag these romantic skeletons out of the closet. Venus retrograde can make things really difficult in the romantic relationship department, unearthing all sorts of ugliness, uncertainty, and unease. But if you prepare to put issues out on the table and deal with them instead of hoping they won't come up and trying to avoid them, you'll actually have a beautiful opportunity to work through the mess consciously with your partner.

Create a budget and get smart about your finances.

Dropping loads of cash on vacations, clothes, and other frivolous and expendable items is tempting during a Venus retrograde, but it is definitely not a good idea. Instead, do the opposite! Challenge yourself to go through your bank statements and make a chart, note, or visual diagram (whatever floats your boat) that breaks down exactly where and how you're spending your hard-earned money. Then, create a budget. You can turn the retrograde energy on its head. Venus rules money and what we value, and during a retrograde we're hitting walls in these areas. Instead of trying to charge through that wall, set up your desk there and map out smarter ways to use your money. Venus retrograde is a time to save—wait until *afterward* to treat yourself and spend.

Up your self-care and self-love practices.

Venus is the planet of luxury, and as she spins backward in her orbit, it's a good time for you to slow down and get in touch with your Venusian sensibilities. Alterations to your appearance during Venus retrograde are a no-no, but there are plenty of other ways to boost your self-esteem and show yourself some love. Indulge in extra luxurious self-care practices during this period. Venus retrograde gives you full permission to burn through your stash of moisturizing face masks and at-home spa kits. Commit to taking a luxurious bath, treating yourself to a massage, or just being ultra-diligent and conscious about your nightly skin care routine during this transit. It can't hurt to have some self-lovin' mantras to repeat during this period, too.

Of course, we want to make the most of Venus retrograde, but let's also acknowledge its power to funk things up when it comes to love, money, and beautifying our bad selves. Here are some quick notes of *caution* when it comes to navigating Venus retrograde's antics.

Pull the reins on your romantic relationships.

When we make big moves in our romantic lives, we want Venus to be giving us her blessing, but she's not well-equipped to do that during a retrograde. That's why astrologers always advise against getting married during this transit. This also applies to taking any other big step in a relationship; making things official with a new partner, deciding to move in with a current partner or start a family, or even *ending* a relationship are ill-advised while this planet is in retrograde. If you can avoid any major moves in your love life during these forty days, do it—and if you're thinking of beginning a new relationship or ending a current one, see if you can't take things slow and give it all a little more time. You'll be more clearheaded about what you want in love once the retrograde passes.

Save the beauty and home makeovers for after the retrograde.

Venus retrograde is not a good time to do any major alterations to your appearance. This means you should avoid any extreme haircuts or dye jobs, shopping sprees at the makeup counter, or any revamp of your personal style (because you might find that you hate every new outfit and lipstick color that you bought post-retrograde). Cosmetic surgery, piercings, and tattoos are also ill-advised, especially anything that hasn't been planned long before-hand. This can even extend to changing the aesthetic of your living space or anything else. Don't redecorate your home or bedroom or invest in any major art pieces if you can help it. If you can postpone these beautifying acts until after the retrograde, definitely do it. You'll have a much clearer idea about what you find beautiful and valuable, will be much more comfortable in your creative vision, and will be more likely to achieve good results.

By being *honest* about the love issues that come up during Venus retrograde, you might realize that a relationship has run its course. Or maybe you'll accept the shortcomings of your relationship, and come out of it even stronger.

Avoid both frivolous shopping and any major luxury purchases.

Venus rules money in general, so spending a lot of it while the planet is in retrograde is likely to prove stressful. But be especially careful when it comes to pleasure-based or luxury purchases—that is, anything you don't really *need*. Now's not the time to book a vacation, buy expensive new clothes or accessories, or splurge on a luxury car. You're likely to regret any big purchases, especially impulse buys, as your sense of what you value is unclear under Venus retrograde. And while retail therapy can be helpful under some circumstances, shopping for fun isn't a good idea under Venus retrograde, either. It's easy to get carried away and overspend, and again, we're more likely to regret our impulsive purchases post-retrograde and find that they actually don't bring us the value we had hoped they would.

Working with Mars Retrograde

Mars is an intense and hotheaded planet. It retrogrades less frequently than any other planet—only once every twenty-five to twenty-six months—and when it retrogrades, it does so for anywhere between sixty and eighty days. Mars rules over anything related to our animal instincts: think anger, physicality, sex drive, rage, passion, and even violence. But additionally, it also rules over our ability to take action. Mars is our defense, our strength, and our initiator—it helps us take charge. It's a planet of great intensity, and thus, its retrograde periods can be rather harsh and unforgiving in nature.

When Mars goes retrograde, it greatly affects our ability to take action on our goals and our willpower. It's not a time to be impulsive, as we won't be on top of our usual Mars-ruled game. Our instincts aren't as sharp, and we simply can't move with the firepower and energy that this planet usually bestows on us when we feel passionate about something, so progress toward our big goals may come to a standstill and temporarily lose steam. Mars retrograde periods may also force us to come to terms with repressed issues we may have regarding rage and sexuality. This may seem frightening, but it's for the best—everything is much bigger and scarier when it's hiding in the shadows, so getting our Mars secrets out into the light can actually be cathartic.

During Mars retrograde, anything we've tried to bandage up or shove aside in these areas is likely to come out in an explosive way that leaves us no choice but to address it.

Mars retrograde can be helpful, as it forces us to slow down and reassess our goals and passions, which in turn, allows us to come out the other side with a renewed sense of energy and a much clearer idea of what we want and how we aim to act on it. Here's what to *focus* on during Mars retrograde.

Use this as an excuse to relax and take it easy.

Mars retrograde asks us to slow down, so try not to rush places or be too hasty or reckless with your physical body, as we can be more accident-prone under Mars retrograde periods. If you don't slow yourself down consciously, then it's possible that Mars retrograde will find a way to slow you down anyway, perhaps by tripping you up somehow and forcing you to take some physical downtime to rest. That said, you'll want to make sure you're still moving your physical body in healthy and gentle ways. Incorporate exercise into your routine (this is important, as Mars is highly physical!), but choose low-impact workouts instead of high-intensity activity—try hitting a yoga class instead of boxing, or using the elliptical at the gym instead of weights.

Focus your pent-up energy toward building your plans.

Mars in retrograde can rain down a lot of restless energy on us. Unfortunately, this stir-crazy anxiety isn't helpful, as Mars retrograde is a crappy time to embark on working toward a new goal. That said, you can channel this restless energy into the planning stages for something new that you're passionate about. Make lists of your personal goals, and start listing potential action steps that you can take to make those goals a tangible reality. Don't act on these things just yet—be patient and wait for the retrograde to end! But once it does, you'll be glad that you took the time to create a beautifully laid-out and solid plan of action to help you conquer these personal missions.

Embrace your Venus-ruled qualities in your relationships and at work.

Mars rules our passion and our sex drive, so it's not uncommon to notice that our wild 'n' burning desires for our sex partners could wane during one of the planet's retrogrades. And this lack of a mojo extends beyond the bedroom: We might find that our passion and ambition in our careers is dimmed as well. Instead of letting your frustration overtake you, embrace the more symbolically feminine and Venusian side of yourself. When it comes to carnal affairs, up the romance factor. Express your desire for your partner during

this period by sharing sensual massages, romantic dinners, and words of affection, putting more emphasis on pleasure and value in your bonding rather than carnal passion. At work, if you're feeling less than motivated, lean into your more free-flowing creative side. Use this time to generate fresh ideas and collaborate openly with others rather than being hyper-focused on conquering a particular goal.

As is true with any testy Mars transit, we should proceed with caution during a retrograde, even if we know the ways to take advantage of it. Here are some quick notes of *caution* when it comes to navigating a Mars retrograde.

Don't physically exhaust yourself.

Mars retrograde can absolutely make us feel low energy and sluggish, both in our physical bodies and in our mental motivation and willpower. That said, any project that requires a major physical output or an intense power of will is best put off until after the retrograde. If you do find that you have to undertake such a project, commit to cutting yourself some slack. Pushing yourself too hard and reaching your limits can actually be dangerous under this retrograde, as we're all more accident-prone, so pay close attention to your body and mind and respect the boundaries of what you're healthily capable of. Now isn't the time to try to prove your strength to anyone else.

Check your impulsiveness at the door and go with the flow.

Mars retrograde is absolutely the worst time to act without thinking. Our ability to charge forward is impaired, yes, but that doesn't mean our brains are! Understand that the vision you hold for your goals at the moment isn't at its clearest, nor is your drive to conquer them at its most ambitious, but this is temporary. You're probably feeling less confident in yourself and your ability to take charge of your life, but if you can let go of the need to take action and simply practice accepting things as they are, you'll be a lot better off. Focusing energy on yourself, going with the flow, and being an observer instead of a performer is a good way to consciously step back from our Mars-ruled need to take action and make a scene.

WORKING WITH ECLIPSES

In astronomy, an *eclipse* refers to any time one celestial body obscures the light (or source of light) of another celestial body during the course of its orbit. In astrology, the eclipses are highly significant, as they are the harbingers of massive and fateful changes and revelations. Eclipses are one of the cosmos's most illuminating and climactic tools. These cosmic events bring massive shifts to our lives, through crises and chaos, as well as powerful truths and realizations.

Eclipses deal with our two powerful luminaries: the Sun and the Moon. Thus, **solar eclipses** and **lunar eclipses** are the two types of eclipses that we consistently refer to.

A **solar eclipse** occurs when the Moon aligns perfectly on the ecliptic in between the Earth and the Sun, hence blocking the light of the Sun from the Earth. This always takes place during a new Moon (as new Moons always occur when the Moon is in conjunction with the Sun), and so its energy can feel sort of like a super-powerful new Moon. Astrologically, solar eclipses tend to bring about new beginnings and opportunities in a large-scale way, whether that comes in the form of a big idea, a new job offer or promotion, or a major piece of news.

Conversely, a **lunar eclipse** occurs when the Earth aligns perfectly on the ecliptic between the Sun and the Moon, hence blocking the Moon from receiving any light from the Sun. This always takes place during a full Moon (as full Moons always occur when the Moon is in opposition to the Sun), so its energy can feel like a super-powerful full Moon. Astrologically, these eclipses tend to focus our energy more on relationships and memories than solar eclipses do, and they usually signify endings, whether that's the end of a job or relationship, the breakdown of a certain belief system, or a revelation that leads you to cut something from your life.

Eclipses happen in pairs (one with a new Moon, and one with a corresponding full Moon), and they occur several times a year. Typically, we'll experience at least four eclipses (or two sets of eclipses) annually, in total. Each eclipse pair takes place on a certain **axis*** of the zodiac (or in a particular pair of opposing signs), and they take place approximately every six months for up to two years, until

No other lunation has quite the dramatic shock factor and action-driving ability that an eclipse does.

their cycle is complete. Once a particular cycle of eclipse sets ends, it won't occur again on that axis (or pair of signs) for another seven to nine years, approximately.

* When I use the term *axis*, I'm referring to a pair of opposing signs on the zodiac wheel that are 180 degrees apart. For example, if an eclipse takes place in Cancer, there will be another eclipse in succession that takes place in Capricorn, which is the sign opposite Cancer on its *axis* in the circle of the zodiac. This is known as the Cancer/Capricorn axis.

The axis on which any given set of eclipses takes place is important, as it colors the energy of the eclipse and shows us the types of revelations, changes, and struggles we may be dealing with under the eclipse's influence. Each eclipse under a particular axis will continue to build on the same themes and bring further action and illumination to the same issues. By the end of an eclipse series, the cosmos should have successfully executed its shifts in our life, outlook, and relationships as pertaining to that area, and that axis's cycle is complete.

Sometimes two eclipse cycles overlap one another (meaning sets of eclipses take place on two different zodiacal axes, or between two different opposing pairs of zodiac signs), and in these cases, we could find ourselves experiencing more than four eclipses in a single year. In all cases, though, eclipses are dependent upon the **lunar nodes**. As a refresher, the north and south nodes represent the two points in space where the path of the Moon's orbit intersects with the Sun's ecliptic. When the Moon hits one of these points, that's when we have an eclipse. That's why you'll notice that the eclipse axis also aligns with the zodiac axis of the lunar nodes at any given time. You may also recall that the lunar nodes are also fittingly known as the Nodes of Fate—and like the nodes, eclipses *also* have to do with the power of fate.

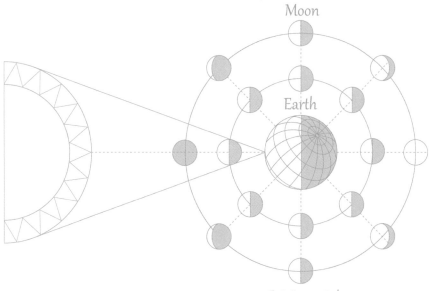

Rotation period

Sometimes eclipses can feel like the cosmic equivalent of the hands of fate swooping in, plucking you right out of the comfort of your current life and tossing you somewhere completely different. While you may not *really* wake up across the globe after an eclipse, it might feel that way.

How Eclipses Affect Us

Eclipses are extraordinarily significant in astrology, and although they always occur on sets of new and full Moons, they are considered much more powerful than those lunations alone. Astrologically, the power of an eclipse is one of those things that we simply can't fight: Eclipses bring the truth, and they bring action. Eclipses are a catalyst for crises, changes, and revelations in very large and swift doses. The earthshaking intensity of these astrological events can cause large-scale shifts in our lives, and can fully alter the path that we thought we were supposed to be on.

Eclipses have the power to bring about major crises, breaking points, big news, changes, monumental revelations, and fated events—but ultimately, in all cases, what they bring is the *truth*, no matter how shocking. Eclipses can shift the way we think, feel, and believe in an extremely short amount of time. If we want to make it through, we must be willing to submit to the eclipse's power.

Eclipse Energy

The chaotic eclipse energy somehow makes planetary retrogrades feel *gentle*. Retrogrades encourage us to slow down, reassess where we're at, make some changes post-review, then move forward feeling stronger—boom, simple and sweet. Eclipses, however, swoop in quickly and with a lot of intensity and pluck us out from wherever we are, only to plop us down somewhere else. It's hard and fast, and we don't have much time to think; we just have to stay on our toes and be ready to roll with the changes.

Because of the immense and ruthless power of an eclipse, these transits (and the many crises and shock moments that they can induce) can make us feel really freaked out and not very much in control of our own lives. But remember: Eclipses are here to help us. Besides, sometimes the changes that eclipses catalyze can be really *good*. You might be surprised at the incredibly positive shifts, revelations, and breakthroughs that an eclipse series can bring! And even if they don't feel good at the time, these shifts are almost *always* for the long-term good at least, so look at the silver lining. The truth is always, ultimately, on our side—and that's what eclipses are about.

Of course, not every eclipse will be so life-altering for every single person. It all depends on the axis of the eclipse sets and where they're hitting us in our birth charts, as well as the degrees at which each eclipse takes place and how that degree aligns with our natal planets. Some eclipses will affect certain people much more than others due to these factors—but no matter what, by the end of an eclipse series, we'll always be transformed in one way or another. Here's how to work with the energy—rather than against it—any time eclipse season hits.

Up your self-care, because you need a solid foundation to support you through the eclipse-induced shifts.

Eclipses are intense, as they bring about a lot of change all at once. In the days leading up to and following an eclipse, take care of yourself! All this cosmic change can manifest in physical exhaustion, not to mention the mental and emotional toll that all the crises can take on us. That said, try not to make your life any more difficult than it needs to be. Get a lot of sleep, take a short social media detox, only make plans with supportive and high-vibrational friends, and nourish yourself with some yummy comfort foods.

Try meditating.

Meditation is always a great tool for grounding yourself and soothing your nerves, but during eclipse season it can become a secret weapon for both staying chill *and* opening up to the eclipse energy. Opening your mind and heart to the life changes that eclipses tend to deliver can be a lot easier with the help of meditation, which can clear your headspace and give you a chance to get in touch with yourself. Even if you have no experience meditating, the eclipse is a great time to try. Plus, it gives you some peaceful and quiet *you* time (which definitely counts as self-care—see above!), with the added bonus of helping you to let go and surrender to the circumstances, a really helpful attitude to take during eclipse times. Meditating is also a great way to calm your nervous system, as eclipses can feel really stressful and can heighten our anxieties. Meditation is a free, simple, and healthy way to combat this.

Think like a cat and be ready to land on your feet, no matter what.

Embrace your inner feline. Eclipses are chaotic, and we simply can't predict how and why these transits will affect us; we should be ready for anything. That said, make like a cat and make sure you're ready to land on your feet, no matter which direction the eclipse tosses you. While you're at it, try to channel the natural feline grace of a kitty, too, because no matter how stressful and unpredictable eclipses can be, these changes are always for the higher purpose of aligning us with our fate, so bringing some grace to even the most awkward of growing pains is helpful. Lastly, keep reminding yourself that, like a cat, you also have nine lives, so no matter how crazy shit gets, you'll be okay.

If you need to fight for something under an eclipse, fight hard.

Eclipses have the power to swoop in and change *everything* we thought we knew about a situation. You can think of this as cosmic fate interfering and readjusting us to make sure we're 1) equipped with the truth, *and* 2) on the right path. That said, if something comes to light (or stands to be lost) under the influence of an eclipse and you feel a need to take action on it, you better act fast and with a whole lot of intensity. In other words, prepare for a fight. Eclipse energy can be very "finalizing" in nature—the events that take place during these periods tend to have lasting consequences. If you need to fight for something, you better come at it swinging and with an equal amount of intensity and passion.

Don't try to manifest anything.

This one is for all you astro-witches (or aspiring ones): Any sort of magical lunar manifestation ritual is absolutely off the table during an eclipse. Don't even try. While the average new Moon is known astrologically as being a good time for manifestation work (or setting intentions about new things you'd like to build up or invite into your life), eclipses are *not*. Putting your intentions out into the universe under an eclipse is useless and counterproductive, because the universe is not really paying attention to you during this time. Instead, an eclipse's focus is on aligning us with our true path. These are intense and sometime-chaotic catalyst events for change. It's a time to *listen*, not to ask. Instead of doing any sort of magic or spells, it's a good time to sit back and do a meditation or journal about your feelings instead.

ASTROLOGY FOR LIFE: LOVE AND SEX

Love life advice: Who *isn't* looking for it? Whether we're in a relationship or just dating around, it can be hard to navigate the trials and tribulations of sex 'n' romance, and sometimes we need a little guidance. Letting astrology inspire you in love is an absolutely gorgeous idea, and believe it or not, there's more to using astrology for love than just reading your crush's horoscope and finding out whether your Sun signs are compatible (although yes, we all do that, too).

Obviously, looking at compatibility between your birth chart and your crush's or partner's is important (although notice I say birth charts and *not* just your Sun signs, because there's *so* much more to compatibility than that!), but if you want to connect with what the planets are up to *now*, you can use certain transits to get an idea of the overall astrological influences that are affecting *everyone's* love and sex lives at any given time. Doing so can help you feel much more in sync with the cycles of our solar system and align your date plans with the cosmic forces that be.

The Love, Sex, and Relationship Planets to Pay Attention to

To start working with astrology in our love lives, let's first look to the planet named for the goddess of love herself: **Venus**. Venus is the planet of pleasure and value, and it rules over all things love and romance. This includes dating, flirting, showing affection, sensual pleasure, and so much more. Venus represents our love language. Obviously, if we want to know our personal love and romance style, we should look at what sign our natal Venus falls in (and same goes for your significant other—look to their Venus sign to see how they show their love). But Venus *transits* can point you toward the energy that's influencing *everyone*. Venus switches signs approximately once per month (and retrogrades about once every year and a half).

We also want to look at what planet **Mars** is up to, as this planet rules over our sex drive. Mars is the passionate planet that's in charge of our animalistic instincts and the primal act of sex. Venus is more about the lovey-dovey side of romantic relationships, but Mars is all about that burning desire inside of us. Venus wants to romantically make love to you, but Mars wants to ravish you in a passionate and steamy all-night romp. This is also the planet of action, so this is what gives us *initiative* to chase after what we want in our love lives, too. Look to your personal Mars sign to get an idea about how you express yourself sexually, as well as the style in which you fight ('cause, that's a big part of relationships, too!). Mars switches signs approximately every month and a half to two months, and retrogrades approximately every other year.

Last but not least, let's not forget about the closest planet to our hearts (and the Earth itself)—the lovely **Moon**. As far as transits go, we're focusing on romantic Venus and sexy Mars in this section, but the Moon deserves an honorable mention when it comes to love. The Moon rules over our emotions, and it shows us the way we want to be nurtured, cuddled, and comforted, all of which obviously ties in very deeply with most romantic relationships. The Moon becomes more important as we get closer to someone, meaning it may not be the most marked influence when it comes to whirlwind flings, random hookups, or the very early stages of dating someone new. But once we enter into a more intimate and trusting stage of a relationship, the way each person experiences, expresses, and processes their emotions (as well as the ways they nurture/need to be nurtured) becomes a big deal. Look at your Moon sign (in Chapter 4) for clues as to the way you're likely to handle emotions in relationships, as well as the way you need to be nurtured by your partner. Conversely, look at your partner's sign to glean the same insight on them!

However, no matter what the influence of an astrological transit may be, when it comes to love and sex, consent is always key. Just because a transit bodes well for high sex drives or making moves *doesn't* mean you should ever move forward on something without asking for consent. For example, maybe a transit has a tendency to make us more direct in love and sex—that *doesn't* mean you should make racy comments or send a sexy pic to someone without getting their permission first, no matter how astrologically emboldened you feel.

Love and Sex Planetary Transits: How to Make the Most of Them

As Venus and Mars each transit through the zodiac, they influence all of us and color the collective energy around how we experience love, pleasure, and value, as well as sexual desire and passion. Keep tabs on where they're at by using an ephemeris or checking trusted online sources. Working with these planetary transits can help you in your love life by inspiring you to make certain moves or plans *and* helping guide you toward areas where the energy will be favorable. Let's look at how it affects our love lives as the sex 'n' romance planets make their moves.

♥ VENUS IN ARIES: Venus in Aries absolutely loves the chase. If you're single, don't be afraid to make the first move—people are *extra* attracted to high confidence at this time. If you're in a relationship, you're probably going to be in the mood to "wear the pants" under this transit, and it's okay to embrace that and lean into your dominant side.

DATE NIGHT IDEA: *Let's get physical.* Aries energy is energetic and loves a challenge, so choose a physical activity (and maybe something slightly competitive), like going bowling or mini-golfing. And don't be afraid to follow your own excitement and take on a leadership role when it comes to deciding what to do. Ask yourself what sounds fun, fresh, and new for *you.* Hopefully, your date will feel equally hyped about the plans.

♨ MARS IN ARIES: Our sex lives are blazin' here! Now's the time to embrace the most emboldened and forward side of yourself when it comes to sex because passionate, action-driven Mars is in its home sign. Impulsive hookups and one-night stands are common, so have some fun and be safe! We'll also be more willing to prioritize our own pleasure. Make sure your partner knows how to satisfy you, and don't forget to return the favor. You're speaking your mind and acting on every impulsive desire that pops into your head and heart, and you should be upping your self-pleasure, too.

♥ VENUS IN TAURUS: Taurus is one of Venus's two domiciles, so the planet of love feels very much at home in this sensual earth sign's territory. If you're single, it's a good time to splurge on a fancy date night with someone new, even if it feels heavy on the romance—this is "treat yourself" season when it comes to love! If you're in a relationship, show your partner how much you care with lots of physical affection and words of affirmation because Taurus energy wants to feel stable and secure, so it's always nice to have verbal confirmation that your relationship is on steady ground.

DATE NIGHT IDEA: *Make it luxurious.* Keep both sensual pleasure and luxury in mind as a priority. Consider reserving a table for dinner at a super-fancy restaurant with your partner, share an expensive bottle of red wine, or book a couple's massage and a spa day. And remember, this is Venus's home sign, so make sure you dress your best!

⬙ MARS IN TAURUS: Taurus is actually the most sensual sign of the zodiac, so now's a great time to up the physical intimacy between you and your partner and maximize your earthly pleasures: Stay in bed all day taking turns pleasing each other and really getting to know each other's bodies. You'll feel super passionate about feeling *good*. Unlike Mars in Aries, though, this is a time when we'll be taking things slower in sexual relationships. While sex is definitely super-hot under this transit, we're also becoming more interested in long-term things, so flings won't be at the top of our priority list.

♥ VENUS IN GEMINI: We're feeling super outgoing, hyper-social, and curious when it comes to romance under Venus in Gemini. This communication-forward sign loves to chat and learn new things, so if you have burning questions to ask your lover, now's a good time! Make it fun: Think game of twenty questions. If you're single, this is *the* transit for speed-dating so you can test the waters.

DATE NIGHT IDEA: *Talk the talk.* Choose an activity that gives you lots of time to converse and get to know each other. Gemini is the chattiest of the planets, so consider grabbing a drink someplace where it's not too loud so you can get deep into fun and stimulating conversations with your date or partner.

⬙ MARS IN GEMINI: Gemini energy gives us a very short attention span, so we'll probably feel scattered and notice our sexual interests are all over the place. That's okay—just go wild and schedule multiple dates with different people to keep yourself engaged! And a little dirty talk wouldn't hurt either, as Gemini energy loves to chat. It's also a good time to mix things up in the bedroom and learn new things about our desires as well as our partners', because Gemini energy is easily bored. Spark a little curiosity in your sex life! Plan a sexy night with your partner where you try something you've never tried before that can show you both a different side of the other.

💜 VENUS IN CANCER:

Venus wants us to cozy up with our lovers and profess our love and devotion for them while it transits through the emotional waters of Cancer. If you're in a relationship, this is a beautiful transit for deepening your devotion to your partner. Make a home-cooked meal for your lover and shower them with cuddles to show you care. If you're single, rely on your closest friends or family for support and comfort if you don't have it in your love life at this time.

DATE NIGHT IDEA: *Embrace your softer side.* Go with something slow-paced and relaxing that allows for emotional connection and feels nurturing. Anything domestic is good. How about you and your date bake cookies at home together, or perhaps plan a fun and cuddle-filled adult sleepover? If you go out, choose someplace with a cozy and casual vibe to maintain the chill.

🔥 MARS IN CANCER:

You're in the mood for something real and emotional, so flings may not be your style now. Your passions and desires will also be a bit more dependent on your mood, but your mood might be a little all over the place! Be willing to ride the moody waves of Mars in Cancer's indirect style of chasing passion. Remember, it's okay to be a little picky and hold off on second dates or hookups until you emotionally connect with someone or really feel in the mood. Stick to self-pleasuring if you're finding yourself frustrated with trying to hook up.

· · · 💛 🔥 · · ·
Love Houses

If you want to be your own best love expert, always keep an eye on what planets in your birth chart are transiting through the areas of your fifth house of love (which can affect how much action your pleasure centers are getting, as well as influence your dating life) and your seventh house of partnerships (which can have a big effect if you're in a committed relationship with someone or potentially getting into one). Also keep an eye on planetary activity in your eighth house, as that concerns sex and intimacy.

💜 **VENUS IN LEO:** We're all looking for love like in the movies when Venus transits through flashy fire sign Leo, and that's exactly what we'll get—high drama, lots of glam, and tons of hot 'n' fiery energy when it comes to romance. If you're single, post your hottest selfies on social media, wear whatever outfits make you feel sexiest, and get your flirt on. If you're in a relationship, now's a great time to go over-the-top when it comes to making your partner feel like royalty. Buy them a luxurious gift!

DATE NIGHT IDEA: *Make it Hollywood.* Don't be afraid to attract some attention. Get yourself majorly sparkled out and hit the town to go clubbing or check out a hot event. Make sure your date gets the glam-it-up memo when getting dressed, too. Whatever you do, make sure you feel sexy and get out in the public eye: Leo energy loves the spotlight!

🔥 **MARS IN LEO:** Sex drives are on high during this transit, so it's a great time to get out there and let your inner sexpot *loose*. This transit makes us all more direct, so if you want someone, tell them! Respectful and consensual flattery can go a long way when Mars is in Leo, because we're all seeking a little extra sexual attention. It's also a great time to get a little performative in the bedroom. Channel your inner actor and try a sexy role-play, or just change up your look with some attention-grabbing new lingerie or red lipstick and treat your partner to your steamiest bedroom getup.

💜 **VENUS IN VIRGO:** Prepare to perfect your love life, because Virgo loves a good project. When Venus is in Virgo, it's considered to be in its *fall*, which means it doesn't feel like its natural qualities are being expressed very well. That said, this transit has its perks. If you're single, you might find yourself feeling picky about your lovers, but you can also embrace this pickiness, as it's simply showing you things that would likely bug you down the road anyway. If you're in a relationship, go out of your way to show your partner love through acts of service; helping with their chores or offering to run an errand can speak volumes under this transit.

DATE NIGHT IDEA: *Go all natural.* Opt for a fun hike or grab coffees and take a walk through a tree-filled park. Doing something wellness-related could be fun, too, like taking a yoga class together. Just remember that Virgo energy appreciates a solid and well-kept plan, so whatever you do, be punctual and clear about your date's itinerary.

🔥 **MARS IN VIRGO:** You're going to be super hyped up when it comes to noticing every little detail, so it might cause your standards for sexual partners to be almost painfully high. It'll be easy to get overly critical of your partner's performance in the bedroom (or their hygiene—Virgo is all about cleanliness and purity!), or alternatively, you might focus these harsh critiques on *yourself*. Don't hyper-focus on flaws; try to let loose! That said, being constructively critical can be a good thing, so this transit is actually a great time to look at your love life with a more critical eye and figure out spots where things could be better. You'll be motivated to make adjustments to anything that seems off or needs improvement, including your choice in partners!

💜 **VENUS IN LIBRA:** Libra is the other sign of Venus's domicile, meaning the planet of love is super happy here and able to show off her most flirtatious side. Social Libra imbues us with great conversational energy and natural diplomacy, so if you're single, put it to good use on the dating scene and mingle—your charm will be off the charts. If you're in a relationship, now's a great time to rekindle the spark of storybook romance. Look at anything that feels off-balance in your partnership and then fix it with the most romantic gestures possible, because Libra energy loves *love* more than just about anything!

DATE NIGHT IDEA: *Get your flirt on.* Do something cute 'n' classy that stimulates your aesthetic senses, engaging both your mind and your eyes with beauty, with *lots* of opportunities to chat and charm each other! Going to an art museum would be a perfect date for this transit, perhaps followed by hitting a bakery for some visually pleasing pastries for dessert and innocent flirting. Make sure your outfit is equally aesthetic, too.

🔥 **MARS IN LIBRA:** Mars is in its fall in Libra, meaning it struggles to express its action-oriented nature here, but that just means we'll be a little more people pleasing in the bedroom. Expect to pay extra attention to what your partner wants, as Libra is the sign that rules partnerships, so there's an added emphasis on duality and balance during these transits. Libra is also the zodiac's charmer, so expect to be super flirtatious in your sexual advances and be upping the charms to degrees you didn't know you had in you! Sweet-talking and flirtation will be big parts of the chase now, although be aware that neither party will likely want to make the first move.

💜 **VENUS IN SCORPIO:** Venus is in its detriment in Scorpio, but that doesn't mean we're not in for a super sexy season. If you're single, there's a chance you could get very deep with someone *very* fast—it's easy to get obsessed with someone under this transit! If you're in a relationship, use this as a chance to deepen your spiritual connection and embrace the truth at all costs. Anything that's lurking beneath the surface should be addressed, or else you risk it coming out in some other (and less-controlled) manner.

DATE NIGHT IDEA: *Prepare to get intimate.* No, I don't mean sex (although I don't *not* mean sex), but I do mean that the energy of this transit is only interested in getting *deep* with someone, so anything superficial will be a huge turnoff. Skip the small talk and keep things super real. It's much less about what you do on a date during this transit and more about being honest, upfront, and willing to go deep.

🔥 **MARS IN SCORPIO:** Mars loves being in Scorpio, so prepare to embrace the most powerful version of yourself in the bedroom. You might even find yourself being drawn to taboo sexual realms, as Scorpio has a magnetic attraction to mysterious and hidden topics. It's definitely prime to lean into your kinky side now. Unleash your inner sex god or goddess under this transit, but only with someone you trust! We are feeling all of our passions and desires with a double intensity now, which is great when it comes to hot, passionate sex, but not so great if we feel threatened, as we're likely fall into the trap of jealousy or possessiveness here. Beware of the intensity of emotion that can come along with sexuality.

💜 **VENUS IN SAGITTARIUS:** Love is an adventure when Venus is in Sagittarius! We're embracing our free-spirited sides when it comes to romance and feeling super idealistic about love. If you're single, it's a fantastic time to date people who are outside your norm in order to expand your horizons—maybe someone from another country or a totally different walk of life. If you're in a relationship, mix things up and add some excitement to your routine by trying something new together (inside or outside the bedroom).

DATE NIGHT IDEA: *Say yes to adventure.* Trying something new and exciting is a must—go eat some exotic food or choose a funky activity you've never tried before, like paintballing or ziplining. Or go with something worldly, like taking in a foreign film or hitting a museum exhibit to expand your mind.

🔥 MARS IN SAGITTARIUS: Sag is a wild child fire sign, and when Mars is here, it wants to party. Expect to be much more spontaneous and wilder in the bedroom—don't be surprised if you find yourself in the mood to try totally new positions or play with some new toys! We're feeling free-spirited with our passions, but this also means we probably don't want to be tethered down, so don't commit to an exclusive situation if you don't really want it. Instead, have an honest conversation about your desires and see if your partner can meet you there.

💜 VENUS IN CAPRICORN: We're all looking for a love to put on lockdown when Venus is in Capricorn. This transit is all about finding someone who is worth putting in the work to make something last. If you're single, you'll probably be choosier about who gets your time. If you're in a relationship, you might sense your focus is shifting onto more practical matters of your partnership. It's a good time to have a conversation about how seriously committed you are to one another, and whether you can envision yourself with the person for the long term.

DATE NIGHT IDEA: *Keep it classy and simple.* As an earth sign, Capricorn loves the finer things in life, so come dressed to impress, as you don't want to look cheap. Traditional vibes are welcome now, so keep things simple with something classic, such as dinner and a movie.

🔥 MARS IN CAPRICORN: We're super goal-oriented under Capricorn transits, and it definitely shows up in our sex life—you're probably going to be less interested in random hookups, as you won't want to waste energy on someone who doesn't fit with your current life goals. But that doesn't mean this isn't going to be a steamy transit—passionate Mars *loves* being in Capricorn. Capricorn is a restricting and authoritative energy, which can definitely be kind of hot in the bedroom (depending on your tastes, of course). Lean into your dominant side and inject a little consensual power play into your sexual dynamic.

💜 VENUS IN AQUARIUS: We're all looking to embrace our individuality and the uniqueness of others in love when Venus is in Aquarius. If you're single, look to your social circle to find love, as this energy is all about making social connections and a potential mate might be hanging among your crew already. If you're in a relationship, practice supporting your partner's independence. Encourage them to go do something they've been wanting to try, even if you don't go with them.

DATE NIGHT IDEA: *Make it social.* Group dates are super fun under this transit, as everyone's feeling more socially and community-oriented, so having the mental stimulation of a whole group of people around you can actually enhance a romantic dynamic. Bring your date as a plus one to a party, or join friends for a night out on the town.

♨ MARS IN AQUARIUS:

Clicking with someone on an intellectual level is what turns us on when Mars is in Aquarius, and we're attracted to people who share our vision of the future. A funky and interesting conversation can be the perfect form of foreplay. Everyone's drawn to the unconventional under Aquarius transits, and your passion is no exception. You might surprise yourself by being willing to embrace kinks or relationship formats that are outside the norm, like trying a threesome. This is also a good transit for a friends-with-benefits situation to develop, so don't rule out the possibility of hooking up with someone just because they're a pal.

♥ VENUS IN PISCES:

Love is but a dream when Venus is in Pisces—the sign of its exaltation. If you're single, this is a great time to plan some dreamy and romantic dates—just beware of falling head over heels for the fantasy of someone rather than who the person really is. If you're in a relationship, you're feeling extra compassionate, which will make you feel even closer to your partner.

DATE NIGHT IDEA: *Flex your spiritual side.* Going to hear some crystal singing bowls or getting your palms read could be fun. But also, expressing yourself through art (or simply appreciating it) is a great way to bond under this transit, too. Hit up an open mic night, an art show, or a bar with live music if the spiritual route is too much.

♨ MARS IN PISCES:

It's hard to express exactly what our desires are under this transit, and it's tough to maintain boundaries around them, too, so be extra careful to stay communicative with your sex partners to make sure everyone is stating their needs. This is one of the more emotional placements for Mars, so you might feel extra intuitive and emotionally passionate now. This could make sex extra romantic, and it could even feel spiritual! Prepare for possibly transcendental moments in the bedroom.

Proceed with Caution Zones: Sex and Love Edition

Certain planetary retrograde periods can heavily affect your love and sex life.

💜 DURING VENUS RETROGRADE

(WHICH HAPPENS ALMOST EVERY YEAR FOR ABOUT FORTY DAYS):

Be wary of starting a new relationship or taking any big steps in love. When Venus isn't shining as her usual self, it's not considered a very auspicious time to seal any romantic deals, so avoid getting married (or popping the question) or even putting a label on a new relationship.

Dating under this transit also calls for added self-awareness, as most new flings that start in Venus retrograde won't be built to last. In fact, we're more likely to attract people who are the *opposite* of what we actually want during this time. This transit also attracts ex-lovers who may be sniffing around for some affection or another shot at romance, so be wary.

💜 DURING MERCURY RETROGRADE

(WHICH HAPPENS ABOUT THREE TIMES PER YEAR FOR THREE WEEKS AT A TIME):

Be aware that the decisions we make in love don't have the staying power they normally would. If you decide to start or end a relationship during Mercury retrograde, don't be shocked if you end up backtracking on the new relationship *or* getting back together with the person you just broke up with post-retrograde.

Exes commonly pop up in our DMs or text message in-boxes during Mercury retrograde, as it's a time that many people seek closure and communication with people from their past. Don't be shocked if someone who ghosted you hits you up out of the blue wanting to talk or touch base, and beware the temptation of hitting up one of your exes, too!

🔥 DURING MARS RETROGRADE

(WHICH HAPPENS ABOUT EVERY TWO YEARS FOR UP TO TWO AND A HALF MONTHS):

This transit is a bit of a sex drive killer. We may experience a lack of passion and desire for our sex partners during Mars retrograde and have a lower libido in general. This could lead to some sexual frustration (or just plain frustration about not being much in the mood), and therefore it's not a great time to find a new sex partner. Even if we *are* in the mood, we might find that hookups may just not be very steamy or satisfying now. If you're already in a sexual relationship with someone, make sure you up your communication at this time so everything's on the table.

Like Mercury and Venus retrogrades, Mars retrogrades are also known for bringing ex-lovers back into our lives, and in the case of Mars, these advances are usually sexually driven. Look out for late-night booty call texts from your ex, and conversely, check yourself before *you* catch yourself reaching out to a long-lost lover just because you want some action.

Best Days for Love

Tuesday is ruled by Mars, making it a super-energized day for taking action and pursuing your desires. Ready to ask someone out? Use Tuesday's energy to amp you up and encourage you to chase your passions.

Friday is ruled by Venus, making this a great day to prioritize romance, affection, and all things love. It's a good time to get glammed up for a date night, too—and thankfully, it falls just before the weekend!

ASTROLOGY FOR LIFE: CAREER

Work takes up *how* many hours of our waking life? Um, a lot. So obviously, we want to make sure we're setting ourselves up right in our careers and making sound decisions in our professional lives. We all want to slay at our jobs, and when we're looking to make big moves career-wise—whether it's to quit a current gig to pursue a dream job or to simply kick off a new project at work—it's normal to seek a little guidance. Who better to consult than the cosmos?

Reading your horoscope and scouring it for career clues is fun, but if you want to connect with what the planets are up to *now*, you can use certain planetary transits to get an idea of the overall astrological influences that are affecting *everyone's* professional lives at any given time. Doing so can help you feel much more in sync with the cycles of our solar system, and can help you align your career goals with the cosmic forces that be. Here are some places to search for cosmic career advice.

The Career-Related Planets to Pay Attention to

When we think of work, we think of motivation, ambition, and our ability to take action, and all of this is totally **Mars** territory. Mars is named for the god of war, but it's not about fighting: It's simply about *action*. This planet is goal-oriented, ambitious, passionate, driven, energetic, and willing to fight for what it wants, making it our ideal astrological ally when it comes to slaying our loftiest career goals and bringing energy and enthusiasm to all professional endeavors. Mars switches signs approximately every month and a half to two months, and retrogrades approximately every other year, and all of these transits affect our energy and motivation to advance in our careers.

There are also a number of other planets that can affect our work lives, depending on what we do, and we can pay more or less attention to them depending on what our current career goals are.

Astrology can be a very useful tool when it comes to helping guide us in our careers, from big things (like aligning our field of work with our higher purpose) to smaller things (like asking our boss for some new responsibilities).

THE SUN rules over self-expression, so if your career goals involve channeling your own creativity or marketing yourself as your brand, you'll want to align yourself with the Sun's energy by playing to strengths of whatever sign the Sun is in at a given time (and of course by fluffing up the feathers of your *own* Sun sign to maximize its power).

MERCURY rules over our intellect as well as all sorts of logistical tasks, so if you have "busy work" to complete, organization to get done, papers or documents to file, or any sort of written communication work on, see what Mercury is up to.

VENUS rules over money, so if your career focus is currently based around boosting your finances, obtaining material possessions, and growing your bank account, Venus is your gal.

JUPITER is the planet of expansion and knowledge, so if you're trying to set shoot-for-the-stars-style goals for yourself or are interested in going back to school to get a higher degree in your field, this is your planet.

SATURN is the planet of discipline, so its energy can affect us in the stress and responsibility department. Saturn is also goal-oriented and all about hard work, so call on this energy to whip you into shape when you need some boundaries and focus.

URANUS is the planet of inspiration and innovation, so if you're trying to think outside the box about your career trajectory or come up with some fresh new ideas, see what's up with creative Uranus to find out how and when its inspo-lightning might strike.

If you want to see the style in which you typically act on your career-related ambitions, you should look at your own Mars sign, but if you're looking for insight into some of these other planets' realms, check out where *they* reside in your birth chart.

Career-Related Planetary Transits: How to Make the Most of Them

Knowing your Mars sign is very useful, but it's also helpful to know that as Mars powers its way through the zodiac, it influences all of us, and it colors the collective energy around how we chase (and hopefully conquer) our goals. Working with these planetary transits can boost your work life by inspiring you to make certain moves, and by helping to advise you on favorable times to do so.

Mars switches signs approximately every other month, so keep tabs on where it's at (and where it's heading next) by using an ephemeris or checking trusted online sources, then work with the energy accordingly.

The Midheaven: The Angle in Your Chart That Can Help You Land a Dream Job

There's a major point in your birth chart that pertains to your professional life, and that's your **midheaven**, aka the cusp of the tenth house, which is the area that rules your public image and career. The midheaven is all about your reputation and your calling. It relates to your career, for sure, but it gets even bigger than that, as it's also about the lasting mark you're going to leave on the world through your work and contributions.

If you want to get an idea about what your ultimate calling is regarding your career, check to see what sign the midheaven falls in within your birth chart. Whatever sign your midheaven is in illustrates the qualities that you should be embracing and highlighting through your work. Leaning into these qualities will help bring you the highest level of success and make you feel the most fulfilled. This can point you in a solidly helpful direction as far as figuring out which types of paths or projects could ultimately bring you the most success, recognition, and personal growth. You should also examine any planets in your birth chart that are forming notable aspects with your midheaven, as they also highlight additional influences or challenges within that realm.

⭐ **MARS IN ARIES:** You've got the energy and the enthusiasm to make big moves in your career under this transit. Mars is ultra-powerful and motivated here, so it's a prime time to take initiative and prioritize your wants. Start new projects, apply for your dream job, and show off your leadership skills wherever you can. And don't be afraid to ask your boss for the raise you know you deserve—this fiery energy will bring the heat.

COSMIC CAREER TIP: Decisions around career stuff shouldn't be taken lightly, so make sure you're thinking through your choices and not just acting impulsively. Patience is a virtue.

⭐ **MARS IN TAURUS:** Embrace a slow but steady attitude at work. There's no need to rush to the finish line as long as you work at a steady pace! Now's a good time to be extra-reliable and solid—this will be a huge help to your colleagues and will impress your bosses simultaneously. But, and perhaps more importantly, it will also ensure that you make some major progress on your work goals without burning yourself out.

COSMIC CAREER TIP: It's good to stick to a plan when it comes to work and projects, but that doesn't mean there's never room for improvement! Try not to be stubborn if someone offers a suggestion.

· · · ★ · · ·
Chart Your Career Goals

Use astrology to gain a professional edge. Check out your own birth chart and keep an eye on which planets in transit are currently within the zodiac degrees that comprise your **tenth house of career and public image** (as this is the house of your midheaven, the major house that dictates your life purpose, career path, and public reputation). Transiting planets there—or transiting planets that are forming aspects with any *natal* planets there—could bring major energy to that part of your life. Look also at what's going on in your **second house of value**, as that house rules money and material possessions and can tip you off to issues that affect your financial life and stability. Lastly, it may help to keep an eye on planetary activity in your **eighth house**, as that concerns issues like taxes, inheritances, and other people's assets, which also tie into your financial life and work.

⭐ **MARS IN GEMINI:** Your energy at work is all over the place, and you're finding yourself more interested in a wider variety of aspects of your company or position. Don't be afraid to ask questions and let your curiosity show—your bosses and colleagues will likely appreciate that you're interested in hearing a variety of perspectives and learning new facts. Gather information while your energy is high, and use it wisely in the future.

COSMIC CAREER TIP: You might find your attention span is lower than usual here, so clear your workspace of distractions to ensure you're not neglecting your responsibilities.

⭐ **MARS IN CANCER:** It's a good time to slow down your work pace a bit now, because when it comes to dealing with professional matters, you may not feel as clear in your wants, as your mind keeps changing and you lose focus. Whether it's riding the wave of day-to-day work drama or the waves of your changing moods, taking on a go-with-the-flow attitude here is helpful. It's okay to take a break from the intensity of building your career to just check in with your heart.

COSMIC CAREER TIP: It may be hard to know exactly what you want career-wise, but make sure you know what you *don't* want. Trust your emotional instincts when it comes to choosing your next move.

⭐ **MARS IN LEO:** Toss your shyness out the window, because it's time to own your confidence and strut your stuff. This is a great transit for putting yourself out there, asking for what you want with no regrets, and making your passion projects a reality. Regardless of your goals, it's a time to believe in yourself. Don't be afraid to show off your shiniest qualities so that everyone you work with knows how valuable you are.

COSMIC CAREER TIP: Confidence is powerful, but cockiness is off-putting. Impress your boss and colleagues by walking the walk, not just talking the talk.

⭐ **MARS IN VIRGO:** Get ready to relish in the details and wrap up the jobs that need finishing, because you're doing the job *right*. This is a great time to scour every nook and cranny of your current position for ways to improve, which will ensure that you're on track to slay your goals. Make sure you're dotting every *i* and crossing every *t* so that when it comes time to ask for a raise or build a resume for another position, you'll be sparklingly prepared.

COSMIC CAREER TIP: Don't become such a perfectionist that you waste time obsessing over every tiny detail of every single project. Finished is better than perfect—don't forget that!

⭐ **MARS IN LIBRA:** Your charm is off the charts right now, so it's a great time to use your heightened people skills to your advantage at work and market your personality wherever you can. The usually extreme Mars seeks some balance in the way it takes action here, so negotiations and collaborations will be more agreeable and pleasant, albeit perhaps less productive. The energy is also auspicious for business partnerships, so open yourself to the possibility of finding a professional partner in crime.

COSMIC CAREER TIP: Being a people pleaser at work has its perks, but it can also get a little toxic. Make sure you're advocating for yourself and not overly placating when someone's in the wrong.

⭐ **MARS IN SCORPIO:** If you want something (and of course, you do!), you're going to go after it with intensity and a laser-sharp focus now. Mars is ultra-powerful and calculated in Scorpio, and will go to any depths, lengths, or heights to achieve what it sets out to do. If you have professional goals or projects that need deep, focused, intense energy to get off the ground, this is the transit that can help you dive into the mess and make it happen.

COSMIC CAREER TIP: You may be feeling drawn to intensity now, but *too* much intensity can be a weird vibe at work. Take little breaks if you catch yourself getting overly obsessive.

Career-Oriented Days

Tuesday is ruled by Mars, making it a great day for taking initiative and charging forward on a new project or endeavor at work. Take the first steps on a new assignment and put your extra energy to good use.

Wednesday is ruled by Mercury, making this a great time to focus on logistical tasks, organization, paperwork, and communication in the workplace. Catch up on emails, remake your to-do list, work on research or data-entry projects, or organize your desk.

Thursday is ruled by Jupiter, making it a perfect day to expand your horizons and think big. If you're going to schedule a brainstorming meeting, do it on a Thursday to encourage bigger and brighter ideas.

⭐ **MARS IN SAGITTARIUS:** Even if you consider yourself an expert in your profession, there's always more to learn, so use the booming energy you feel during this period to expand your knowledge within your field and gain some new skills and perspectives. If you want to switch careers, it's a great time to start learning a new skill or finding a mentor who can share their wisdom.

COSMIC CAREER TIP: It's good to be optimistic, but temper your lofty goals with a healthy bit of realism, too. If you take on too much, you'll be tempted to abandon it all.

⭐ **MARS IN CAPRICORN:** There is no goal you can't conquer under this transit, so get to work. Mars is at its most ambitious here, so it's not a matter of *if* you'll reach your destination—it's a matter of *when*. Take advantage of your hyper self-discipline and your ability to work super hard right now in order to reach your long-term goals. Long hours of overtime are no match for your goal-focused determination to get to the top.

COSMIC CAREER TIP: Working hard and planning for the future are great, but throwing your work/life balance out the window to reach your goals isn't ideal. Don't forget to take breaks.

⭐ **MARS IN AQUARIUS:** Networking can bring you major success right now, as you'll find it easier to make genuine connections with people in your field (or the fields you *want* to be in) and actually follow through on working with them. You'll also find a lot more value in working collaboratively with others, so don't shy away from group projects and remember to bounce your ideas off your colleagues—you're feeling like a team player.

COSMIC CAREER TIP: It's good to problem-solve at work by thinking outside the box, but don't toss aside traditionally successful ways of doing things simply for the sake of being unique.

⭐ **MARS IN PISCES:** Lean into your creative side to help you blossom at work, even if you don't work in a creative field. It may be hard to make traction on your goals during this period because the linear path in front of you has turned into a nebulous cloud. That's okay—just float along with it and allow your creative thoughts and intuitive readings to guide you toward your next moves in an almost spiritual fashion. Who knows? It could even lead you to your higher calling.

COSMIC CAREER TIP: It's harder to be direct at work under this transit, but make sure that doesn't stop you from maintaining boundaries. If you're feeling depleted, say so.

Proceed with Caution Zones: Career and Work Edition

Certain planetary retrograde periods could heavily affect your work and career life.

★ DURING MARS RETROGRADE

(WHICH HAPPENS ABOUT EVERY TWO YEARS FOR UP TO TWO AND A HALF MONTHS):

Going to work sucks under this transit, as we're likely to feel drained, physically and mentally exhausted, and totally burnt out on our job. Expect to lose a lot of motivation and steam when it comes to a gig or work project that you previously felt super-inspired and pumped about. It might feel like all the wind has left your sails, or that you've totally run out of gas and are sputtering to a full stop in the middle of the freeway. Obviously, this isn't ideal if you happen to be in the middle of a large endeavor at work, nor is it fun to dread getting up and going to work each day. Try to cut yourself some slack, get lots of rest, and take things slower at work where you can. Your energy will build back up again.

Avoid making any rash or impulsive decisions around work at this time. You may be tempted to suddenly quit your job out of sheer frustration or propose a huge new project to your team that you haven't fully thought through yet—but don't. Temper your impulsiveness with well-thought-out plans and lots of reflection time to be sure you're making the right decision and not just getting swept up in the heat of the moment. Taking action on new things is difficult under this transit, and attempting to do so (especially on impulse) is not advised. Take deep breaths and muster up all the patience you can.

★ DURING MERCURY RETROGRADE

(WHICH HAPPENS ABOUT THREE TIMES PER YEAR FOR THREE WEEKS AT A TIME):

Everything logistical in nature is a total mess under this transit, so expect to hit all sorts of frustrating snags when it comes to scheduling meetings, crunching numbers, getting to work on time, and even thinking clearly. Communication and technology are haywire, too, so you'll want to double-check work emails for typos or missing attachments (and make sure you're sending your message to the right person), and don't be surprised if your laptop is running slow as molasses or your Wi-Fi keeps going out.

It's really inadvisable to sign contracts or agree to anything binding in nature during Mercury retrograde, as this transit heightens the chances that we overlook important details or that the terms of the offer aren't being presented clearly. This could manifest in signing a contract that isn't actually favorable to you, for example, or taking a job that isn't what it was made out to be. Try to avoid job hunting during Mercury retrograde if you can help it, as the energy doesn't support us starting something new. If you do get a dream offer, make sure you spend extra time reading every bit of fine print and getting all of your questions answered before accepting.

ASTROLOGY FOR LIFE: SOCIAL LIFE

Our social lives comprise a big part of who we are, and this can include our friendships, our relationships with our family members, and the way we interact with other people. Social connection is about so much more than having fun (although it's certainly great for that); it's also deeply important when it comes to bringing fulfillment and joy into our lives. Astrology can be a very useful tool to both examine and enhance these social relationships.

Using astrology to examine the compatibility between you and your friends or family members' Sun signs can be interesting and fun, but there are many other ways to work with astrology to enhance your social life and enliven your relationships. Whether you're looking to find ways to bond more closely with your friends and fam, or just want a little cosmic guidance when it comes to planning your social calendar and weighing your weekend options, astrology is here to the rescue.

The Social Planets to Pay Attention to

There are several planets that illustrate different parts of our social life and relationships, and they all work together to build a full picture of the complexities of this part of our life. We'll start with chatty **Mercury**. Mercury rules over a whole lot of things, but it is also the planet of communication, so when it comes to making social connections, this planet takes up lots of bandwidth. Mercury is all about taking in information and then sharing it, which is sort of just a fancy way to describe a conversation. Mercury governs all types of communication—it's our manner of speaking, our style of texting, the way we show up in a conversation.

Mercury is all talking, texting, small talk, gossip, and any other form of basic communicado. We can look to our Mercury sign to see our social style and how we express ourselves, and we can also take a look at where in the zodiac Mercury is transiting at any given time to see what the overall influence on the current social landscape might be.

Then there's **Venus**. It's best known as the romance planet, but Venus is also the planet of love and pleasure, and both of these things are important when it comes to social relationships, too! While Mercury represents the very literal social element of social relationships (i.e., communicating with each other), Venus represents the *pleasure* in our social lives. It's the fun we have, the parties we go to, and the affection we show each other. Of course, that's what Venus is famous for: love. Venus is the queen of romantic love, but the love we have for our friends and family counts here, as well. Look to your Venus sign to see the way you seek pleasure and value within your social relationships, as well as the way you show your love and affection for your friends and family.

Then there is the **Moon**. This planet is in charge of our emotions, which often come into play within our closer relationships, but it's especially important when it comes to looking at the relationships we have with our families or the people who are in our closest inner circle. The Moon is all about nurturing, so we can look to this planet when it comes to examining how we operate within our closest familial relationships (and yes, this includes the friends whom you consider family, too!). How we nurture, want to be nurtured, and connect emotionally with others is ruled by our Moon sign. The transits of the Moon can affect our day-to-day moods (as this planet switches signs every few days), which in turn colors the way we interact with the people closest with us, like our families. While we may not show these fluctuations in feelings to our colleagues or even our friend group, we feel comfortable being vulnerable with our families or most intimate friends.

Social Life Planetary Transits: How to Make the Most of Them

As planets like Mercury, as well as Venus and the Moon, travel through the zodiac, they influence all of us and affect the way we approach our social lives, communicate with our friends, function as part of a community, and bond with our families. Our social lives are complex and involve a lot of different parts of our lives, including friendships, familial relationships, working relationships, our free time, and so much more, so it's no surprise that multiple planets work together to create the current vibe of any given moment.

While several planets hold various influences over our friendships and other non-romantic relationships, we're going to focus on Mercury, because Mercury rules over our communication style as well as our everyday relationships. Mercury switches signs every three to four weeks, on average, and as it transits it changes up the energy of our day-to-day social landscape. Keep tabs on where it is in the zodiac by using an ephemeris or checking trusted online sources. Becoming aware of the energy of the Mercury transits can help you make social plans, align yourself with the cosmic energy at play, and gain a better understanding of your relationships with friends and family.

··· ☺ ···

Specific Houses Can Offer Major Social Life Insight

Check out your own birth chart and keep an eye on which planets in transit are currently within the degrees of the zodiac that comprise your **third house**, which rules over the way we communicate as well as the friends, siblings, and peers that we spend time with regularly. Transiting planets there—or transiting planets that are forming aspects with any *natal* planets there—could indicate major energy flowing toward that part of your life.

Look also at what's going on in your **eleventh house of friendships and community,** as this house focuses more on social groups and the dynamics, power, and community that build within them. Any natal planets here indicate that a lot of energy exists within this area of your life, and any transiting planets here can light up your friendship groups as well.

Lastly, your **fourth house** is in charge of home and family, so transiting planets hitting that area could either help or hurt your relationships and dynamics with your family members or the people you share your home with.

☺ **MERCURY IN ARIES:** Our social lives are always on fire when Mercury is in fiery Aries. We're confident, direct, and straightforward in our communication style, and we're all more likely to initiate some fun plans within our social circles. Reach out and include everyone! Get out and be active with friends and family during this transit.

☺ **MERCURY IN TAURUS:** Hitting the town with a big group might not be your speed during this transit, but that doesn't mean you're not looking to connect socially! You'll probably just be in the mood for more chilled-out hangs with closer friends: Think dinner parties, movies nights, or coffee dates instead of nights at the club.

☺ **MERCURY IN GEMINI:** Your social life is on speed! Your communication abilities are off the charts. Prepare to feel extra chatty and more curious and interested in other people's thoughts (which makes us better conversationalists!). Use your amped-up social energy to fill your social calendar with all different types of plans.

☺ **MERCURY IN CANCER:** This is an awesome period to spend more time at home connecting with the people closest to you. There's an emphasis on family under Cancer transits, so try to prioritize quality emotional-bonding time with your family members and longtime close friends. We're all in the mood to connect and nurture each other.

☺ **MERCURY IN LEO:** I hope you're ready to put your social life first, because Mercury in Leo is all about a good time. This is a great vibe for socializing and embracing your inner extrovert. We're feeling super social and likely in the mood to go out and hit the town with friends—say yes to the invites! Just don't let yourself get caught up in social drama.

☺ **MERCURY IN VIRGO:** Tighten up your social group now and let yourself be a little choosier about where you channel your energy within your social life. If you feel you have toxic or draining friendships, now's a good time to pull away and start prioritizing energy toward your healthy, fulfilling, and energizing relationships!

☺ **MERCURY IN LIBRA:** Our social lives are the center of attention under this transit, so turn on the charm and have some fun! Every convo you have with someone—from your best friend to your barista—will be extra sweet and diplomatic. This is a great time to bring balance and energy to both our social circles *and* one-on-one relationships.

☺ **MERCURY IN SCORPIO:** You're more interested in intimate and real conversations now. Socially, this is a more reserved time. You're a little more wary about opening up to people, and you'll probably want to spend more time with your most trusted crew. Look forward to lots of deep and existential convos!

☺ **MERCURY IN SAGITTARIUS:** Are you ready to party? Because we're feeling excited, optimistic, and highly social in our friendships here and will want to have some fun! This is an ideal time to be spontaneous, go on adventures with friends, and meet new people who can expand your horizons. Just be sure not to leave your old friends behind!

☺ **MERCURY IN CAPRICORN:** Our social life may take a little bit of a back seat to our personal and professional goals. It's easy to take on a more serious, hardworking, and less social approach to your friendships, so you might naturally minimize any frivolous hangs and find yourself being more intentional with your spare time.

☺ **MERCURY IN AQUARIUS:** Prepare to get trippy and have some fun! Conversations move to fascinating topics about ideals and global issues. We're more socially conscious and aware of social justice now. We feel more community-oriented and want to spend time with our most like-minded friends, family members, and colleagues.

☺ **MERCURY IN PISCES:** This is a sensitive time when it comes to interacting with friends and family, as we're focused more deeply on our emotions: Feelings are running strong! This can make us feel sensitive and overwhelmed, but can also be a great time for creative, spiritual, and emotional connection with the people closest to us.

Polarities of Zodiac Signs and How They Affect Us Socially

Polarities of zodiac signs (which are explained in depth in Chapter 2) represent the yin and yang energies—or masculine and feminine energies—of the twelve signs. Masculine signs are outward focused, while feminine signs are inward focused. We can look at the polarities of the signs to tip us off as to whether the transit will bring energy outward (toward other people and outside energy, i.e., social) or inward (toward ourselves and our emotions, i.e., less social).

While some relationships can certainly help us turn inward and be in touch with our emotions, we're generally going to be more social and interested in connecting with the people, friends, and ideas within our environments during the masculine or yang seasons, the fire and air signs. During the feminine or yin seasons, the earth and water signs, we'll be a little less focused on other people and more invested in our own feelings and experiences.

You can see this on a broad and general scale by examining one planet that we haven't even mentioned in this chapter yet: the Sun. The Sun is the center of our solar system, and when it travels through the zodiac, the energy is experienced by all. Sun seasons have a huge influence on the overall energies that we all collectively experience, and thus, during fire and air sign seasons, you'll probably feel much more social.

The masculine and feminine seasons take turns in the zodiac—every other zodiac sign is one and then the other—so there's a natural balance, and aligning with this energy helps bring some order to our lives. After a month of the Sun being a yin or feminine sign (which encourages us to focus our energy inward), it moves into a yang or masculine sign (which encourages us to focus our energy outward). The same is true for any planet's cycle through the zodiac, and we can keep the polarities of the signs in mind when we want to know how a planet's transit might affect our social lives and the relationships we maintain with our friends and families.

 ## Proceed with Caution Zones: Friends and Family Edition

Certain planetary retrograde periods can heavily affect your social life and interpersonal relationships.

☺ DURING MERCURY RETROGRADE

(WHICH HAPPENS ABOUT THREE TIMES PER YEAR FOR THREE WEEKS AT A TIME):

Communication is a struggle here. We're all more likely to misinterpret someone's words and take offense, and the opposite is true, too. Being extra aware of having clarity in both verbal and written communication is the key to avoiding hurt feelings and drama with friends and family. It also doesn't hurt to do a triple-check to ensure you're not texting the wrong person or accidentally sending something embarrassingly personal to your office group chat thinking it was just your best friend!

Social Connection Days

Monday is ruled by the Moon, which makes it the type of day where you'll want to connect with your family and enjoy the nurturing feeling of home. If you're going to be social on a Monday, it should be with people who make you feel nurtured, safe, and secure, and this could certainly include friends who *feel* like family if your actual family isn't an option. Heart-to-hearts are well received on this day.

Wednesday is ruled by Mercury, so it's the perfect vibe for lighthearted social interactions. Use the energy by catching up with friends, sharing some gossip, chatting on the phone with a faraway pal, and otherwise focusing on connecting through communication and conversation.

Friday is ruled by Venus, and it's also the kickoff to the weekend, making it perfect for fun social events! Friday vibes are all about getting dressed up and having a blast with friends in a sweet and love-filled way. It's a great time to go to a party.

Sunday is ruled by the Sun (obvi), and it can also be a great day for socializing, as the Sun is all about self-expression. We're feeling very much ourselves under the Sun's influence, and this can make socializing feel more genuine and fun. It can also make us feel a little brighter and more social all around!

Remember, timing is totally off under Mercury retrograde, so everyone is more likely to show up late to events, misunderstand the details of where and when you planned to meet up, or have frustratingly incompatible schedules. Try to be flexible if you run into this kind of thing, and hope your friends and fam will do the same for you! And always confirm plans before heading out to make sure you've got them right. Give yourself a little extra time to get from place to place, too, in case you hit traffic or a map malfunction on your phone sends you in the wrong direction (all of which is typical of Mercury retrograde).

ASTROLOGY FOR LIFE: SELF-CARE

Life is stressful. Between long hours at work, navigating our love lives and friendships, and dealing with the constant news cycle that can be *so* draining, prioritizing self-care isn't a luxury. It's a necessity. Setting time aside away from our stressors and allowing our mind, body, *and* soul to rest is essential for our well-being—and a must if we want to be in touch with ourselves enough to connect with the surrounding planets.

Self-care isn't just about "treating yourself" or going over the top with pampering; sometimes it's a matter of mental health. Sure, it can look like a fancy spa day full of glamorous selfies, or it can look like closing your laptop for five minutes at work and doing yoga breaths to keep yourself from having a panic attack. Self-care isn't selfish—it's necessary. We need to check in with ourselves regularly and make wellness as much a part of our daily routine as we possibly can.

Even small things help: The feeling of wholeness and interconnectedness that astrology offers can bring a lot of light and joy, even on days when we're feeling dark.

You can always call on your inner Mother Moon when you want to offer yourself some really worthy and nurturing self-care.

The Self-Care Planets to Pay Attention to

There are certainly a number of places in our chart where we can look for self-care advice, but one in particular stands out. **The Moon.** Think about it: Anxiety tends to come at night, and where can we look to soothe our worries and remind us that we *all* look up at the very same sky? This is one of the most familiar planets to us Earth dwellers, as we see her every night. This luminary rules over the sensitive and vulnerable part of our hearts, like our emotions and our memories. But the Moon is also the planet that's concerned with nurturing. This planet is astrology's mother figure—she's here to comfort us, nurture us, feed us a healthy meal, and give us blankets to cozy up with.

When it comes to setting time aside in our schedule to care for ourselves, it can be helpful to keep our natal Moon sign in mind. Check out Chapter 4 for information on looking up your Moon sign, then read about the description as well as how that Moon sign likes to be nurtured. Then, go look through the section in Chapter 2 that describes the qualities and energies of that zodiac sign. Synergize this information to help you create a cosmic care package for yourself. Think of the ways in which that vulnerable, private, sensitive inner self of yours wants to be nurtured and taken care of. Now, commit to actually doing those things for yourself!

Self-Care Planetary Transits: How to Make the Most of Them

Looking at our personal Moon sign is a great way to get in touch with the ways our cosmic self wants to be nurtured, but we can also plan our self-care routines around what the Moon is up to right *now*. As the Moon moves through the zodiac, its gentle influence impacts our emotional state (this is astrology's explanation for why our day-to-day moods can change so easily—the Moon's fast pace through the zodiac switches up the vibes on us every few days!). If we align ourselves with the intuitive and emotional lunar energy, we can find better ways to take care of ourselves that feel *right* at any given time.

Here are some ways you can work with the energy of the Moon in each of the zodiac signs in order to make your self-care routine more astrologically in sync. Feel free to adjust, as these are simply jumping-off points! Look to your natal Moon sign for insight into yourself, and blend that energy with whatever zodiac sign the Moon is transiting through right now. Most importantly, take a beat and listen to your inner self. That part of you will always tell you what you need to hear and how to take care of yourself.

Look to astrology to inspire new ways to care for yourself or to simply remind you to take a quick break. Because sometimes, caring for yourself feels somehow more significant when you've aligned your practices with the cosmos.

☽ SELF-CARE UNDER A MOON IN **ARIES**:

Being physical and breaking a sweat right now is good! Any way you can move your body during an Aries Moon will actually bring you *more* energy, so dance in your room, hit the gym, or go on a brisk walk with a friend. Get your blood pumping and your heart rate up.

☽ SELF-CARE UNDER A MOON IN **TAURUS**:

Sensual healing is what's called for now, so embrace sensual pleasure and lots of it. Book a deep massage or ask your partner to oil you up and treat you to one! Or light some beautifully scented candles, eat a delicious meal, and have a nice glass of wine to wind down.

☽ SELF-CARE UNDER A MOON IN **GEMINI**:

Conversations and human connection are a great tool for self-care. Get together with an uplifting, supportive, and trusted friend who will listen if you need to share whatever's weighing on your mind. Bonding and supporting each other through kind words is the way to heal.

☽ SELF-CARE UNDER A MOON IN **CANCER**:

Retreat into your personal shell and listen to the sea of your heart. The Moon is in her domicile here, so go full-on nurture mode on yourself. You have per-mission to stay in bed, order your dinner for delivery, and watch however many episodes of a good show as you feel like.

☽ SELF-CARE UNDER A MOON IN **LEO**: Glamour

healing is real, and this is a great time to go out of your way to feel beautiful. Primp yourself up in whatever way feels special. Maybe that means blowing out your hair, splurging on a manicure, or spending a few extra minutes in the morning doing your sexiest cat eye.

☽ **SELF-CARE UNDER A MOON IN VIRGO:** Cleanse, cleanse, cleanse. Cleaning out your closets, drawers, and every other corner of your home feels damn good under a Virgo Moon. A clean and tidy space leaves room for a lighter spirit, so use this energy to organize your belongings and clear out anything you don't want or need.

☽ **SELF-CARE UNDER A MOON IN LIBRA:** Pay attention to the beauty that's all around you—or create it! Do something to make your space more aesthetically pleasing, like buying a bouquet of fresh flowers to set on your table or finally framing and hanging a pretty art piece that's been leaned against a wall.

☽ **SELF-CARE UNDER A MOON IN SCORPIO:** We're drawn to the mystical and mysterious sides of life under a Scorpio Moon, so get in touch with your inner witch and set the stage for a grounding ritual. Look up rituals for self-love and self-care online, gather your supplies, and give it a shot. You'll feel empowered and enlightened.

☽ **SELF-CARE UNDER A MOON IN SAGITTARIUS:** Expanding your mind can truly soothe the soul, so do something that makes you think philosophically or teaches you something new. Pick a book off your shelf you haven't read yet and spend a couple of hours with your phone off, just enjoying the book page by page.

Days for Self-Care

Monday is the Moon's day, making it a good day to be extra gentle on yourself, honor your emotional side, and spend time with people who bring you comfort. Jumping into a new week after a nice weekend can be hard, so prioritize this as a self-care day, no matter how hectic the rest of your week might get.

Friday is ruled by Venus, making this a great day to prioritize your pleasure. It's definitely the week's "treat yourself" day in astrology. Do something fun, luxurious, and social—it's Friday, after all!

Tough Love from the Universe

Feeling drained? It helps to take a peek at your natal chart and then cross-reference it with a chart you make for today's date. Take a look at the signs and the *degrees* of the signs that the planets are in—are there any transit planets forming aspects to your natal planets? If so, are they hard aspects? Or are any of the tougher planets involved on either side, like malefics Saturn and Mars, or even unpredictable Uranus or intense Pluto? If the answer is yes, cut yourself some slack.

Transiting planets—especially ones that can induce tough life lessons, intensity, upheaval, or conflict—can make life difficult and stressful for a period of time. If you're seeing some tough aspects, plan to up the self-care and remind yourself, using the ever-changing symbolism of the Moon, that all things shall pass and you are learning lessons through each moment of your existence.

☽ SELF-CARE UNDER A MOON IN **CAPRICORN:** Christmas comes but

once a year, but sometimes we all need to treat ourselves. If you can spare the cash, splurge on a little something special that you've had your eye on. It feels good to buy ourselves something new once in a while, so allow yourself to give you a gift.

☽ SELF-CARE UNDER A MOON IN **AQUARIUS:** Give to yourself by giving

to others and do something that makes you feel connected to humanity. Perhaps you can attend a volunteer event or even just browse the web for ideas on ways you can be more sustainable. Feeling interconnected with the planet and other people feels good.

☽ SELF-CARE UNDER A MOON IN **PISCES:** Creativity and spirituality are the

language of caring for yourself during this period. Try a guided meditation or visualization to get in touch with your higher self, or take your mind off things by doing something artsy—painting, doodling, making jewelry, playing music, or even writing a poem.

Self-Care in the House

To get a good read on when self-care is needed, you can also try looking into which planets are transiting through the degrees in the zodiac chart that comprise your **sixth house of wellness**. This is the house that rules over our day-to-day habits, practices, and health—in other words, this is the premiere house of self-care. Transiting planets visiting this realm could either inspire you to up the self-care or make you feel drained and off your wellness game.

Also look to your **fourth house of home and family** for insights, as this is the house that represents your emotional, inner core—the side of yourself that could often use some soothing. The Moon is the natural ruler of this house, so if aligning your practices more with the lunar cycle is part of your routine, it might help to get in touch with the goings-on of your fourth house at any given time.

Lastly, keep an eye on what's happening in your **twelfth house of subconscious**, too—action here often calls for us to do a little soul-searching.

ASTROLOGY FOR LIFE: PERSONAL GOALS

We're all out here trying to be the most badass version of ourselves and build the life of our dreams, and whether you want to call it manifestation, intention-setting, or goal-setting, it's an equally important part of our lives and our hustle. Our personal goals are all individual. Whether we're focused on professional ambitions, health goals, or building the love life of our dreams, we can use astrology to support our goals in a much more involved way than simply reading about our future fate via a horoscope. We can actually *align* ourselves to the ever-shifting cosmic energy to help support our goal-setting and manifestation. It's really easy, even if you're a total newbie to astrology.

What's great about working with astrology to conquer our personal goals is that when we align our goal time lines to the moves 'n' vibes of the planets, we have something measurable and *real* holding us to a schedule—a schedule that is even bigger than us. Sometimes, if we're on our own, we can be less inspired. But if you have the surrounding solar system on your side? Who knows, you might be more inclined to stick to your plan.

The Personal Goal Planets to Pay Attention to

There are a number of planets that can factor into the way we set and conquer goals (which is no surprise, as planets work together just as different parts of *ourselves* work together to create our reality). For example, **the Sun** is our self-expression and our creative core, so it can drive our life purpose, which ties in with our goals. Energetic **Mars** shows us how we *conquer* our goals and go after what we want. Expansive **Jupiter** helps us think big and think of things in terms of idealism, which can take our goals to new heights. And even **Saturn** is there to throw us challenges and teach us to work harder to overcome life's hurdles.

But there's one planet that can perhaps be most useful to us when it comes to goal-setting, and that's **the Moon**. The Moon is a super-personal planet: It governs our emotional sides and the parts of us that are most vulnerable. The Moon is the keeper and protector of our inner child, the part where our *hope* grows from. When we're all alone and our Moon sign is shining brightly, that's when we envision and fantasize about our biggest, brightest, loftiest dreams in life—the ones that, perhaps sometimes, we're too self-conscious to share with others and release into the light

of day. The Moon's energy changes quickly (she spins through the zodiac approximately every four weeks), and thus it can be very helpful to align with when it comes to working on both short- and long-term goals.

> Under the new Moon, without all the distraction of the full Moon's light, the cosmos is more likely to listen.

Working with Lunations and the Lunar Cycle

Tracking the energy of the Moon as it moves through each sign of the zodiac every few days is definitely helpful, as that energy colors our day-to-day moods, feelings, and inspirations. But it's actually the *phases* of the Moon that we're going to work with when it comes to goal-setting. So as the Moon waxes and wanes in the sky, serving us its visible and nightly transformations throughout the month, we, too, will wax and wane our energies to align with this ever-intuitive and sensitive planet.

Working with the phases of the Moon makes conspiring with the cosmos a little more visual and immediate. While you may not be able to see the zodiac right in front of you, you can look up at the Moon every single night (weather permitting, of course) to see the current state of the Moon's cycle! Once you realize how to actually work with the lunar energy, it opens up a whole new world of manifestation possibilities.

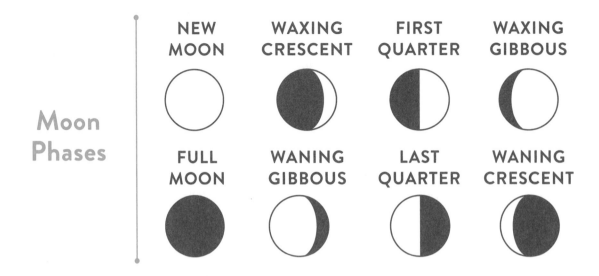

Moon Phases

| NEW MOON | WAXING CRESCENT | FIRST QUARTER | WAXING GIBBOUS |
| FULL MOON | WANING GIBBOUS | LAST QUARTER | WANING CRESCENT |

What Are Lunations?

Lunation refers to either a **new Moon** or a **full Moon**, which happen about two weeks apart within each lunar cycle. The Moon's energy is especially potent and powerful during these points in the monthly cycle, as they represent the Moon in its most extreme states of visibility: in full view (full Moon) or completely invisible (new Moon).

A **new Moon** typically occurs when the Moon is in a conjunction with the Sun (which means both luminaries are near the same spot in the zodiac). Visually, this is when the Moon has gone black and looks to have disappeared from the sky (which is why it's also called a *dark Moon*). This marks the beginning of a brand-new lunar cycle—the Moon is just a little baby here, beginning a new journey.

From there, the Moon **waxes** (or grows larger) for about two weeks until it becomes a **full Moon**. A full Moon typically takes place when the Moon is in an opposition to the Sun (meaning that it's in the *opposite* sign) and, well, we all know what a full Moon looks like. This is when the Moon's face is fully lit and within full visibility from the Earth. After the Moon reaches its peak fullness, it begins **waning**, or growing smaller.

The influence of each lunation mirrors its descriptions above symbolically. So as the new Moon begins a new lunar cycle, its energy, too, represents that of a new beginning. This designates it as a time to start something new, begin a project, or otherwise manifest something. From the time of the new Moon on, the energy grows and grows, imbuing your goals with the energy of "growth." The full Moon, however, is a time of fullness and illumination. It's a time to bring something to its peak. This time also holds the energy of impending release (as the Moon wanes from that point forth, through the end of the lunar cycle).

Full Moon for Release

There are some cases in which setting your intentions on the *full* Moon instead of the *new* Moon actually makes the most sense. While we'll want to utilize the energy of a new Moon for new beginnings, we can use full Moons for any sort of *release*. New Moons have impending built-up energy: If you're beginning a new project or adding something to your life, new Moons are best. Full Moons have impending release energy: If you're bringing something to fruition or releasing something, full Moons are best.

Personal Goals and the Lunar Cycle: How to Make the Most of It

Think of the energy of a full Moon. Many of us have experienced a shift in energy during these periods, or at least heard of some of the folklore around it, right? Anecdotes about the Moon affecting our behavior come from all over the world and have existed through history.

It makes sense, then, that when it comes to setting goals, we can use the energy of the lunations to guide us. Each stage between the new Moon and the full Moon and the end of the lunar cycle carries its own energy, and we can use every shift in energy to guide us and support us in reaching our goals.

○ **NEW MOON:** If your personal goal involves beginning something new or expanding something in your life, the new Moon is the moment where you begin. Your intention is born here, just as the new lunar cycle is born. This is the very first step and the laying out of the initial foundation. Now's the time to clear the slate and create space for your new undertaking. Make room for your intention to breathe as you release it into the universe! You don't want to cramp its style.

This lunation marks the beginning of a new cycle, and the energy is full of *growth potential*. That said, its energy is highly fertile, and this is the time to plant energetic seeds. If you want to add something to your life, build upon something, grow something, or begin something, now is the point in the lunar cycle that you should state your intention and put it out into the universe.

◗ WAXING CRESCENT MOON: So the new Moon birthed your intention. Now the waxing crescent Moon is at the point in the lunar cycle where you must begin clarifying your goals. At this point in the cycle, the Moon has just begun to illuminate with a crescent—it continues to grow, as your goals will, but allow this first sliver of light to ignite your plan and set it into place. At this moment in the lunar cycle when the Moon is very close to the Sun, we see the energy of the luminaries working in conjunction. There's a harmony here that's very conducive to setting new goals and being in touch with ourselves. Think about every part of your goal: What are the actual steps you must take, one by one, to get there and make it real? Use the hopeful energy of the waxing crescent Moon to refine your intention and create the *plan* that can help you get there.

◗ FIRST QUARTER MOON: At this point, you have your intention as well as your plan to make it real, but this part of the lunar cycle is about taking action on those plans. With the Moon halfway to full, there is much more energy being put toward your goals, which could, of course, present you with some challenges, too. The light of the Moon always illuminates things for us symbolically, so here is where we may begin to see the hurdles that must be jumped in order to stick to our plans. Stick to it, and keep working toward your prize.

● WAXING GIBBOUS MOON: As the Moon continues to illuminate and show more of its face, our energy and traction on whatever projects we're working on grows as well. At this point, you've likely faced some obstacles and had to refine bits and pieces of your plan. Perhaps that was because you lost focus or fell behind, or maybe it was due to outside factors and certain things simply not working out as hoped. That's okay, and it's normal! Keep your focus and accept the course; don't give up hope and stay optimistic. That's the important thing. Remain flexible in the process.

● FULL MOON: Ah, finally we reach the full Moon, illuminated in all her glory! Just as the full Moon illuminates the night, so it illuminates our minds and goals and spirits. We are able to see things more clearly and can spot everything that stands in the way of meeting our goal. What a gift it is to have all the lights turned on, even if it's only temporary! There's a big buildup of energy that's been taking place since the start of the new lunar cycle, and the full Moon absolutely peaks and brims with it. This moment in the lunar cycle is when the Moon and the Sun are opposing each other in the zodiac. This causes some pull and friction for us. This is the energy of a climax, an explosion and the release that comes along with it.

This is also the point where our labors should start bearing fruit. Sure, we have work to do, but the first half of the lunar cycle's energy helped us get somewhere. Working from the new Moon to the full Moon, you've brought a goal from its infancy to its first stage of release. You've grown it, and now you're at a point where all is illuminated and you can see the lessons you're learning as you make progress.

WANING GIBBOUS MOON: You've experienced the exciting, wild, and possibly chaotic climax of the full Moon, and now it's time for the Moon to begin its descent back into invisibility with the waning gibbous phase. Now is the time to open yourself up. Become a sponge and soak up every bit of energy and knowledge you've gained from the past weeks of work toward your goals. Energy exchange is good here: It's helpful to show the universe how thankful you are for its support by sharing what you've created. But this isn't a time to slow down or get lazy on your goals—just because you've reached a milestone doesn't mean there's not more work to be done!

LAST QUARTER MOON: Here is where we begin to slow down—not in giving up on our goals, of course, but rather understanding that it's all about the cycle of the process. The full Moon is always a shock to the system of sorts, full of energy and illumination, but just like the Moon, we can't be in waxing or "going hard" mode 24/7. It's vital that we rest and recoup. Now's the time to take a deep breath and check in with your goals as well as yourself.

WANING CRESCENT MOON: With this lunar phase, we are on the precipice of the coming Moon cycle. There's an energy of an ending—we're wrapping up and finishing something—but there is also the anxious energy of the impending new beginning that's yet to come. Now's the time to allow yourself room for self-reflection. Think about your goals over the past month's Moon cycle and what you've accomplished. This reflection isn't just to milk all you can from your current goals, though; it's also to offer you clarity on what's next, as you're about to embark on a whole new Moon cycle in just a few days.

Proceed with Caution Zones: Personal Goals Edition

There are always going to be lunations that are more auspicious than others when it comes to setting intentions and planning your goals, but a good rule of thumb is that new Moons are good for manifesting, and full Moons are better suited for releasing things. However, the series of eclipses that take place a couple of times a year are definitely an exception to this rule. You do *not* want to try to manifest your goals or start a new project under the energy of an eclipse. Eclipses are all about fate, and they sweep through our lives to put us back on track. Skip all manifesting work during these periods and instead just sit back and let it run its course.

Goal-Crushing Days

Monday is the *Moon*'s day. While it has a reputation in society as being a "back to the grind" day, astrology feels a little differently. Because it's ruled by the sensitive and emotional Moon, this is a good day to go inward, nurture yourself, and allow your feelings to take center stage. Don't push yourself or expect to get too far on your goals today; instead, listen to your intuition and allow yourself to daydream.

Tuesday is ruled by Mars, so *this* is astrology's true "back to the grind" day. Mars is all about action, so capitalize on this ambitious go-get-'em vibe as much as possible (especially since you rested up yesterday!). You're likely to feel more energized, determined, and willing to make big and courageous moves right now, so hop to it.

Wednesday is ruled by Mercury, and it's a time to immerse yourself in the details. While yesterday was a day of action, today is a day of sorting out the logistics. If your plans need tweaking, use the clear-minded and objective energy of Mercury's day to help you make those adjustments and tie up loose ends.

Thursday is ruled by Jupiter, which is the biggest planet of them all, so it's here to expand your goals. This is a great day to dream big, but it's also an ideal moment to seek knowledge. If you realized, thanks to Mercury's eye for detail, that you need to gain some wisdom in order to make your dreams a reality, Thursday is the day to make that magic happen. Influenced by Jupiter, our minds are more open to new knowledge and paradigm shifts.

Friday is ruled by Venus, so when it comes to setting goals, ask yourself about your desires. What brings you pleasure? What is valuable about your goals, and why does it mean something to you? Focus on what brings meaning, pleasure, and enjoyment to your life, and how that ties in with your goals. Being clear on how your goals will add value to your life will help bring clarity and focus to your going after them.

Saturday is Saturn's day. While we may think of Saturday as the happy-go-lucky first day of the weekend, astrology is here to whip you into goal-achieving shape. The planet of responsibility knocks a little reality into our weekend by reminding us that we should use some of our free time to get on top of our obligations and make sure we're working toward our goals.

Sunday is the Sun's day. If you spent Saturday working toward making your personal hustle a reality, then good for you—time to enjoy the creative self-expression of Sunday! This is a great time to get creative and let the artistic juices flow. It's possible some of your most authentic ideas could come to you on a Sunday, under the Sun's trusty guidance and confidence.

Working with the Zodiac and Longer-Term Goals

We may have shifted our focus from the energy of the zodiac to the energy of the lunar phases, but don't think we've forgotten our gorgeous gaggle of signs! If you *really* want to align your goals with the lunar cycle, it is still important to consider where in the zodiac each lunation takes place. The placement of each lunation colors the energy of its powers. So for example, if a new Moon takes place in Leo, we may take advantage of that by setting intentions that are related to our passion projects and creative endeavors, as this is Leo's realm. If the new Moon takes place in Libra, our goals might be more powerful if we focus them on our one-on-one relationships and bring balance to our lives.

This leads into how to use the lunations for *longer*-term goals. Because obviously, not everything can be achieved in a single month! When you set intentions on a new Moon in any given sign, in addition to working with the energy of that particular four-week lunar phase cycle, you're also working with a much larger series of cycles of the zodiac. This means that whatever sign the new Moon was in when you set your intentions will have a corresponding full Moon in the same sign approximately six months later. This will, on a larger and more long-term scale, circle back to the themes of the new Moon six months prior and bring that energy to fruition. From there, it will slowly pass through long-term versions of the same cycles over the coming six months, until the new Moon takes place within that same zodiac sign once more. Keeping a goal journal that aligns with the Moon cycle makes this process much easier.

ASTROLOGY FOR LIFE: STYLE

We're all unique, one-of-a-kind individuals—we know this based on the incredibly complex mosaic of our birth charts alone! And every single day, one of the many ways that we express ourselves takes place before we ever leave the house: via our personal style. This includes the clothes we wear, the makeup looks we gravitate toward, the hairstyles we choose, and the accessories we adorn ourselves with. Our personal style is an important facet of who we are, even if we don't consider ourselves that stylish.

Even if you do have a well-defined sense of style, it's always fun to branch out of the usual box and get dressed for something other than the weather, so why not look to astrology as your fashion muse? If we can use astrology to inspire us when it comes to planning date nights, socializing, self-care practices, and career goals, then we can certainly use it in relation to our personal style. And there are so many different ways to do this.

However, not everyone is interested in fashion—that's okay! I have endless respect for those of you who get dressed purely for function. But whether we like it or not, the way we choose to present ourselves does make an impact on those around us. Use this advice if you'd like some astro inspo to help you take control of that image in a more serious way—or not! Either way is a-okay.

Where can we find our fashion guidance in astrology? Several places. Follow me.

The Personal Style Planets to Pay Attention to

There are many different ways you can use astrology to inform or inspire your personal style, and there are a few places to look that will *always* guide you in the right direction.

If you're able to obtain your birth time and thus look up your **rising sign**, or ascendant, this is perhaps the first place you'll want to check out (read all about it in Chapter 4!). You can look to this point throughout your life to inspire your style. Your rising sign is basically your brand and your aesthetic. It illustrates the qualities of the surface-level you; it's the person you *appear* to be or embody at first glance. While there are lots of influences in your birth chart that could affect the way you dress and accessorize, the ascendant marks the cusp of your first house, which rules your physical appearance, so it'll perhaps be the biggest and most consistent influence.

The lovely and pleasure-centered planet **Venus** is another planet you can look to if you want some cosmic style inspiration. Venus is best known for being the ruler of all things love and romance, but this is also the planet that rules beauty and aesthetics, which, of course, applies to the way we beautify and adorn *ourselves*, such as styling our hair, putting on makeup, or exploring different fashions. We can look to our Venus sign to illustrate what we value when it comes to beauty and style.

Personal Style Planetary Transits: How to Make the Most of Them

There are a few ways you can use the following information. If you're interested in exploring a more long-term interpretation of your personal style's energy, look to your rising sign. Read the fashion tips for your sign below, then read the section for your rising sign in Chapter 2 to get an even deeper idea of its energy. Work with this energy any time you're planning something related to your personal style, aesthetic, or brand—this is *you*.

If you're interested in more seasonal style changes, instead of looking at your own chart, look to Venus in transit. As the planet of beauty moves through the zodiac, she influences all of us when it comes to our aesthetic, so we can use these transits for more fluid advice. Venus switches signs approximately every month, so keep tabs on where it's at (and where it's heading next) by using an ephemeris or checking trusted online sources. Her regularly shifting energy can help move us through our closets and give our items of clothing a little more use and variety.

Last but not least, if you're seeking *daily* fashion inspiration, look to the trusty Moon. The Moon influences so much about us, especially as it relates to emotions and our inner selves. While it's not necessarily a "personal style" planet, its energy can certainly be used for day-to-day fashion advice, as we *all* feel the Moon's influence daily. The Moon moves through the zodiac in less than a month, meaning it's only within each sign for up to a few days—again, you can keep tabs on where it's at by using an ephemeris or checking trusted online sources.

You can use the following tidbits for advice for either your rising sign, the current Venus transit, or the current Moon transit. Let yourself get creative and be inspired accordingly!

ARIES STYLE INSPIRATION: Highlight your courage. Fireball Aries energy is all about action, so whatever you wear, make sure you can run, jump, and do splits in it. Athleisure is definitely a look—style up a hoodie, track pants, or leggings for a leisurely yet fashionable outfit. Or pair something girlier with a pair of sneakers to give an otherwise cutesy look an on-the-go edge. Red is definitely the power color here—don't shy away from a bold red lip.

TAURUS STYLE INSPIRATION: Highlight your luxuriousness. This Venus-ruled sign is all about the sensual pleasures, so choose clothing made from fabrics that are silky and soft to the touch. Anything that bridges the gap between luxurious and comfortable is very much up the Taurean alley. Indulge in a fancy perfume or other body products to make yourself feel extra special. Taurus is an earth sign, so stick to natural tones rather than bold colors. Florals are always welcome here, too. Rule of thumb: Say yes to anything and everything velvet.

GEMINI STYLE INSPIRATION: Highlight your excitement. Gemini, represented by the twins, is all about duality, so bring that energy into your personal style, too. Think of the qualities of the looks you typically wear, then incorporate something that feels the *opposite*. It's about tension. Do you wear lots of girlie things? Throw on a boxy men's jacket over your dress. Typically the leggings and sweatshirt type? Wear a fancy blazer over your leggings. Find yourself sticking to muted colors? Grab a scarf or a pair of shoes in a neon shade for a streak of color.

CANCER STYLE INSPIRATION: Highlight your comfort. Cancer weather calls for your old favorites. What's your most loved, most nostalgic item of clothing? What item of clothing or type of accessory simply makes you feel at *home* in your style? Wear *that*, and things like it, and treasure it under a Cancerian mood. Your style here should be inspired by the familiar things you love. Silver accessories are always nice, as they pay homage to Cancer's ruling planet, the Moon. Also, up the cozy factor! Fuzzy sweaters and oversized knits are perfect. Oh, and don't forget pajamas. Cancer energy is *not* opposed to wearing pajamas or pajama-esque clothing in public.

LEO STYLE INSPIRATION: Highlight your sparkle. Gold lamé? Check. Bold eyeliner? Check. Leo energy? Also check. This fire sign's vibe is all about being flashy and *loves* to be the center of attention. If your look can grab all the attention without you having to say a word, that makes life even easier. Embrace all the gold accessories you can to show homage to Leo's ruling planet, the Sun. Make some bold and brave fashion choices here—this is not the time to be shy about being "too much." Nothing is too colorful, too sparkly, or too flashy for a Leo influence. Be a sartorial maximalist.

VIRGO STYLE INSPIRATION: Highlight your natural beauty. Earth sign Virgo is represented by the virgin maiden, so think of natural hippie looks here. Flowy tops, long skirts, and beautiful floral dresses are lovely. Natural fibers like cotton and hemp, free of artificial dyes, are definitely the way to go—Virgo loves purity! Carry a larger purse or bag so you can fit all the things you feel like carrying with you (you never know, you might need a book, a box of Band-Aids, and a hairbrush today!). Don't be afraid to throw a flower in your hair for an added earth maiden vibe.

LIBRA STYLE INSPIRATION: Highlight your aesthetic sense. High fashion finds its home with Libra's classy yet cute energy. Ruled by luxurious and beauty-lovin' Venus, this sign wants everything to be gorgeous, and it knows that sometimes, beauty is pain. This means you might be willing to wear those too-small shoes if they happen to go perfectly with the rest of your outfit. Balance is a theme here, though, so you'll be drawn to matchy-matchy accessories from head to toe. Pay attention to color palettes, too; if it clashes, it probably doesn't feel balanced.

SCORPIO STYLE INSPIRATION: Highlight your mysteriousness. Okay, we know that not all Scorpios are goth (and most Scorps are probably sick of everyone stereotyping them as such), but this energy *does* embody the dark and mysterious parts of life. Therefore, you can channel Scorpio energy by going with dark and mysterious looks. This is easily achieved by dramatically wearing all black, but you can get symbolic with it and be "mysterious" with your look in other ways, too.

SAGITTARIUS STYLE INSPIRATION: Highlight your free-spiritedness. Fun, vibrant, and spontaneous, Sagittarius is stylish *and* free-spirited, making a boho-chic vibe very applicable. Pull inspiration from different cultural fashions (without culturally appropriating, please!) or commit to picking up wardrobe items and accessories on your travels, then layer, layer, layer. Exotic and colorful fabrics and out-of-this world prints are all fun, flashy staples of the Sagittarian vibe. Top it all off with some fun, eclectic jewelry!

CAPRICORN STYLE INSPIRATION: Highlight your classic beauty. Capricorn energy wants to look like it has its act together even if it doesn't, so make sure you look polished. Simplicity and classic silhouettes are definitely the key. Find a classic but flattering cut and stick to it! In fact, because Capricorn is associated with older energy, it's a great time to look to vintage styles for inspiration, too. Less is definitely more here, so take after Coco Chanel and remove an accessory before you leave the house, even if you feel like you'd already pared things down.

AQUARIUS STYLE INSPIRATION: Highlight your uniqueness. Now's the time to get weird with your style. Don't be afraid to stick out in the crowd; showing off your individuality through your style is the whole point here! Dig through your closet and find something funky that you haven't worn in a while (or perhaps have *never* worn), and find a new way to style it. Aquarius energy is all about being inventive and embracing the unique, one-of-a-kind aspects of yourself, so that's exactly the approach to take with your style. Commit to trying new and different things. Some things might miss, but others will hit, and it'll be a whole lot of fun.

PISCES STYLE INSPIRATION: Highlight your dreaminess. Everything is a fantasy with Pisces energy, including the wardrobe, so get imaginative. Choose ethereal pieces that feel otherworldly to you (whether you interpret otherworldly as being fairy-like or just vintage is up to you). Let your actual dreams inspire your outfit or fashion look. Keeping a dream journal can help you remember the details so you can pull from it for bits of inspiration. Oh, and don't forget the waterproof mascara—a Piscean *must*-have.

Conclusion

I hope you learned what you came to learn here, and that this book will continue to be a resource for you when it comes to building personal relationships with each of the planets and the energies of the signs within the zodiac. Astrology is vast and virtually endless. It has adapted and shifted throughout history, and will continue to do so into the future, perhaps for as long as we humans exist within this corner of the universe. One of the joys of this mystical art is the sheer amount of historic, present, and future insight it continues to offer astrologers. The archetypes, systems, and symbols used within astrology are so varied and run so deep that there is a seemingly endless amount of interpretation there for the taking. And guess what? Now you have just as much access to this mystical world as anyone else. You can start making your relationship to astrology much more personal and unique.

Let this book be something fun to whip out when you have a friend over, or, you know, when you *really* want some extra outfit inspiration or date night ideas. Some people enjoy peeking beneath the surface of astrology, but that doesn't mean you have to. There's no pressure to, for example, master an ephemeris. There are plenty of wonderful professional astrologers who would be happy to consult with you on any outstanding astrology questions that pop up as you live your life. I recommend that everyone hire and support astrologers. Getting different opinions from different astrologers is as helpful as getting different perspectives on a situation from trusted friends. They will most likely be different but equally good viewpoints, and *all* of them will broaden your understanding.

This book can also be a jumping-off point, the beginning of a cosmic journey that extends far beyond your Sun sign and your horoscope and what you might have thought astrology was limited to before. True astrology, as I hope you've discovered, is the opposite of limiting. It's the opposite of confining you to any single box. Instead, it's expansive, vast, all-encompassing, and endless. We've yet to find the border of astrology because, like the universe itself, it is in flux, ever changing, and ever adapting to our lives.

So go off! Dive into your birth chart. Google every aspect on it. Read astrology books. Hire an astrologer. Hire *multiple* astrologers. Follow astrology accounts on Instagram. Read your daily horoscope. Read an ephemeris. Check the transits of the planets every morning. Immerse yourself in this world in a way that works for *you*. Do whatever feels right for *you* with astrology—but above all, use it. For life.

Index

money, 49–50. *See also* finances

Moon, 15–17, 20, 22–23, 37–42, 74, 83, 87–88, 99–100, 128–130, 177, 214, 223, 231, 272, 292, 297, 299, 310, 314–315
    nodes. *See* lunar nodes
    personal goals and, 305–309
    power of, 233–234
    self-care and, 298–303
    transits and, 252

Moon sign, 200–201, 232–240, 272, 299

mutable signs, 108, 111, 124, 126, 136, 138, 150, 162

natal chart. *See* birth chart

Neptune, 26–29, 70–75, 80–81, 115, 162, 164, 185, 215, 223, 230

Neptune return, 75

new Moon, 305–307, 309, 312

ninth house, 150, 182

Nodes of Fate. *See* lunar nodes

Nodes of the Moon. *See* lunar nodes

north node, 192–194

opposition, 198

orbits, 21

orbs of aspects, 195

Pallas, 83, 94–95

personal signs, 114–115

Pisces, 29, 47, 55, 70, 100, 107, 111, 113–115, 120, 162–165, 185, 215, 223, 230–231, 240, 248, 280, 289, 295, 303, 317

planetary returns, 21, 59, 64, 69, 75

planetary transits, 250–252, 273–280
    career-related, 285–289
    and love and sex, 273–280
    self-care and, 299–303
    and social life, 292–295
    and style, 314–317

planets, 19–20, 97–99, 167–170. *See also* specific planet
    aspects. *See* aspects
    career-related, 283–284
    co-ruling, in decans, 206–207
    dignities, 29–30
    dwarf, 83, 87. *See also* Pluto
    generational, 26, 115. *See also* Neptune; Pluto; Uranus
    inner, 22–25, 69, 75, 81. *See also* Jupiter; Mars; Mercury; Saturn; Venus
    modern, 26
    natal, 172–173, 250–252, 286, 293
    outer, 26–29, 69, 75, 81, 115. *See also* Neptune; Pluto; Uranus
    personal. *See* planets, inner
    personal goals and, 304–305
    retrograde. *See* retrogrades
    self-care and, 299

social, 25, 115. *See also* Jupiter; Saturn
    social life and, 291–297
    transcendental. *See* planets, outer
    transit vs. natal, 250–252. *See also* planetary transits
    transpersonal, 23, 25. *See also* Jupiter; Saturn

Pluto, 20, 26–29, 71, 75–81, 115, 145, 148, 181, 215, 222, 231, 250–251, 302

points, 19–20, 170, 187–192

polarities, 102, 112–113, 296. *See also* feminine signs/femininity; masculine signs/masculinity

quadruplicities, 108

qualities, 108

relationships, 89–91, 180, 260–262, 264–265

retrograde cycle, phases, 255–256

retrogrades, 21–22, 253–265, 281–282, 290

returns. *See* planetary returns; solar return

rising sign, 169–170, 174, 187–189, 200–201, 241–248, 314

romance, 48–49, 53, 89–91, 178, 262

rulerships, 29

Sagittarius, 55, 103, 111, 113, 150–153, 182, 209, 217, 224–225, 238–239, 247, 278–279, 289, 295, 301, 316

Saturday, 60, 311

Saturn, 7–8, 23, 25–26, 54, 60–64, 84–85, 115, 154, 157–158, 161, 183, 211, 219, 226, 250–251, 284, 302, 304–305, 311

Saturn return, 21, 64

Scorpio, 29, 51, 65, 76, 107, 110, 113, 145–149, 181, 215, 222–223, 231, 238, 247, 278, 288, 295, 301, 316

second house, 121, 175, 181, 286

self-care, 92–93, 261, 269, 298–303

seventh house, 140–141, 180, 189, 275

sex and sexuality, 53, 80, 148, 181, 271–282

sextile, 197

signs. *See* zodiac signs

sixth house, 136, 179, 185, 303

social life, 291–297

soft aspects, 196–198

Sol, 36

solar eclipse, 266

solar return, 21, 36

south node, 192–194

square aspect, 197–198

stellium, 173

style, 313–317

Sun, 20, 22–23, 27, 32–36, 59, 97–100, 132–134, 178, 209, 216, 225, 284, 296–297, 304, 311

Sunday, 32, 297, 311

Sun sign, 6, 11, 23, 33, 200–231, 244
    importance of, 204
    individuality and, 205–206

Taurus, 23, 47, 88, 100, 104, 108, 110, 113–115, 121–123, 126–127, 143, 156, 175, 210–211, 219, 227, 235, 245, 250, 273–274, 286, 294, 300, 315

technology, 260

tenth house, 154, 157, 183, 190, 286

therapy, astrology as, 8–9

third house, 124, 127, 176, 293

Thursday, 55, 288, 310–311

transcendent signs, 114–115

transit planets, 250–252, 273–280, 286, 292–295, 314–317. *See also* planetary transits

trines, 197–198, 251

triplicities, 102

Tuesday, 51, 76, 282, 288, 310

twelfth house, 162, 164, 185, 303

Uranus, 26–29, 44, 65–69, 75, 84–85, 95, 115, 158, 160–161, 184, 213, 221, 228, 284, 302

Uranus return, 69

Venus, 23–26, 47–50, 53, 58–59, 70, 75, 83, 115–116, 121, 140, 143, 175, 180, 210–211, 213, 219–220, 227, 229, 250–251, 264–265, 271–272, 282, 284, 292, 297, 311, 314–315
    transits, and love and sex, 273–280

Venus retrograde, 260–263, 281–282

Vesta, 83, 92–93

Virgo, 23, 42, 88, 100, 104, 111, 113, 136–139, 156, 179, 211, 218–219, 227, 237, 246, 250, 276–277, 287, 294, 301, 316

waning moon, 306, 309

water element, 107, 113, 128, 145, 162

water signs, 24, 102, 107, 112–113, 129, 131, 146, 162–165. *See also* Cancer; Pisces; Scorpio

waxing moon, 306, 308

Wednesday, 42, 65, 288, 297, 310

work. *See* career

Zeus, 56, 89, 94–95

zodiac signs, 19–20, 96–167. *See also* specific sign
    ascension of, 114–115
    in astrology charts, 170
    energy of, 99–101
    fundamentals, 97–116
    personal vs. transcendent, 114–115

zodiac wheel, 19, 21, 120, 170, 188, 242, 267